C000006580

WEDNESDAY EARLY CLOSING

NORMAN NICHOLSON

WEDNESDAY
EARLY CLOSING

faber and faber

This edition first published in 2008
by Faber and Faber Ltd
3 Queen Square, London WC1N 3AU

Printed by CPI Antony Rowe, Eastbourne

All rights reserved
© Irvine Hunt, 1975

The right of Norman Nicholson to be identified as author of this work
has been asserted in accordance with Section 77 of the
Copyright, Designs and Patents Act 1988

This book is sold subject to the condition that it shall not, by way of
trade or otherwise, be lent, resold, hired out or otherwise circulated
without the publisher's prior consent in any form of binding or cover other than
that in which it is published and without a similar condition including this
condition being imposed on the subsequent purchaser

A CIP record for this book is available from the British Library

ISBN 978-0-571-24327-3

For
JOHN EDWARD FISHER
to give him
something else to grumble about

NOTE

Some of the Christian names have been changed.

N.N.

CHAPTER ONE

"Your mammy has gone to join the angels," my grandmother said, her old face creased like a shrunk potato.

"When will she be back?" I asked.

I had sensed that I was to be told something of importance. My father had winced off into the shop, where, under no circumstances, was I allowed to follow, and we were sitting in the middle room behind the shop, my grandmother with her back to the window, and I, on my four-legged stool, beside the fire. Somewhere in a blurred, now-forgotten corner of the room was my Auntie Lizzie. It must have been afternoon, for my grandmother had removed the coarse apron she always wore until dinner time. It was fairly early spring, and I have the impression that it was a fine day with the light bright in the back yard. The year was 1919 and I was just turned five.

On my eight-inch stool I was about the right height to stare level into the fire. I have always been a great starer into fires. And this fire was framed like a picture by the old fire-place of black marble, or what I thought was black marble, though I now know it to be of polished and painted slate. Set round it were three long panels – one, upright, on either side, and one, horizontal, above – all of red marble, like red grained wood or red ink running on blotting paper. A few years later I would see the pattern as a map of unendingly explorable archipelagos. The canopy or hood was of iron, embossed with lily stalks, heart-shaped leaves and snakes knotted like bow ties. Similar bows appeared again, red on green ground, on the square tiles my father had set into a kind of entablature on either side of the fire. In the half-light, before the gas was lit, the fire-place turned into a cave, glowing red and green deep down in its gullet, where my fancy could tunnel and hide and lose itself for hours and hours.

But this is surely far too much for a child to remember in his grief! The truth is that I cannot remember any grief. I can remember my grandmother's words, and my answer, but not what I felt about it. As for the fire-place, I do not have to remember that at all.

For, though my grandmother and my aunt are long dead, the fire-place is still there. I stare into it every night. Except that the red and green tiles have been replaced by bronze, it is still just as it was when my grandmother was alive. So, too, are the doors, the window, the shape of the room. Even the little stool still stands in more or less the same place. My childhood is not safely locked off from the present, a world to be revisited or forgotten but never, in either case, to be altered. My childhood is built into the everyday life of today, into the bricks of the house where I live and the walls of the room where I am writing these words. When, a couple of years ago, decorators stripped off the wallpaper in that same middle room, they brought to light the mud-brown, twined-waterweed pattern that must have been there when my grandmother spoke to me – a pattern I had not seen since I was eight years old and had completely forgotten. When at the same time, they burnt off the paint on the stairs, they uncovered, not just the old pasche-egg-coloured grain and varnish that I could faintly recall, but also the original green, laid on bare wood, that had been put on when the house was built in 1880. If I pause in my writing and look out of the window, across St. George's Terrace, I can see the Post Office that is no longer there, and Seth Slater's tailor's shop that was there before it was a Post Office, and, through long-demolished windows opening on to what is now empty air, I can still watch Mrs. Slater and Rosa and John carrying the tea-things from the kitchen to the dining room.

It is not just that the past persists into the present: the present pushes back into the past. I cannot separate what I think I saw from what I know I must have seen. Sometimes the present may even reshape the past. I have memories that seem to be set, quite vividly, in this room, beside that chair, outside that chemist's shop or along the verge of a public footpath – yet second thoughts compel me to admit that, at the time remembered, the chair had not been bought, the chemist's shop was a greengrocer's, and the path had not been laid down across the Park that was then just a field.

And quite apart from such falsifications, the past takes much of its meaning from the present. The whole of my life, in a way, is a follow through from those first five or ten years, and, whenever I think of them, I see both what they were and what they came to be.

"Your mammy has gone to join the angels" – and the tone of my reply suggests that I suspected she had gone somewhere. I was what my father called "sharp", and I must have been aware that something was being kept back from me. I know now that the three of us – my mother, my father and I – all fell ill, simultaneously, of the "Spanish 'flu" which killed more people throughout the world in eighteen months than the War had killed in four years. Our terrace house was of the typical Victorian plan, three rooms up and three rooms down, with a two-room attic, and, since the downstairs front room was the shop, the room above it became our sitting room, which meant that, apart from the attic, we had only two bedrooms – the middle room for my parents and the little back room for me. And what makes me able to remember all this is the fact that when my mother's condition worsened, my father was moved into the back bedroom with me. The whole scene remains vaguely in my mind, the two of us lying close to the window, the gas lit on its bracket above the bed. There must have been many whispered messages and consultations, unexpected visits, bumpings and shufflings on the stairs. Somehow, my father must have made the decisions which had to be made. There was much that I could not understand; maybe I was mercifully too ill to take notice.

But the next memory is as clear as a photograph. After a few days my father moved back into the middle room, but I was told that I must not see my mother until she was better. Then, one day, when my own door was open, I saw my father walk up the stairs and lay his hand on the door of the middle bedroom. I was well enough by this time to sit up and play on the bedroom floor, so I quickly jumped up and ran to my father, expecting, at last, to be allowed to enter with him. My father put out his hand to hold me back, then opened the door about a foot, edged himself carefully inside and closed the door after him. He had not said a word to me nor to my mother, whom I believed to be lying ill in the room. I can still feel the suspicion, the apprehension that came upon me, and my father must have felt it too. That was why my grandmother had to tell me about the angels.

With that closed door my mother was shut out of my memory for ever. I know that neighbours and friends looked on me as a poor, motherless child, and I can still see how my grandmother's face, under the strain of contrary emotions, would crack into a broken-toothed smile that half-teetered into a sob. But, apart from one moment some months later, I have no recollection at all of having missed my mother.

Yet a ban or block was set up in my mind, for in the very few memories that come from the time before her death, my mother has been cut out of the picture as if with a pair of scissors. That part of the scene where she might have been is a gap or a blank.

With one exception, all these early memories are associated with the War, which, even for a child of five, was the weather in which we all lived. Only one of them is set away from the house. And not very far away. I was standing at the corner of St. George's Terrace and Lapstone Road, outside the shop that was then Miss Crellin's, Millinery – and later on became Seth Slater's, when he moved to our side of The Terrace. My left hand was held by somebody – here the picture is a blank – and in my right I clutched a small Union Jack on a stick. Somebody else bent down towards me and asked why I was carrying the flag.

"Peace," I said.

It cannot have been the Armistice, or the somebody would not have asked. I think it may have been an anticipatory rumour of peace, some short time before the 11th of November. But, at least, I had the right impulse.

So, too, in the matter of War Savings. There was a belief, at that time, that even tiny tots should be encouraged to feel that they were helping Our Brave Lads and Etc., and, in this case, they were asked to empty their money-boxes and put their pennies into National Savings. I have no doubt that what my father intended to do was to buy in my name a small batch of Savings Certificates, or whatever they were, and that all I was being asked for was a token subscription of half a crown, or, at most, ten shillings. But I did not like the idea at all. For hours I went about the house clutching my money-box to my miserly chest and howling my eyes out. My father relished the incident and kept on giving a comic imitation of my behaviour for the entertainment of friends, and my repeated shaming, as I pushed my head into cushions or hid behind a chair, no doubt helped to stamp the occasion on my mind. But I still have the money-box, and, looking back, I am glad that I refused to be a War Profiteer.

There may have been a touch of conscience in my father's financial patriotism, for, though he was as pro-War as any man and venerated Lloyd George, he was determined not to be called up. He was thirty-seven when the War broke out and nearly forty when men of his age began to be conscripted. He was, moreover, an undersized man, who would have been useless in the services, though he was delighted when a doctor once called him "a wiry little devil". It was not, however, on his own account that he insisted on staying home. He had a wife, he had a child, he had a shop, and he felt a moral obligation to all three. And not least to the shop. When he said he kept a shop he did not just mean that the shop kept him. He was bound to the shop as he was to his wife and looked on bankruptcy as almost the same as adultery. For years afterwards, right up to the time of the Second World War, he would keep on telling how he had faced up to the Chairman of the tribunal or committee before which he had to appear.

"I'm not going to the War," he would say, tilting back his head and sticking out his chin towards the brother or friend or commercial traveller whom he had trapped into listening:

"I've got a business to look after," he would continue. "You build it up, you look after it, you go away and where is it when you come back?"

He would stand quite still, leaning slightly backwards as he had to do to look almost anyone in the face – his spectacles sparkling with indignation, his small paunch pushing out his waistcoat as if he were pregnant. Then, dropping the righteous pose, he would begin his word-perfect, Harry-Tate-like monologue of how he and the other call-ups were marched through the streets of Lancaster, hobbling, limping, contorted with arthritis or doubled-up with a hump.

"'By Lad, Billy,' I said, 'if this is what we've got to fall back on, God help England.'"

The upshot was that my father was not called up but was ordered to work at the Millom Ironworks for three days a week. It was, of course, a complete waste of time. He had not the physical strength to be a labourer, nor the skill to be a furnace-man, nor the education to be a clerk. He and his two or three fellow industrial conscripts seem to have spent much of their time finding a quiet spot behind the furnaces, where they were out of the way and could catch some warmth from the tapped slag. Yet nobody called him a shirker. He was well liked by both the men and the bosses, and many of the latter became his customers in the post-War years. Sometimes he would seek out one of the foremen to ask if he could find him anything to do.

"You mooch off home," the foreman would say. "I've never seen you!"

But on one occasion, at least, they did find him a job and then he managed to drop a wooden plank on his foot and sprain his ankle, and was brought home in the Ironworks car. Perhaps it was the car that makes me remember this so well. Cars were still very rare in Millom. When they passed along the street we did not run after them and cheer, but we stood and watched. I remember, too, how my father limped into the living room and sat beside the fire, and how someone brought the small zinc bath with a handle at either end – *my* bath, in fact – and how my father peeled off his sock, turned up his trouser leg and bathed his foot in the hot water.

From that time onwards the Ironworks belonged to the world in which I lived. Before then, I have no recollection of them whatever, though I could scarcely have helped seeing them almost every time I went outside the house. But now they had become real to me: they were the place where my father sprained his ankle.

It is said that a child's use of language depends, to a great extent, on his verbal relationship with his mother during the first five years of his life. So maybe the very fact that I am writing this book is due to the influence of the mother I cannot remember. I have no photograph of her; no visual image whatever. All I have is a few dates and data.

She was thirty-nine when she died in March 1919. Like my father, she was one of the first generation to be born and bred in the town of Millom. Twenty years before their time there was no town to be born in. Her father was a butcher who died before I was born – I did not, in fact, see either of my grandfathers – but the house where they lived still stands in the older part of the town, much of which is already derelict. Cornthwaite, my mother's maiden name and my own middle name, has a true Scandinavian ring about it, meaning the *tveit* or clearing of the corn. Indeed, my great-grandfather, William Cornthwaite, was, as you might say, a "corn thwaiter", belonging to Osmotherley, near Ulverston, in a part of North Lancashire much colonised by the Vikings, where he kept a scratching of a farm at Boretree Style. He is described on the birth certificate of my great-uncle Tom as an iron-ore miner, and must have worked by day at one of the little mines near Lindal, leaving the care of the cows and the pigs to his wife. Three boys were born to him at Boretree – my grandfather who came to Millom; a second son who became a bookbinder and of whom I know no more;

14

and Tom who lived at Kirksanton, a few miles north of Millom, and worked as a maltster at the Brockbank Brewery, which, for scores of years, provided all the local brew of South Cumberland. The old brewery building stood close to the railway line, and, once, in the 'forties, I passed it on my way to give a W.E.A. lecture at Whitehaven, and when I returned the next morning it was no longer there. A gale had flattened it during the night.

My grandmother sometimes used to take me to Kirksanton to see my great-aunt, and I suppose we must have walked all the three miles, except when I was young enough to ride in my push-chair. The cottage still stands on the way from the pub to the shore – set back from the road, and darkly environed by slate barn-walls and rheumaticky sycamores that look dead in winter and dying even in spring. But, from that early time, all I remember is the cobbled yard at the back, where, after much pushing and shoo-ing and Go-oning, I was persuaded to scatter a few handfuls of corn to a flock of vicious little hens that pecked and darted like a swarm of gigantic, angry, feathered bees.

There was, indeed, a certain smell of animals, dead or alive, about my mother's family. Her brother became a butcher like his father, and opened his own shop in Preston. Her mother, the butcher's widow, spent her last years at the end of a terrace next to a slaughter-house, and on my annual visits to her, I would sometimes hear the beasts bellowing and bumping up against the kitchen wall. My mother's elder sister married a carter, one of the very last of his calling in the area, and there were cousins, too, on my grandmother's side, who farmed near Kirkcudbright on the Scottish side of the Solway.

It was to the house of one of these cousins, my godmother, known to me as Auntie Pop – I cannot imagine what her real name can have been! – that I was taken for a holiday during the years of the War, when I was not more than three or four. My Auntie Pop had done well for herself by marrying a Captain Stanhope of the Merchant Navy, and she lived, not at the farm, but in a large villa, bolt upright, all by itself, on the banks of the estuary of the Dee. Any memories I still have of the villa and garden, the railway embankment and the mudflats, must come from a slightly later visit – if not from the pages of Dorothy Sayers's detective novel, *The Five Red Herrings,* in which, or so I have persuaded myself, the villa becomes the house where the murderer lived.

The one memory drawn without question from that first visit is far more fantastic than anything in Dorothy Sayers, and for years I refused to credit it. I remember, then, or think I remember, that I had tea with a duchess. As if I were emerging from a black mist I find myself in a carriage full of women, driving across a long bridge with much water beneath. Somehow I am led from the carriage into a house and up dark stairs. There, in a small room, beside a small fire, a tiny old woman, bunched up like Queen Victoria, leans forward in her chair, nodding metronomically, down-up, down-up, as if her neck were on rockers. The whole scene is packed-tight and scaled-down, an Old Master on a postage stamp, as if everything had to be reduced in size to fit it into my small head. Though the season must surely have been summer, it all seems dusky, darkly-shadowed, the figures high-lighted and haloed in the flickers of the fire. After more than fifty years time has not rubbed out that picture. Yet, for most of those years, I refused to credit it.

Then, round about 1955, my godmother, then a very old woman, visited Millom and came to see me. And I asked if there were any truth in the duchess.

"Oh yes," she said. "Only she was a countess – the Countess of Selkirk. We used to go to Gatehouse-of-Fleet to see her, over the Dee Bridge. And that summer we took you and Edie." – My mother's name was Edith Maud Mary. – "And I remember that Edie just couldn't get over the thought of meeting a real live countess. She was so excited. She talked about it for weeks."

And, of course, she talked about it to me. For my mother, as I'm told, was a gentle person. If the word did not carry a sneer, I would be tempted to say "genteel". To her, a countess must have seemed to belong to an almost mythical order of creatures. There was no snobbery about this. You can be snobbish about being friends with the Vicar but not about knowing a mermaid or a gryphon. Anyway, the very few people who have talked about her to me – my father rarely mentioned her after her death – have all assured me that she was of an exceptionally sweet disposition, with not the least taint of envy or uppishness. To present her son to the countess was like presenting him to the Bishop to be confirmed into a state of grace and gentlemanliness.

She had never been really at home with the cows and sheep and horses which were the everyday companions of the rest of her family. Before she married she had trained as a dress-maker, which was about the most ladylike occupation that was open at that time to a girl of her upbringing. Her ideas of gentlehood were, of course, long out of date, even in 1919, for she had spent the first twenty-one years of her life in the reign of Queen Victoria, and I doubt if her outlook had changed very much in the eighteen years since the Queen died. My father's certainly had not. He used to say that he always found it odd to have to sing "God Save the King."

My parents were married, just after the beginning of this century, in St. George's Church, Millom, and lived for a time in the old village of Holborn Hill which was then just beginning to turn into the residential part of Millom. Here their first child was born and died only six months later. They called him Harold, and when strangers sometimes ask me if I'm related to Harold Nicolson, I reply that he was my brother. The following year my father took over the shop in St. George's Terrace and soon he and my mother moved into the house behind it. I feel that I have lived at this address since even before I was born.

It cannot have been easy for my parents in those first years behind the shop. There was no bathroom, of course, and no hot water. My father had an unshakeable distrust of gas cookers so that, though there was a small gas-ring to boil a kettle, all the cooking had to be done on the old iron range in the cramped room we called the back kitchen. Personal washing was at a cold tap in the sink; the family wash was in a huge built-in copper that had to be fired and stoked from the bottom like the furnace of an old steam-engine. All this was taken for granted by my parents, without thought of complaint, since it was the normal lot of everyone they knew. Indeed, even to his death in 1954, my father looked on tapped hot water as an up-to-date luxury he could justly boast about.

If, however, I rightly understand certain faintly remembered hints and innuendoes, there was a sadness in my mother's life during that Edwardian decade because of the death of her first child. She waited for seven years before a second child came, by which time she was already middle-aged, and my father, three years older than her, was settled down in his groove, the day-by-day revolving routine of shop and home. Then, on the 8th of January 1914, when I was, perhaps unexpectedly, born, I turned out to be a sickly child, with not much chance of living even as long as my brother. And when, after all, I did manage to survive those first six months, the War broke over us, with all its privations and hazards, making it a struggle to bring up even a healthy child. My father was convinced that most of the illnesses of my youth and early manhood were due, primarily, to the "war bread".

So it is not surprising that I was coddled as a child, fussed over by

17

middle-aged and elderly women, my mother, my aunt, my grand-mother. I was lagged in layers of clothing like a water-pipe protected from frost. Young women were paid small fees to wheel me out in my pram, and there are still some elderly ladies in Millom who claim to have had that honour. Even the dog was taught to stand guard over my push-chair when the few square inches of me that were not muffled and scarfed out of sight were allowed to take the air. The dog, indeed, and my father were the only male creatures I can recall from those first four years, though most of the time the dog was confined to his box in the wash-house and my father to his shop, sent to Coventry by the intense Trade Unionism of the women. As for other children, I can recall none of either sex. For I was not encouraged to play with other children; I was not allowed out into the street; I was cossetted, comforted, protected, and I grew up, as I could hardly help growing up, pale, timid, dependent, self-absorbed and rather girlish – one of my early photographs shows me with a short skirt, like a kilt, and long curls. I never had a chance to grow up rough, tough, noisy and untidy like an ordinary boy, and I do not in the least regret it.

What I thought and felt about my mother is now quite unknown to me. What she thought about me can be guessed from the evidence of one photograph. It is by Hargreaves of Dalton-in-Furness, and must belong to my fifth year, probably to the autumn of 1918. At this time the most popular work of art in all England was Sir John Millais's portrait of his grandson blowing bubbles, which had entered every home on post-cards, on calendars, and, above all, as an advertisement for Pear's Soap. The faintly epicene, brown-silk-clad boy became part of the folk-mythology of early Twentieth-Century England. So the photographer persuaded my mother to allow me to pose in the manner of the picture.

I was wearing a white sailor suit, with bare knees, white ankle socks and black pumps. I was perched on a wooden bench or table, shaped and painted to resemble a bridge. I was made to cross my legs, was given a clay pipe and a small white basin, was told to stare at a point about two feet above the camera. All this from the evidence of the photograph itself. But memory also recalls one item on its own account, for I know that the basin felt very cold against my bare knees and I set up a great howl about it, until the photographer tore off a piece of newspaper and set it between the basin and my bare skin. A scrap of the paper protrudes in the photograph to prove the truth of my story.

There I sit, not so much myself as a child in a middle-aged woman's fantasy – cherubic, dreamy-eyed, surprisingly round-faced considering what was to be my later bill of health. I am gazing upwards, with hypnotised attention at a huge soap bubble which, in fact, was not there, being painted in afterwards by the photographer. Yet, to my mother, that bubble was perhaps more real than anything else in the picture – the hopes of twenty-five years of girlhood and young womanhood floating off into what at last seemed a predictable future. It was fortunate that she did not live to see the bubble burst.

At my mother's death my father was left stunned and bewildered. The child had to be looked after; the shop had to be kept going – that was about all he could really grasp. To help to tackle the immediate problem, my grandmother – Grandma Cornthwaite, as I called her – came to look after us. I was moved into the big double bed in the middle room with my father, while my grandmother set herself up in my old small back bedroom. I fancy that my father regarded this only as a temporary measure, but before long my mother's family began to take us over altogether. My grandmother clearly felt that she was settled in St. George's Terrace for the rest of her life. My Aunt Lizzie, with whom she had been living before she came to us, assumed the position of general adviser, inspector, unofficial godmother and taker for walks. My Uncle George, who much approved of the new arrangement so far as my grandmother was concerned, played his part by taking me with him on his horse-drawn lorry as he went about his carter's business of shifting furniture and delivering goods for the local shops. Sometimes he would let me hold the reins on those stretches where the horse knew the road as well as he did, though never on the journey back, when, about two miles from home, the horse would sense stable and feed and set off" in race-winning trot, with the heavy lorry banging and skidding behind it along the empty road.

Everyone, in fact, took pity on the poor little lad and everyone expected his poor little father to live a kind of posthumous existence, dedicated to the memory of his wife and to his duty towards his wife's son. I dare say that my father himself saw it rather like that in the first shock of bereavement, for, during the summer that followed, he took me on what really amounted to a memorial pilgrimage. We went first of all to my mother's cousin at Kirkcudbright, and then, by Shap from Carlisle, to her brother at Preston. (It was the only time I have ever crossed Shap by train and, alas, I can remember nothing whatever about it.)

Of Kirkcudbright, however, I *can* remember something – the railway at the back of the garden and the wild strawberries on the embankment, but, above all, I remember that the children of the town went barefoot, and, in particular, that one little girl came, barefoot, each day to the house to deliver the milk. There was a long cinder path leading through the back garden, and, after she had come through the back gate, she would walk along the side of the path, keeping to the grass edging on the margin of the cultivated soil. But, when she came level with the door, she had to cross the full width of the path, and I can still see her feet picking their way among the cinders, snuffling a little before she trusted her weight to them, the toes clawing cautiously round each pumicey lump. My Auntie Pop told me that in Kirkcudbright the bakers kneaded their bread with their bare feet, and, to this day, I don't know whether to believe her or not.

Preston yielded three memories, markers on the way out of infancy. I was taken to my first film, my first play, my first museum. The film was *Little Lord Fauntleroy* with Mary Pickford playing a dual role, of woman and boy – a fact which, when it was explained to me, puzzled me greatly. Indeed, I was puzzled by the whole idea of the film, and worked out a theory that the actors were really performing at the back of the stage in front of a bright light and that what we saw was their shadows. I was good at theories from the first. It was not very long after this that I told my father that I knew what the stars were: they were made of the gas burned in street lamps. After all, the lamps were burning nearly all night and the gas must go somewhere.

The play was a melodrama of sex and martyrdom called *The Sign of the Cross,* about a Roman soldier in love with a Christian maiden who was going to be thrown to the lions. I think my knowledge of the plot must have come from some later acquaintance with the play, but the sight of the Roman chasing the girl all around the stage was exciting enough to remain in my mind, even though I understood very little of it. The Museum, however, remains in my mind precisely because I did not understand. We were passing through a room where Greek and Roman statues stood about the floor. I pointed to one of them.

"Why has that gentleman got a leaf there?" I asked.

The question was whispered round from mouth to mouth, giving rise to much giggling and nudging and furtive glances at the other people in the gallery. I was aware of a susurration of suppressed mirth, about two feet above my head. They fobbed me off with some answer but I was not deceived. There was obviously some joke in the air that I was not supposed to know about and I suspected that the joke was rather at my expense. I never asked a question of that sort again.

It is round about my sixth or seventh year that our house first begins to take on a clear outline in my memory. The address was significant, St. George's Terrace, for it took its name from the church, built in 1877, the sign of Millom's claim to be recognised as a new community. Before that, it was not so much a town as an improvisation. Thirty years earlier it had been only a marshy, muddy, sand-and-shingle peninsula, moored like a raft between the mouth of the River Duddon and the Irish Sea. Millom existed then neither in fact nor in name. When iron ore first began to be mined at Hodbarrow, in the 1850s, the cottages for the first miners were built at the old village of Holborn Hill, nearly two miles away from the mines, and the station, when the railway first came, was called Holborn Hill. But with the opening of the Ironworks in 1867, streets of black-slate houses began to be shovelled together on the marshy fields as fast as the builders could cart the stone from the quarries. Suddenly the two or three ironmasters who were responsible for it, began to realise that they were watching the growth of a new town. They decided, first of all, that it must have a new name. "Duddonville" and "Lonsdaletown" were considered, but "Millom" was chosen because the town lay in the outer periphery of the estates of the old Millom Castle, which stands, some miles away, at the foot of the hills.

Next they needed a church, so the new parish of St. George's was budded off the former country parish centred on the Old Church beside the castle. Having got their parish, they chose a site: a seventy-foot-high, smooth, clay gumboil of a hill – a glacial drumlin, in fact – among open fields about quarter of a mile from most of the houses. The setting is superb. On its low, isolated hill, St. George's is the most conspicuous church in the Lake District, the only spire, except for All Saints, Cockermouth, that is not dwarfed by neighbouring fells. From the shore, from the hills, from all along the Lancashire side of the Duddon Estuary, and even, if you know where to look for it, from a point on Kirkstone Pass, St. George's steeple spikes up against the sky, graceful as a larch tree and bold as Blackpool Tower. 332, the number of

"There is a green hill" in the old *Hymns Ancient and Modern,* was, by a happy mnemonic, the telephone number of the Vicarage.

But the building of the church, and the opening of a new railway bridge, threw the whole town on to the wrong foot. Till then, most of the houses had sprung up close to the Ironworks, like a British settlement round a Roman fort, but now the builders began to raise their eyes to the slopes of the church hill. St. George's Terrace runs right up this slope, and for a long time I believed that it was called a "terrace" because it was built on the side of a hill like the terraced vineyards in Italy. Not until years later did I discover that a terrace of houses was what we called a "row". "We live in The Terrace," we would say, taking St. George's for granted, and, as a small boy, I felt the address was much superior to the streets and roads of the older part of the town.

Certainly, when it was built, The Terrace was equally sure of its superiority as the first residential road in what was then almost a suburban area. The houses were built of brick, for one thing, and brick was felt to be far more respectable than the local stone. And each house had its own garden in front, about the size of a large hearth-rug, surrounded by a two-foot wall, topped with freestone, which threw the black soil into everlasting shade. What can have grown behind those walls I can scarcely even guess, for, by the time I was a boy, only three of them were left, their soil buried ankle-deep under dank, sooty pebbles. Now there is only one. Every other house has lost its wall, its garden and its little bay-window, and the garden space has been enclosed into a shop-front. For, as I said, the building of the church upset the plan of the town, which soon began to reassemble round a new focus, so that, by my time, what was to have been a superior residential area had become the main shopping centre.

The effect, so far as I was concerned, was to push my childhood into the back of the house. Our shop, like the others, had been made by knocking down the indoor wall between the lobby and the front parlour. The old vestibule door had then been set back, almost to the foot of the stairs, and, immediately inside this, a door opened into the middle room which we called the dining room. I write all this in the past tense but, structurally, it is scarcely altered to this day. From the middle room a door led into the back kitchen and another from thence to the scullery or wash-house, so that these rooms, while each kept a separate function, were really a kind of corridor, and, except in cold weather, the doors between were nearly always open.

This, for a year or so, was my entire world. The middle room comes the more clearly into view. I remember the gas-brackets, on either side of the fire-place, each with a glass globe like a goldfish bowl. I remember the red plush curtains, hung from a rail at the top of the door, which automatically swished backwards and forwards as you opened or closed the door; the chairs, stiff as pews, with arms of turned wood, upholstered in a dark khaki corduroy that zithered like a comb when you ran your fingernail along it; the rectangular Edwardian over-mantel, one large mirror fitted with a dozen struts and ledges, with little niches and shelves, where, as before a shrine, could be displayed a whole generation's votive offerings of photographs and shells. It was in this room that I played on the oilcloth, being much addicted to dolls and tin tea-sets and other unmanly toys.

Here, too, I began my literary education. For one day, some months before I was ready for school, my grandmother and my Aunt Lizzie started to teach me my letters. They had no alphabet book or cards or blocks, but made do, instead, with the illuminated capital letters at the head of each paragraph in *Home Notes*, the monthly in-set in the St. George's Parish Magazine. Large Gothic letters, they were, much curled and crocketted and seriffed, printed in red and decorated with twining bindweed or honeysuckle and with a little cherub's head peeping over the middle stroke of the "E". Even today, I have to think for a moment or two before I can spot the letter under the embellishment, yet soon I was recognising the "T"s and "D"s and "P"s, and calling out their names to my grandmother's delighted nods. In her younger days, as I was to find out later on, it was not everyone who learned even that much.

The back kitchen and the old wash-house were once entirely separate, but one of the previous owner-occupiers had been a chemist who needed extra space for his pharmacy, so he had knocked a new door in the wall and enlarged the wash-house by adding a corrugated iron roof and sides and a long horizontal window, till the room looked more like an outsize potting shed than part of the house. In my grandmother's days the place was almost as Mr. Dixon, the chemist, had left it. In one corner was the built-in, brick boiler for wash-day, covered on the other days of the week by an unpainted wooden lid like a vast straw hat with a handle instead of a bow. Beside it was the one cold tap and the old slop-stone, a rectangular, horse-trough-like basin, only about three inches deep, made of some coarse brown earthenware that weathered under soap and water to what looked like petrified potted meat. And, alongside the window, was the huge bare table, solid as a stone altar, which remained there until it disintegrated into sawdust and woodworm only a few years ago. It was here, in summer, that I painted and scissored and pasted and fretsawed until, eventually, exercise books and homework claimed the whole of the evenings.

But already I am beginning to over-load my infancy with recollections of a later date. In fact, from my fifth year to my eighth, these two back rooms are almost entirely obscured by the presence of my grandmother. She was only a little woman yet she seemed to overcrowd the house. In figure she resembled Mrs. Noah, constructed like a wooden skittle of solid spheres and cylinders – a round-ended cylinder for the base, a large sphere for the middle and a smaller sphere for the top. She wore nothing but black, hooked-and-eyed and laced in at the waist and bulging upwards in a solid curve from middle to top. So much did this seem to me to be the standard shape of a woman that I don't think it was until I was about twelve that I felt any curiosity as to the cause of the bulge.

My grandmother lived a very sedentary life, rarely moving outside an area of a few square yards during the whole course of the day. Yet she managed to be unceasingly active like a tense, irritable, continually fidgety, broody hen. All the morning she was on her knees, scrubbing the oilcloth or polishing the furniture; or bending down, blacking the kitchen-range; or sitting backwards, out of the window sill, her lap wedged safe by the lower window frame, her arms working like a two-legged spider, chamois-leathering the outer panes. All afternoon she was baking – sleeves rolled up, hands dipping deep into the flour, kneading and scooping and trowelling as if she were digging a hole big enough to plant an oak. All round her was an ironmonger's shop of tins and floured plates and basins waiting ready for dough and pie-crust and plain cake-mix. "Plain" was a word of great moral approval in my grandmother's vocabulary. The fire in the kitchen-range was stoked to furnace heat; the dog was banished to the yard and my father to the shop; and I staggered apprehensively among the obstacle-course of pots and pans, being invited, at one moment, to taste, and having my head snapped off at the next.

Yet, when my grandmother was in one of her baking moods or went on the rampage with duster and floorcloth, there was still one retreat which I shared with the dog – the back yard, which, in those days, was a little Eden, a Garden Enclosed. Even today I survey it with a complacency equal to that of any Duke of Devonshire looking out from Chatsworth. It was divided by a wall from the yard of the next house, and as this was the office of a solicitor who lived fifteen miles away at Kirkby-in-Furness and as his upstairs windows were blocked up with cardboard and dirt, our yard was never overlooked from that side. (By an odd coincidence, the next door house is once again occupied by a solicitor, a friend of mine from almost the days of which I am now writing, though, his profession being what it is, I had better make it clear that he does clean his windows.)

Nor were we overlooked from over the way, for, on the opposite side of the back street, the one building was the windowless wall-end of Christopher Walmsley's grocer's shop. Elsewhere, seen from the yard, there was only the sky, broken by two telephone poles and a pulley for a washing-line. And when you looked out of the window of the little back bedroom, you could see the explanation of this emptiness, for the whole length of the other side of the street was taken up by the wall of the playground of the old Millom Secondary School, almost every corner of which could be kept under watch from our house.

Today that playground – now, a playground without a school – comprises the whole extent of our back-of-the-house view, and has done so since 1921, when the County Education Committee bought one of the wooden huts which had housed Belgian refugees during the War, and set it up in the schoolyard as a school gymnasium. Many times my father said he hoped it might be burned down in the night, but, in fact, it survived him and survived the school and still stands blocking our view as the Meeting Hall of the Girl Guides.

But if I climb up to our second storey and push my head out of the fanlight in the back attic, I can look over the roof of the hut and see what I used to see: the St. George's Hall, the scraggy, slag-clogged fields, the old mines at Hodbarrow, the hills of Low Furness across the estuary, and – though this is now partly obscured by the slag bank that was laid down in the late 'Twenties – Barrow-in-Furness, with its cranes and spires and its Town Hall Clock. My father was very proud of that view. On a clear day, he used to say, you could hear the clock strike.

But Barrow and the view and even the school playground were all too far away to mean much to me at that age. I rarely ventured out into the street, which, apart from the (to me) nearly grown-up Secondary School boys and girls, was empty of children. I stayed behind the back door, teasing the dog, trotting up and down the slate slabs that paved the yard or dibbling a fork into the few clods of soil we called our garden. For when my father first came to The Terrace, he had up-ended a row of black tiles, cemented them to the slate paving about a foot away from the wall, and filled in the space between tiles and wall with soil dug up with a pen-knife on his walks around the fields and carried home carefully in brown paper bags. In this he had planted a few cuttings of Virginia Creeper and half a dozen wild ferns, fixed hoses spraying the yard with green. I have, from time to time, added more male and lady ferns from the hedges of Hodbarrow so that I cannot now be sure which is which, though one Royal Fern is certainly older than me. Of the Creeper there can be no doubts, for it has routed its black arteries all over the walls, giving them the withered, sinewy look of an old coal miner's arms. Every year, out of less soil than would be needed to fill a couple of beer barrels, it processes a huge cubic-footage of sappy and tangled leaf. Neglect it for one season, and you would have to hack your way through the yard as through a jungle. This very spring, nearing its seventieth year, it still flourishes fresh enough to induce a blackbird to build and lay.

Here I lived my childhood's last, almost childless years in a kind of court mourning which everyone was conscious of but no-one referred to. I was the little boy whose mother was never to be mentioned. And then, one Sunday, my grandmother and my aunt decided that it was time for me to be taken to church. It was in 1919, at one of the Children's Services, held once a month, to which several hundred Sunday Scholars marched up from St. George's Hall. That must have been the first time I smelt the peculiar St. George's smell of those days – the effect of warm stagnant air seeping up from hot pipes among dusty hassocks in a completely unventilated space. It may have been the smell as much as the hush which numbed and scared me. I looked up at the window near our pew and saw angels. In window after window there were angels – green, brown, petunia-red, with palms, with banners, with scrolls, with all manner of musical instruments. Some hung or floated with gigantic, hideously-foreshortened wings, in the volcanic smoke of glass that the afternoon sun had not yet reached. The voices of the children, wailing up in Mrs. Alexander's most sanctimonious misery, wheezed and spluttered as if the painted smoke had got into their lungs.

I began to whimper and my grandmother quickly shushed and hustled me out of the church.

"What was the matter, son?" she asked me as soon as we were safely out of ear-shot in the porch.

"It was the angels," I said. "They made me think of my mammy."

I have had no further use for angels from that day to this.

CHAPTER TWO

My father had not much use for angels either.

If was now the main word in his religion: "The good Lord – if there is one; Adam – if there was such a person; Heaven – if there is such a place." The *if* was his protection. He did not want to look far into the future – the immediate prospect was enough to worry about. He saw his son, mollycoddled by an ageing grandmother, barred off from other children and not allowed to grow up. He saw himself housekeepered for ever by a conscientious but cantankerous mother-in-law, the house in perpetual mourning, the memory of his dead wife stacked on the mantelpiece beside the clock. I think he must have hoped that when I started school I would somehow begin to solve my own problem. What he cannot have guessed is that I would help him to solve *his*.

Had my mother lived, I was to have started school at Easter, 1919, but because of her death and my illness, school was postponed until either the autumn of 1919 or the spring of the next year – I am not sure which. There was a choice of two schools: Lapstone Road in the new part of industrial Millom, known as Newtown, and Holborn Hill in the older part. Each was about the same distance from home, but Lapstone Road was regarded as the rougher of the two and my mother had long made up her mind that Holborn Hill was to be the school for me.

The three hundred yards which I walked four times a day – up The Terrace and over the railway bridge – took me into a world far removed from the one I knew. Holborn Hill itself was a two-hundred-foot-high outcrop of Lake District rock separated from the clay hill of St. George's by the dell or level along which ran the railway line. The school lay at the very foot of the hill in a little corrie hacked out of the slope, and on two sides the rock towered above it higher than the roof – from the road you could look down through the windows into the classrooms, which caused much distraction at times. On a third side, the land slid away dead flat into the cricket field, beyond which there was not a brick between you and the Irish Sea.

The school was built of stone quarried out of the hill on which it stood – a black Silurian slate with grey "Kirkby round heads" from Furness on the roof, and blocks of mouldering St. Bees sandstone for doorsteps and window sills. In style it was midway between an almshouse and a prison. The roofs were narrow and steep and always meeting others at right-angles to themselves, so that the roof-scape was slotted and compartmented with buttresses, gable-ends and chimney-shafts, making dozens of gutters and nooks where a cap could be thrown and remain lost for ever, though still visible to anyone from the road. Everywhere there were ventilators, pushing up like periscopes, and porches with high-peaked roofs and pointed-arch doorways. The windows were vaguely in the manner of Early English lancets as copied by a boy with a fretsaw, more wood than glass, letting in the least possible light and air. And above the whole building, from the porch of the boys' school, there spiked up a vinegar-bottle turret for the school bell.

Boys', Girls' and Infants' schools were all under the one roof, disposed round a central quadrangle, which may originally have been left open to the sky, like a prison exercise yard, though long before my day it had been roofed over with glass and partitioned into two class-rooms, one for the boys and one for the girls. The windows in the party-walls were all blacked out so that the boys could not look at the girls and vice versa. All of this is now pulled down, except, oddly enough, for the Infants' school block, which has been patched and rough-cast and shored up to make a rehearsal room for the Amateur Operatic Society.

If I remember anything at all of my first day, it must surely be the smell. It was what biologists call "a culture" – a smell forced and fertilised as in a hot-house, airless, humid, fungoid, an attar of unwashed clothes, unwashed hair, sweat, spittle and mucus, adulterated with chalk-dust, stale ink and fumes from the coke stove. For six years that smell was as much part of school as the desks and the blackboard. Later on, when I went to see my old headmaster, I nearly retched as the air belched out at me from the porch, but as a boy, I wore the smell for five days a week, putting it on each morning as you put on an overcoat for the day's work.

I began my education under the care of a little girl about two years older than me – Vera, daughter of the chemist who had formerly owned our house and shop. She led me to and from school for about a week and looked after me in the playground shared by both infants and girls and divided from that of the boys by a low wall and a decorated iron fence. After that I had to manage on my own.

I soon found that there were more things to be adjusted to than just the smell. We sat in twos on benches at low, flat desks, very like a short-legged table, and the girl on the desk immediately in front of me had bright red hair. And one day I saw three or four head-lice grope and blunder out of that hair, crawl across the nape and burrow back into the hair again. Now for six years I had been scrubbed and towelled and laundered until I was conditioned to regard even a speck of dirt as a moral fault. "And make me a clean boy, oh Lord, Amen" might have been my nightly prayer. Yet what I felt was not the disgust that my grandmother would have expected me to feel: it was more a kind of detached, observant fascination. I had not even known that head-lice, or any other kind of lice, existed. But I had been sent to school to learn.

In a class photograph taken about this time I can be seen in a white, fresh-washed, buttoned-to-the-shoulder jersey, leaning against a wall as if to put the greatest space between me and my neighbour. Yet this, I am sure, is merely a sign of my shyness, so far as the other children were concerned. I was not worried about the teachers – theirs was, on the whole, the predictable behaviour of adults to which I had already learned to adapt myself. But I was painfully aware of the mockery of my contemporaries. More than once in the early weeks I peed in my pants because I did not dare to hold up my hand to ask to be excused.

"Please, Miss, Norman Nicholson's wet himself again," my helpful neighbour pointed out. I'm sure it must have been a girl.

The third or fourth time this happened I was led by my class teacher to the headmistress, a Miss Sharpe, who was also head of the Girls' school and came into our school only once or twice a day. She was tall, thin, straight as a stick, with her brown hair wound so tightly round her long bobbin of a head that she looked like a bullrush in a collar and tie. She had about the most severe eye I have ever had to meet, but I don't think that she was particularly severe with me on that occasion. In fact, she showed more patience and more understanding than my class teacher.

"Why didn't you ask to leave the room?" she queried.

"Because I don't know what to say."

But of course I did know what to say: it was just that I was scared at the thought of saying it.

This kind of predicament did not often recur. Soon I had learned to control my bladder so that I did not need to be excused. And I learned also that to any self-respecting boy the lavatory was the piss-house, and that this building had a special, male privacy about it, shunted up against the wall by the old orchard, round the back of the school and seventy or eighty yards from the school porch. I remember that once, when I had moved up into the second or third class, a small boy was pushed through the door from the next room, his eyes bulging, his face red as a tomato, his hands pressed against his flies, holding his little cock as if he were trying to stem a leak in a Dutch dyke. He hobbled desperately across the floor, quite oblivious of the shushed crescendo of giggles, and managed to wriggle out of the door on the other side. I doubt if he got any further than the porch.

Before long I came to realise that for certain functions and parts of the body, there was one vocabulary for home and one for school, but I did not think of this second vocabulary as being bad language or swearing. Nobody, at that time, would have persuaded me to say "damn", but "cock" and "piss" and the rest were part of the normal playground conversation. When, years later, I first read *Lady Chatterley's Lover*, I did not feel that I was being liberated into a new frankness of manhood: I felt that I was returning to baby-talk.

In the same way, I was soon taking "biddies" as much for granted as the sparrows in the gutters, so that before long my grandmother found it necessary to put my head down over a newspaper and rake a small toothcomb through my hair with as much vigour as if she were trying to scrape old paint off the yard door. The lice split open with a gratifying pop as she cracked them with her finger nail.

The old pre-industrial village of Holborn Hill – the Ship Inn, a smithy, a few cottages, a couple of farms – straddled right across the hill from which it took its name and became the Main Street of the oldest part of Millom. The first miners' rows were strung along the line of the road, and then, later, more imposing houses were built out at right-angles for the mine managers, the council officials, the prosperous shopkeepers of the rapidly growing town. But it began as a village and Holborn Hill School began and, to some extent, remained a village school. There were gaps between the houses. Whether a boy came from one of the more decrepit old terraces or from the bourgeois villas, he could look out from his windows, either at the front or the back, on to kitchen gardens, allotments, old orchards, hen-huts and hen-runs or open fields. Holborn Hill boys behaved like country boys. They did not play in the back streets, they rampaged out into the woods and fields and hills. They bird-nested and blackberried; they gathered tadpoles in jamjars and mushrooms in handkerchiefs; they hacked sticks out of the hedges, stole apples from the orchards, whacked the cows round the fields and scooped caves and dug-outs in the old sand pits.

I lived too far away in Newtown to join in such pursuits. Yet I was not entirely locked off from the country, for the country came into the school with us. We had a day's holiday in early autumn at the time of the local agricultural show; we had a week's holiday in October at the time of the potato-picking. Some of the boys took days off at hay-time or harvest; and we all wore an oak leaf on:

> "Royal Oak Day
> The twenty-fourth of May" –

though I doubt if any of us knew that we were honouring King Charles. Nearly all the farmers and farm labourers within two or three miles sent their children to Holborn Hill, and there were in my own class two farmers' sons, both of whom grew up to take over their fathers' farms.

I shared a desk with one of them at one time, and it happened that, in a drawing lesson, we were asked to draw a turnip from memory. Nearly all of us, including me, drew exactly the same shape – a fat football with an aspidistra growing out of it. But when I glanced at Harry's drawing on the desk beside me, I noticed that he had given his leaves a wavy shape, more like a fern than an aspidistra. I had no great respect for his artistic talent, but it struck me that he probably did know what a turnip looked like. So I made my leaves wavy, too. Afterwards I was commended for my observation – a commendation entirely justified – and my drawing was held up to the class as an example and encourage-ment. Harry's drawing was not commended: I think the teacher suspected that he had copied from me.

I had found school something of a disappointment. Having learned my letters in less than a week, I expected to be able to learn to read in not much longer. I was soon bored with sand-trays and coloured tiles and counting frames. Yet learn to read I did, for when I was ill in bed at the age of seven, our doctor lent me Ruskin's *King of the Golden River*, and I most certainly read *that*. It is, in fact, the first book I can actually remember having read at all and John Ruskin, of all people, is the first author to have written his name on my mind.

Perhaps what mattered most about the Infants' school was just that for five hours a day it took me away from the back kitchen. Though, to begin with, it was largely a case of going from one cramped, stuffy room to another. I was scarely aware of what lay in between. So that, until it was pointed out to me by the daughter of the Methodist minister, I completely failed to notice that, in the Market Square, on one side of the Market Hall and the clock tower, there was an umbrella shop kept by Charlie Norman, while, on the other side, was a newsagent's shop kept by the Misses Nicholson, so that the name "Norman-Nicholson" was painted in large letters right across the principal place in the town. And when I crossed the railway bridge, always I am told at a trot, I could have seen, if I had chosen to look, the long, serrated skyline of the Lake District, peak after peak, from Scafell Pike round to the hills of Westmorland. I even knew the name of at least one of the peaks, yet it was all quite vague in my mind. Once my father called me into the shop to introduce me to a customer.

"This is Mr. Vincent," he said. "He comes from Coniston."

"Oh," I said, as I shook hands, "are you Coniston Old Man?"

For round about this time a new awareness of the shop began to come to me. In the first place, it was very small and reduced even further in size on three sides by a foot-deep lining of shelves. It was also dark, lit at night only by hanging gas globes. The back of the shop window was built up more than half-way to the ceiling and in the gap my father hung mufflers and scarves, blocking out nearly all the daylight that filtered through the plate glass. There was a polished mahogany counter, its graining faintly empurpled with ink; there was my father's till and his shelf of a desk, hidden from the customers by a standing mirror; and there was a cane chair so tall that I had to be lifted on to it and would sit there with my feet dangling far above the floor. Above all, there was a sort of worsted stuffiness about the shop, the smell of bales of cloth and men's caps and socks and jerseys, and, in winter, the smell of the oil stove. I did not much like the shop, but from it I gained my first awareness of the street outside, and the topography of that street was to shape – and had already shaped – my life more than I could understand at the time.

Our house was the third from the bottom in St. George's Terrace, number fourteen of sixteen original houses. The end and corner shop was that of Miss Crellin, milliner, and next door to us Sandham's, fruit and vegetables – at least this was so until 1920, though a change was soon to take place which was to be of tremendous consequence to me. On the other side of us, beyond Dickinson, the solicitor, were four or five more shops, interspersed with as yet unconverted houses – Sheward's, watchmaker and tobacconist, who were there before my father came into The Terrace and are still there today; Withington, an outfitter, like my father; Mr. Cartwright's saddler's shop, a dark grotto where fungoid strips of leather hung down from the roof like stalactites; and on up to John Mills and Sons' huge furniture shop and Mr. Benson's high-class groceries which continued the line of The Terrace and also made up one side of the Market Square.

On the other side of the street there was only one building belonging exclusively to The Terrace: Miss Danson's bakery, café and commercial hotel, which also housed Mr. Bennett, the barber who gave me my first haircut. Further up the street was Mr. Dixon, the chemist, whose corner shop had a frontage on the Square, while below Danson's, and divided from it by the back street along which I went to school, was the corner building which housed the Post Office. It also housed the business premises of Seth Slater, tailor, immediately opposite us, while the Slater family lived upstairs above the shop.

Mr. Slater's had been about the largest tailoring establishment in Millom in the days when ready-made clothes were worn only by working men and everyone else had their suits made locally. On a photograph taken around the turn of the century, the first-storey walls are to be seen emblazoned with trade slogans, painted in bold capitals and enclosed in embossed plaster frames:

S. SLATER
TAILOR AND BREECHES
MAKER
LADIES COSTUMIER

---

and:

> DOCTOR JAEGER'S
> PURE WOOL
> UNDERCLOTHING

even the chimney carried the sign:

> SLATER
> TAILOR
> & C

By my time the slogans were painted out and the facade had taken on a sober brown, appropriate both to the cautious sobriety of post-Victorian Millom and to Mr. Slater's own growing status in the town – for by now he was a respected and influential leader of the Wesleyan Methodist Church. But there was a strangeness about the Slater home which I could not altogether understand. For one thing I had never been inside it. Nor, so far as I then knew, had my father, my mother or my grandmother. Again, though Mr. and Mrs. Slater had five or six children – of whom the youngest, John, was exactly my age – I met none of them as a child. From our sitting room window I could see them moving about in their house, but they never came into our back street and rarely appeared even in their own. By the time I had reached the age of seven, I had got to know John since, like me, he attended Holborn Hill School, but at first we established no more than a distant official recognition between the families.

One incident stays clear in my mind. It was on one of the rare days, other than Christmas and New Year, when my grandmother and I went into the sitting room above the shop. The time was late afternoon, just before tea, and I was standing near the window, looking through one of the volumes of a garish and expensive *History of the World War* which my father had bought from a door-to-door salesman who had persuaded him that "it would be very useful for the little boy's education". Some illustration in the book – a photograph or drawing of a battleship or aeroplane or shell-burst or trench warfare – must have caught my fancy, and, as I noticed that John Slater was looking out from his window on the opposite side of the street, I held up my picture against the glass so that he might see it. The street was narrow enough for anyone with good eyesight even to read the caption if it were printed in large enough letters. John nodded and promptly held up a picture in a book *he* was reading. I turned over a page or two and then held up another picture. John responded. And soon we found ourselves caught up in a competition, a long-drawn-out, cross-street tennis rally, in which neither side was ready to concede a point. I had the advantage of the twelve volumes, but before long John's mother and his sister, Rosa, were busy searching for illustrated books and magazines to keep the pot boiling. Next, John's elder brother, Charlie, arrived back from the Secondary School and began tearing down the pictures from the walls and carrying them one after the other to the window. We were all so excited in the end that none of us so much as looked at what the other held up for display, but merely nodded a formal acknowledgement and slapped our own next offering up against the glass.

How it came to an end I cannot remember. Presumably either my grandmother lost patience or the walls of the Slater house were entirely stripped of pictures. But I'm sure that we all enjoyed it because we knew we were breaking a ban, like German and English soldiers fraternising across No Man's Land on Christmas Day. For by that time even I knew what the ban was; knew that for twenty years my father and Mr. Slater had faced one another across the street and not once exchanged a word.

This is how it had all come about.

When Mr. Slater had first set up business in Millom, it was not in St. George's Terrace, but in the older part of the town, at Main Street, Holborn Hill, in what later became the office and printing shop of *The Millom Gazette*. And it was there somewhere round about 1890 that my father was bound to him as apprentice.

My grandmother, like many girls brought up to the hard labour of the land, had a great respect for the retail trade and its ancillaries. Another of her sons, my Uncle Bob, was apprenticed to the other main clothes-maker of the town, Elias-My-Tailor, who counted among his apprentices a boy who was later to become three times Mayor of Bournemouth, a little Dick Whittington of the clothing trade.

But I don't think my father really trained as a tailor. He learned to sew, of course, and to carry out minor alterations, making buttonholes or lengthening sleeves and trousers. He learned how to press and clean and smarten up a suit, and how to measure and fit on. He knew how to judge the quality of cloth. When he draped his tape measure round his neck and stuck a hedgehog of pins in his lapel and took a wedge of marking chalk in his hand, he had the air of a professional, of a man who knew exactly how it should be done. But his ambition from the beginning had been in the retail side of the business, in the shop rather than the sewing room, and by the time Mr. Slater moved into new premises at the foot of the railway bridge, my father had become his chief counter assistant, well capable of attending to customers and dealing with commercial travellers and of supervising the running of the shop and the ordering of stock.

From Mr. Slater, straight as a pew-back in character and carriage, my father learned to take his work as seriously as the members of the Young Men's Bible Class were expected to take their religion. To be punctual, to accept long hours, to be ready to oblige – these became moral duties. Similar rules applied to personal appearance. His boots were scrubbed and rubbed and polished till they shone like black lacquer; he put on a clean starched collar every morning; he sponged and brushed his jacket, pressed his trousers, trimmed every fraying edge, sewed on every button – and all this in a house where the ten sons slept four to six in a room, and every penny had to be accounted for.

I have a photograph of the Bridge shop, togged up with flags for the Diamond Jubilee of Queen Victoria, with my father, in a straw hat, standing in front of the window in a group of postmen and telegraph boys. For Mr. Slater was not just a tailor, he was also Sub-Postmaster, and the Post Office, though it was housed in a separate shop, moved about with him as he shifted from one area of the town to another. My father, indeed, for the rest of his life, tended to look on the Post Office as a normal sub-section of tailoring, and he always watched over the postmen and Post Office clerks as if they were his own employees. In fact, one of his jobs, in later years, after Mr. Slater's death, was that of measuring the postmen and telegraph boys for their official uniform, for which service he received a regulation fee of three old pence.

One rather odd reminder of those days remained in our house for many years – a large collection of used Victorian and Edwardian stamps, English and colonial, of all values, packed away in the square, white cardboard collar boxes we used for storing things. How they came into his hands I cannot think – unless the postmen tore the stamps off the letters and parcels before they delivered them! My father gave them to me when I first began to show an interest in stamps. Alas, he gave them too soon. For I thought they looked untidy and trimmed off all the perforation with a pair of scissors. Undamaged, they would by now have been worth hundreds of pounds.

It was while he was at the shop on the Bridge that my father began to act as Mr. Slater's country representative. Once or twice a week he would go out with a pack of samples on his back to call at farms and cottages, making measurements and taking orders, He would go by train to one of the little country stations – Green Road, Foxfield or Broughton-in-Furness – and then continue by foot along the Duddon Valley or up among the fells. Many a time, he told me, he went to Swinside, passing the great Megalithic stone circle that used to be called Sunken Kirk, and not once did he climb over the stile to go and look at the stones. To have done so would have been wasting his employer's time, and, anyway, he felt no curiosity. Few people in those days thought of walking the fells for pleasure, and my father regarded his journeys purely as a matter of business, keeping strictly and con-scientiously to the shortest and most convenient route. But at the same time he got to know the lanes and moorland tracks in all weathers, and made friends with the farming families, some of whom remained his customers for life.

When, in my schooldays, I read H.G.Wells's *Kipps*, I recognised it as in some ways a portrait of my father. He was about Kipps's build, short, slight, rather flat-chested and, because of the immensely high collars he always wore as a young man, he looked as if he had a perpetual stiff neck. His face was pale and wore much of the time a surprised, rather scared look. Yet, in fact, he knew very well how to take care of himself and would not be put upon by anybody. Those were the days when the country gentry were still held in exaggerated respect, at least by the shopkeepers of the town, and the boys were expected to raise their caps and bow when Squire Lewthwaite drove down the street. This my father resolutely refused to do.

"I'm kowtowing to nobody," he told Mr. Slater.

He even carried his independence into church and would not join in the "bobbing and bowing" introduced by a High Church vicar's wife. I have many a time seen him straighten himself at the beginning of the Creed, tighten the muscles of his neck and maintain a deliberate level stare at the pulpit, while the rest of the congregation bowed the knee at the name of Jesus. He did not say a word about this to me, yet I often noticed a look of satisfaction come over his face, and I thought that once again he had quietly shown the Church of England that he would kowtow to nobody.

For nearly fifteen years my father worked for Mr. Slater, and all that time he was planning, scheming, getting to know the commercial travellers, and putting by every week out of his small wages. Then, in 1905, by which time both tailor's shop and Post Office were established in St. George's Terrace, he saw his opportunity. A shop at Number Fourteen, immediately opposite Mr. Slater's, fell vacant. He applied for it, sank all his savings in it, used his friendship with the commercial travellers to procure an account with the wholesalers, and set up a business which lasted until he died in 1954. Some of Mr. Slater's customers crossed the road with him; some stayed with the old firm. Chris Walmsley, who owned the grocery shop behind us, found himself in some embarrassment. He was a colleague of Mr. Slater's at the Wesleyan Chapel and did not want to cause him any offence. He spoke to my father one day.

"I'd like to patronise you now and again, Joe," he said, "but you know how it is. So maybe if I'm wanting something from the shop, I can come in by the back door, and then the old man won't know."

My father squared up the whole five foot five of him:

"If you can't do business with me at the front door," he said, "you needn't do business with me at all."

There is one shop in The Terrace which I have scarcely mentioned so far – Number Fifteen, next door to us on the lower slopes. For round about 1919 or'20, Sandham, the greengrocer, left the premises, which were then re-let, the house separately, and the shop to J. T. Hall, a piano and music firm from Whitehaven, whose local manager was Miss Sobey, a local-born young lady – she would have been indignant at any other description – who was well known as pianist and accompanist at concerts, children's parties, church services and the like. The shop sold sheet music, violin strings, gramophone records and, now and again, a banjo or a mandolin, but all this was mere window dressing. The real business was that of selling the upright pianos which stood, opposite the fire-place, in the little front room of every house with a proper self-respect. The sales averaged perhaps two or three a month, so that most of the time Miss Sobey had nothing whatever to do, except on the days when she went about collecting the monthly payments. Her friends often came to see her in the shop, to learn the gossip and the popular tunes of the day, but for many hours Miss Sobey was on her own, and when she had read the morning's letter from J. T. Hall and made up her small accounts and dusted the pianos and looked out of the window for half an hour, she would sit down at one of the pianos and play. She played nearly all day. She played the songs of the early 1920s, the ballads of the Edwardians. She played hymns, polkas, Gilbert and Sullivan overtures, extracts from *The Merry Widow or Messiah, Henry VIII* dances and "Pomp and Circumstance" marches, and simplified versions of Beethoven and Chopin from albums of selected classics for the drawing room. She played – though, of course, I could not appreciate it at the time – with enormous pleasure and a natural panache, always bright, lively, rhythmic. She played sometimes with little regard for what the composer actually wrote, but with a great deal of intuitive invention, decorating the line of the tune with little *arpeggios* which she called "twiddly bits", as if she were hanging tinsel on a Christmas tree. There may have been times when she did not let her left hand know what her right hand was doing, but she could play accurately enough when she wanted to. It was just that she mostly could not be bothered. The most derogatory remark she could make of another pianist was that "she just plays the notes".

So now, for hour after hour, our house was filled with music – loud in the shop, fainter in the dining room, and dying away altogether in the back kitchen. Up to that time, I had heard a piano only at school; I don't think I had heard a gramophone at all; while practically the only other music which had reached my ears was that of the Salvation Army and the other brass bands in the street. So I was drawn as to a Pied Piper. Soon, on Saturday mornings and on school holidays, I was regularly finding my way to the next door shop, sitting on one of the piano stools, letting the music drench me like a glittering fountain. And when the music stopped I began to talk.

I have called Miss Sobey a "young lady", though, at that time, she was about thirty-four. She had striking, dark, deeply-set eyes, arched over by wide, dark eyebrows, giving her a pensive, introspective, almost pre-Raphaelite look. But the rest of her face had been drawn by quite a different kind of artist, for there was a sharpness about her features, even a touch of caricature, that hinted at impatience. Sometimes, coming upon her suddenly, you surprised a faint redness about her nose and mouth, as if she'd just been crying and was annoyed with herself about it. She belonged, I supposed, to that generation of women whose potential husbands had been lost in the War, though I don't think that this had worried her greatly. The War – in the memories of her old age – was seen, not as a time of privation, but as one of dances, concerts, bazaars, a time when she was always in demand. She had been adored and petted by her parents and admired by everyone for her piano playing, and throughout her twenties she seems to have looked on marriage and home-keeping and child-rearing mainly as the resort of women who were not capable of anything better. But now that the War was over and a dull post-War slump was hanging around the streets like a sour, dirty mist, the thought of an old-maidish middle-age was beginning to drift vaguely round the piano stools in her empty shop. Already the streets seemed to be full of what she called "bits of kids", by which she meant anybody ten or even five years younger than herself.

To me, however, she was still young, lively, laughing, welcoming. She even seemed, as I thought, fashionable, in her V-neck blouses and long strings of wooden beads – a complete contrast to all the other women I came in contact with. The contrast intrigued me and I must have talked about it.

"What is your grandma doing?" she asked me one afternoon.

"Working," I said.

"She's always working," she said. "I can't think what she finds to do all day with only you and your father to look after."

It struck me as an interesting comment and I repeated it later on to my grandmother. I can still feel my astonishment at her reaction. She went pale as floured dough. Her old jaw wobbled with anger. She managed to keep her hands off me, she struggled hard to keep patience, but her voice croaked and gasped as if she were fighting an attack of asthma.

"You can tell her", she said, the sounds wheezing out like wind from a puncture, "that I'm working to keep the house nice for you, and baking your pies and your cakes and all the things you like. You can just tell her that."

So, of course, since it seemed a reasonable request, I told her, and she half-laughed in an embarrassed way and said no more about it. And for my part the correspondence was closed. But the next day my father came rushing into the house, his tight little body rumbling with rage.

"What have you been saying to your grandma about Miss Sobey?" he asked.

I could not, at first, remember having said anything, but, when at last I realised what he was talking about, I started to explain. He would not listen.

"You come and apologise," he said.

He seized me by the neck of my jersey and shoved me through the door into the shop. I was scared and bewildered, but I had no feeling of guilt. I had said nothing I should not have said, and, anyway, I could not understand why my father thought that it had anything to do with him.

Miss Sobey stood there, silent and embarrassed.

"Apologise to her," said my father.

I began to feel a humiliating and debilitating sense of shame flooding through me, as if, once again, I had wet my pants in public.

"Go on," said my father, angry and insistent. "Apologise to her. Tell her you're sorry."

I had no idea what on earth I was to be sorry for, but in some dim way I felt that I had offended one of the three or four people in the world I least wanted to offend. I burst out hopelessly into noisy tears.

I can just manage to remember that Miss Sobey twisted awkwardly on her feet, pulling at her beads. I suppose in a different way this must have been nearly as distressing to her as it was to me.

"I didn't want this," she said.

"He's got to apologise," said my father, in a tone of Shylock demanding his pound of flesh.

"No," said Miss Sobey, "let it go. I didn't want any of this."

She pushed me through the open door into the street and let me run back to my grandmother.

And I suppose my father did let it go, for I can remember nothing more being said about it. But now I began to realise that a new situation had come about. It was a situation, as I saw it, that lay entirely between my grandmother and Miss Sobey. My father's part in it – or so it seemed in the beginning – was merely that of an umpire. It was a situation which was to be dealt with by pretending that it was not there. I no longer mentioned Miss Sobey to my grandmother; I did not mention my grandmother to Miss Sobey. My grandmother did not ask me where I had been when I came in from the shop, though she always asked me where I had been when I came in by the back door. And Miss Sobey did not ask me if my grandmother knew where I was.

Gradually I began to realise that my father was not just neutral, as I had thought previously; that there was a tenseness between him and my grandmother which was somehow connected with Miss Sobey. There was, I imagine, an agreement not to say anything in front of the boy, but the boy could not help but notice that nothing was being said. I remember vividly how, one day, my father laid the housekeeping money on the top of the desk and my grandmother did not pick it up. From my three foot of height, I looked up at a silence as menacing as a quarrel. My father pointed threateningly to the money. There was another clashing silence, and then my grandmother picked up the notes, pushed them in her purse and almost jerked her fat little body out of the room.

It must have been very soon after this that, one Sunday morning, my father took me for a walk along the footpath through Dowbiggin's Fields which border the town on the south-west. The place is scarcely altered to this day – a footpath with a ditch and a hedge on the left, and on the right, pastureland swelling slowly up to the top of the hill, from which the steeple of St. George's church sticks up like the spike on a German general's helmet. As we walked, my father explained to me that Grandma Cornthwaite was going to leave us and live in another house, that he and I were to spend the next six months with Grandma Nicholson, at my father's old home, and that, when we returned to The Terrace next spring, Miss Sobey was to come and look after us. He may also have mentioned that he was going to marry Miss Sobey, but this was not of sufficient interest for me to have remembered it. I learned, years later, that my father was intensely nervous about this interview with me.

"It was worse", he said, "than proposing."

He need not have worried. Far from being upset by the prospect, I was delighted. The idea of spending Christmas at Grandma Nicholson's was exciting in itself, and I was even more pleased to know that Miss Sobey would no longer be a person whose name could not be mentioned in the back kitchen. About my Grandma Cornthwaite's future I had, I fear, very little thought at all. It did not occur to me that we were condemning her to a disappointed, lonely and penurious old age.

CHAPTER THREE

THE human landscape of the Lake District, its character and ver-
nacular, did not really begin to take shape and sound until the Vikings
arrived there in the ninth and tenth centuries. Those Vikings were not
pure-bred Norse: they came from Ireland or the Isle of Man rather than
from Norway or Iceland. Many of them had Irish mothers and Irish
wives; some of them may have had Irish grandmothers. The Cumberland Vikings, in fact, were the product of the cross-fertilisation of two
cultures, Viking and Celtic, and in Gosforth churchyard, a few miles
from the Cumberland coast, you can see the two strains pictured side
by side – Norse myths and the Christian crucifixion carved into the
same sandstone. I might almost take that cross as my family totem pole,
for a thousand years later, my grandparents repeated the same cross-
fertilising process.

My grandfather came from Cartmel in the little limestone peninsula
that juts out into Morecambe Bay between the estuaries of the Leven
and the Kent. *His* father was a farmer at Hard Crag, a quarter of a mile
or so from the village, and that is about all I know of him. But Nicholson is a common and long-established name in Cumberland, while
the map of the Cartmel district is overprinted with Scandinavian
place-names: Haverthwaite, Allithwaite, Finsthwaite, Rusland, Grize-
daie, Witherslack and so on. No landscape in Cumbria evokes more
reminders of the sagas than this triangle of the old Lancashire, balanced
upside down above the Sands, so that – though some believe we are a
branch of the Clan Nicholson of the Isle of Lewis – I am convinced
that my grandfather's family came from the true Viking stock of the
dales.

My grandmother, on the other hand, was half Irish. Her father, whose name was Brennan, had come from Ireland in the first half of the nineteenth century to be gamekeeper at the Dallam Tower, near Milnthorpe, on that short stretch of Morecambe Bay where Westmorland staked a right-of-way to the sea. Dallam was once a pele tower but the building of my grandmother's day and ours is a handsome, seven-bay house of about 1720, coolly contemplating a deer park that slides down to the Bela, just before the river wriggles into the marsh as into a sleeve. Today a metalled road runs from the Lower Lodge Gate, past the front of the House and out by the Upper Lodge, where, in the 1840s, my grandmother was born. She herself was employed as a maid in the House but her father and her brothers all worked on the estate. Dallam Tower, at that time, was a great centre for the gentlemanly killing of beast and bird. Beagles and otter hounds were kennelled in the grounds, and the foxhounds often met there, while there were pheasants and partridge to be shot in the park, and geese and snipe and all the other wild fowl on the immense sands and mosses of the Bay.

It was a great centre for poaching, too, and what with the poachers, the deer, the dogs and the game, my great-grandfather must have had a busy time of it by day and by night. I don't know if any of his descendants still live around Dallam, but descendants of the deer and the game certainly do, and I like to think, when I see a pheasant in the park, that it may be in the direct line, egg to egg, from those my great-grandfather hatched out under the farmyard hens. And as, to my mind, the man who preserves the game has as much right to the land as the man who kills it, I feel entitled to claim Dallam Tower as my ancestral home.

Dallam is only about seven miles from Cartmel, in a straight line, but that line is cut by the estuary of the River Kent, with its long slats of sea and sand and the soggy acreage of the Foulshaw Mosses on the opposite shore. In the mid-nineteenth century, this was one of the loneliest places in Westmorland. On the east, the park was moated in by the Bela, all the way from the Lodge Gates to Beetham; on the west, thick woods swambled up the steepish limestone slopes, curtaining off the winds from the sea. After dark, when you stepped outside the Lodge Gates, you stared out on nothing: either the marshes were muffled up in mist, or you looked across to the black emptiness of the Witherslack and Newton fells. Only on the clearest nights could you see the faint household glimmers from Low and Middle Foulshaw; and though they were no more than a mile away, you could reach them only after a nearly ten-mile walk round by the Levens and the Gilpin Bridges, followed by a groping, sludgy trudge along lanes that in winter turned into ankle-deep, unflowing ditches and canals.

It is a wonder to me that my grandparents were able to meet at all. Yet meet they did – I suppose at some fair, or sheep sale or dale sports – and in the middle 'sixties, they were married at Cartmel Priory, the cathedral of Southern Cumbria, with its two limestone towers, one set diagonally across and within the other, looking as if God had designed them when He was still a baby, playing with a box of bricks. The fact that they were married there, rather than at my grandmother's parish church at Beetham, suggests that the Brennan family were not enthusiastic about the match. I don't think the Nicholsons approved either. They may even have thought that my grandfather was marrying beneath him. At any rate, he left his father's farm and went with his wife to Flookburgh, about two miles away, where their eldest son, my Uncle Bill, was born. Maybe the early birth of that child explains some of the disapproval. My grandmother also used to tell a story about a dispute over a will, mentioning a member of a family still well known in the Cartmel area: "That was the old bugger that was to blame," she would say. What truth there was in all this I have now no way of knowing, but my grandfather certainly seems to have had nothing more to do with his own family after his marriage, and all my ancestral memories come down to me from my grandmother's side, from Dallam and the Brennans and all the uncles and great-uncles scattered about farms and parklands from Kendal to Bay Horse.

In any case, my grandfather did not stay long at Flookburgh, but left the land, like thousands more, to find work on the industrial coast, then at the beginning of its great nineteenth-century expansion. He went first to the booming new town of Barrow-in-Furness, and then, after a few months, across the Duddon to Millom. Millom began to develop rather later than most of the iron towns of Furness and West Cumberland, and, at the beginning of the 'sixties, was still no more than a few cottages and pubs haphazardly spilled around the first small iron-ore mines, the enormous potentiality of which had not yet been realised. It had no church, no schools, no real streets, not even a name. But by the time my grandfather came, in 1867, the mines were yielding over a hundred thousand tons of ore a year, the Ironworks were smelting it, and the first streets were mushrooming up on the marshy fields round about. Millom was already looking like at least the beginnings of a town.

But not enough to suit my grandmother. She followed her husband a few weeks later, bringing my Uncle Bill and her few bundles of belongings with her. They crossed from Askam-in-Furness by horse and cart over the estuary of the Duddon at low tide, following the old cross-sands route. And when she saw what Millom looked like – the ramshackle furnaces, the grey anthills of slag, the half-made-up roads, the tight, huddled, half-grown streets with slate walls still raw from the quarry – she told the carter to turn the horse's head round and go back. But the tide had turned and she had to stay.

My grandfather soon found employment at the Ironworks, and, because of his farming experience and knowledge of horses, he was put in charge of the haulage, which was then, of course, except for the railway, quite literally a matter of horse-power. It is said that he helped to cart the hundreds of tons of gravel and stone needed to lay the new road from the Ironworks to a town centre that had not yet been built. He must have been a man of resource and natural ability, for before long he was taken into the productive side of the works, and eventually became one of the furnace foremen. My father once told me that, when the Millom firm opened new furnaces at Askam, my grandfather was offered the job of works manager. He refused, my father told me, "because he was no scholar".

My father paused for a moment, and his face took on something of the dreamy, wistful, end-of-century look that stares out of photographs of him as a young man.

"If he had accepted", he added, "it would have made a difference to us."

By "us", he meant himself and his brothers, and there were plenty of them to have made a difference to. Like that first crossing of Viking and Celtic strains in the ninth century, my grandparents' union was notably fruitful, for in fifteen or sixteen years, my grandmother gave birth to thirteen more sons – fourteen boys altogether, and not a girl among them. Three of them died in infancy; one died in his teens; but the oilier ten were all reared in a small terrace house in Lord Street, part of the new dwelling-house property planned when Millom first realised it was going to be a town. "Planned" is hardly the word. The builders simply bought up the almost-worthless reedy pastures beside the new slag bank, and then slapped down rows of houses side by side, as if they were laying railway sleepers. The stone of the walls came from the quarries of Holborn Hill; the slates of the roofs came from Kirkby-in-Furness; the kitchen ranges and little cast-iron fire-places were brought in by train. Eventually, as one street was laid beside the other, the new town took the shape of a gridiron – seven or eight short parallel streets, split down the middle by King Street and bounded, on the side away from the Ironworks, by Queen Street. (Street names of the time were almost invariably royal, patriotic or aristocratic: King Street, Queen Street, Albert Street, Victoria Street, Crown Street, Wellington Street, Nelson Street, Earl Street, Duke Street, Lonsdale Road.) As the population grew, the builders bought more job-lots of land and extended the parallel lines away from the Ironworks, in blocks of ten or twelve houses, as required. And as the town prospered, so the houses improved and became larger, with three instead of two storeys, with front doors that opened into a lobby instead of straight into the parlour, and with, here and there, little apron-gardens between house and road. To walk today along Albert Street, the longest of them all, from the slag bank to the railway sidings, is to walk through fifty or sixty years of social change.

It was towards the end of this period that the Nicholsons moved themselves upwards about half a mile and half a class, and when I remember her, my grandmother was living in what she still thought of as the new house at the top end of Albert Street. She had lived in Millom for sixty years, and the move from Lord Street to Albert Street was the only one she ever made. I doubt if, in all those years, she slept more than one night or two away from her own home, and when she died, in 1928, *The Millom Gazette* said of her that she had never once travelled in a train.

For, whatever she may have thought of Millom when she first saw it, she was immensely proud to be a Millomite. She had seen the town grow out of almost nothing, its population doubling and then doubling again in ten years, and she felt like a pioneer opening up a new colony, writing the name of the Queen on an empty space in the map. When she first arrived, the only church in Millom was the lovely old parish church of Holy Trinity nearly two miles away, close to Millom Castle. The oldest of my uncles used to walk there every day, through the fields to the school beside the church, paying one penny a week for his education. But as soon as the new St. George's was built, my grandmother and grandfather switched their allegiance to the town church. My father, indeed, was born in January 1877, only four months before the consecration of the new church, and neighbours tried to persuade my grandmother to delay his baptism, so that he might be the first child to be christened in the new building. But, with the warning of three infant mortalities behind her, she decided not to wait.

So, from his baptism to his marriage, my father was a member of the St. George's congregation. My grandmother saw to that. She was not, as she said, what you would call a religious woman, but she was going to bring her sons up respectable if she had to knock respectability into them with a clothes brush.

St. George's seems to have been one of the most sought-after parishes of the Carlisle diocese at the end of the nineteenth century. Its stipend was not large, but Millom was a growing town, and the living was seen as a good stepping-off place for preferment. And those early vicars – remote and upper class as they must have seemed in their vast Victorian vicarage, surrounded by servants and gravestones – nevertheless had a conscience about the weekday needs of their parishioners. They built a Parish Hall, and founded the St. George's Men's Institute, which ran among much else, a Chess Club, a Debating Society, Roller Skating on Friday evenings, a Harriers' Club, and Junior and Senior Gymnastic Classes. That is where my father came in. He was a runner and a gymnast, winning prizes for cross-country and long-distance road walks, and demonstrating the manliness of the Low Church ethic on the horizontal bars and parallel bars, in human pyramids and among the criss-cross of Indian clubs and dumb-bells.

It was here, in the years before he opened his shop, that my father began to find his own small niche in the town. It was worth more to him than money. He became Secretary to the Gymnastic Class and its assistant instructor, and he began to arrange concerts, displays, sports days to raise funds for the Club, or to help pay off the debt on the Parish Hall. On 5th February 1903, there was a Rummage Sale, Promenade Concert and Ping-Pong Tournament. And on Pay-Monday Off, 4th July 1902, there was a Carnival and Gymkhana in the Cricket Field, with Grand Cycle Parade and Athletic Sports, Maypole Dance and Comic Cricket Match. (Pay-Monday Off was an institution peculiar, so far as I know, to the Hodbarrow Mines, where the men were paid on a Monday morning, once a month, and took the rest of the day off to celebrate.) At such events the Junior Gymnastic Class would parade the town in a decorated cart, with the boys displayed, like goods in a shop window, in three layers, and all wearing white shirts, white shorts and long, black cotton stockings. My father preserved many programmes and photographs of such occasions, and in all the photographs he stands at the side, in a collar so high that he could scarcely swallow, very pale, very serious and very proud. When he resigned from the secretaryship he received a gold watch, elegantly engraved with scrolled and ornamented letters:

"Presented to
JOSEPH NICHOLSON
by the members of
ST. GEORGE'S GYM, MILLOM
as a token of APPRECIATION for
HIS 8 YEARS GOOD WORK
as HON: SEC:
April 29   04."

He wore it until he died and it always kept – and still keeps – good time. He would have been surprised if it hadn't. My father asked no wonders of himself nor of anyone else. But he expected us to keep good time.

In those years round the turn of the century, my grandmother was in the full pride and power of motherhood. All ten of her surviving sons were still at home, though three of them were soon to leave Millom, and three more – my father, my Uncle Jim and my Uncle Jack, who was killed at the mines before I was born – were soon to be married.

Over the remaining four my grandmother held a matriarchal rule until the day she died. There is a photograph of her, round about 1918, taken with my cousins, Billy and David, sons of Uncle Jim. She sits in a chair in Sammy Lamb's studio, her back straighter than the back of the chair, her black skirts barrelled round legs splayed wide apart. One hand, clenched in emphasis, is pressed on one knee, and she glares steadily at the photographer, as if daring him to take the picture at all. Her grey hair is raked back from her forehead tight as a skull cap. Her large ears angle out like chimney cowls, and her lips are snapped to, leaving the mouth not enough play, it would seem, to speak let alone to smile. She was tall, bony, square-chested, so masculine that most men looked effeminate beside her. "Bring forth men children only," said Macbeth to his wife:

"For thy undaunted mettle should compose
Nothing but males."

He ought to have married my grandmother.

The days of her uprightness were over, however, when I came to know her, for, just beyond the bounds of my memory, she slipped on the slate flagstones outside her own front door and broke her hip. For a while she was very ill indeed.

"It's the beginning of the end," said the doctor.

But for me it was just the beginning. For when I went to live at Albert Street in the autumn of 1921, she was a cripple, moving about awkwardly with a long wooden crutch under her armpit, and her free hand grasping at the furniture or the banisters of the stairs.

Sometimes she would hobble into the backyard or would stand at the front door and look out into the street, but I do not think she went out of the house again until she left it in her coffin. She governed the home, now, from the back kitchen, sitting all day on a plain, cushion-less wooden sofa, with the crutch lying beside her, ready to hand. All the work had to be done by a niece, Annie Brennan, from Dallam, who had come to Millom as a young girl, and lived at the same address until she died in 1973.

But Grandma Nicholson still ran the house. She would sit almost on top of the small kitchen range – the large range was in the middle room – and supervise the cooking like a five-star chef. My Uncle Bill, who was a blacksmith at the Ironworks, had forged for her a whole series of iron pokers and long-handled ladles and hooks, so that without shifting from her seat, she could poke the fire or lift the kettle from the grate and adjust the lids of the saucepans and stir the contents.

The back kitchen was so small that she could stretch out and touch all four walls of it with the ferrule of her crutch, almost without moving from her sofa. In the mornings, she would be there in the same place, peeling potatoes into a bucket of water or shelling peas into a bowl, while Annie prepared the meal at the table. Each chopping up or mixing or larding or peppering or sugaring had to be handed across the room for my grandmother's inspection before it was put into the oven or on to the gas. The sink or slopstone was even closer to hand than the table, and it was here that we queued up to wash in the mornings, with a little hot water from the kettle for my uncles to shave with, and a splash of it for me, in winter, to take the chill off the cold tap. I was given a bath once a week in front of the fire, after much boiling of kettles and pans, but the whole process took so much trouble and so disturbed the household that, for the others, I think it can only have taken place before important events, such as going to the doctor or getting married. The weekly household wash, of course, was carried out in the wash-house, entered only from the back yard, but when the washing was over, there was the ironing to be done and the airing, all under my grandmother's eye. A clothes line was strung across the kitchen just below the ceiling, from which, like a man-o'-war dressed over all, there flew a perpetual bunting of shirts, vests, underpants and socks. After a wash-day, the kitchen steamed like a boiler house, and all the rest of the week the air tasted of warm flannel.

The back room, in fact, was the kitchen, the laundry, the workshop, the bathroom, the dynamo of the house, and, so far as I was concerned, my grandmother was always there. In all the six months that I lived in that house, I cannot once remember her to have been in bed when the rest of us were up. Even when seven of us sat down together, in the middle room, for Sunday dinner, my grandmother, who could not easily sit at the table, ate in her usual place on her own. The room seemed empty without her, and none of us spoke. Even the linnet in its cage beside the window was silent. And, as soon as the meal was over, I would be back in the little back kitchen again, helping my grandmother to her cup of tea.

There was a toughness about her that I had not met at St. George's Terrace. She could flick out a rebuke like a whip crack, and when she banged her crutch on the floor in annoyance, the whole of Albert Street shook with apprehension. Yet I was not afraid of her. I trusted her roughness as I did not trust the smarmy smiles and head – pattings of some of my other grandmother's friends. For one thing, I was seven, now, nearly eight in fact, and she did not treat me as if I were only six. I had left the Infants' and entered the Boys' School to find out that life was rowdier, dirtier and a lot funnier than I had ever dared tell my Grandma Cornthwaite. But I could tell my Grandma Nicholson. She knew all about little boys. She knew what they did and how they talked, and if I used a bit too much of that talk, she might come a crack across my bottom with her crutch, but she would not be shocked or threaten to tell my father. My grandmother was not in the habit of going to fathers when she had trouble with boys – it was more likely that fathers would come to her.

I remember once reciting to her the words of a song which, according to the boys at school, had been sung the very night before at a concert in the Palace. It was one of those now-you-see-it-now-you-don't pieces, where the mildly naughty rhyme word is replaced at the last moment by some unctuous phrase. I hesitated before daring to repeat it, but risked it in the end:

"All the girlies in the town
Wear pretty short frocks,
And when the slightest breeze comes down
You can nearly see their –
BEAUTIFUL EVENING STAR."

My grandmother laughed and laughed and laughed, but it was not until years later that I realised what she was laughing at!

At the time when I stayed in Albert Street, my grandmother had been living among streets and slag banks for fifty-five years, yet she was still essentially a country woman. She never lost the Westmorland clack in her speech. Her mind was stock-full of memories of the country life; her conversation sounded at times like an encyclopaedia of country cracks and crackers. When my Uncle Jim played the flute it was "worse than the tune the old cow died of"; when my father was preoccupied with his forthcoming marriage, he was "scratting about like an old hen that wants to lay an egg and can't find where to put it". And once, when I came in soaking wet from a sudden shower, my grandmother enquired sharply:

"Why didn't you take your coat?"

"I thought it was going to be fine."

"You know what Thought did?" she asked.

"No."

"Messed in the bed and thought it was the midden."

Sometimes she would talk about her girlhood at Dallam – of the pet lamb she had reared, of the hounds, the deer, the walk through the Rookery. She told me also of the Treacle Mines at Ulpha in the Duddon Valley, and of the Fairy Steps, a little staircase cut in the limestone cliff near Beetham. It did not occur to me to doubt the Mines, though I was somewhat dubious about the fairies.

Sometimes, too, she would talk to her caged linnet with a tenderness she never permitted herself to show to any of her sons once they were past the age of twenty months.

"Pretty Dick," she would say, "pretty, pretty, chuck, chuck, pretty Dick!"

The bird itself was a sadly drab, dull, brown creature, cooped up in a space not much bigger than a biscuit tin. Unlike its species in the wild, it never put on the cocky spring plumage, the russets and terracottas, but spent the whole year disguised as a female. Yet, whenever my grandmother walked into the room, the song would begin to trickle and trill from its throat until it filled the whole dark house with the sound of hay-time and hedges.

"We never fed our cats at Dallam," she once said to me. "We just tellt 'em: H'away into the garden and catch yoursel' a bird."

It was a sign of her country upbringing that she was quite content to be what she was and gave no thought to climbing the social ladder. For society, in the Westmorland she knew, had changed very little in two centuries. There was no harm in bettering yourself if you could manage it, but, on the whole, you were likely to be what your great-grandfather or your great-grandmother had been many years before, and it was no use pretending anything else. The fact, therefore, that the four sons who stayed at home had bettered themselves rather less than those who had left did not in any way lessen my grandmother's pride in them. They had been good sons to her and that was what she asked. She had given them all the same start, opening for each, on the day of his birth, a penny-a-week insurance policy which she had paid until he started work, after which it was his own responsibility. As for her married sons, they were welcome to come and see her whenever they liked, but what they made of their lives after they left home was their wives' concern, not hers.

The four bachelor sons who remained her concern included both her first born and her last. Uncle Bill, the eldest, was getting on for sixty when I knew him. By trade he was a blacksmith, working in the fitting shop at the Ironworks, where he forged small attachments and replacements to the machinery, though I think my grandmother always thought of him as working in an old-fashioned village smithy. Of all the males in Albert Street he was the kindest. I think the younger brothers found me something of an embarrassment in the house, needing too much hot water, and always sitting about reading.

"You want to get his nose out of them books, Joe," they would say to my father. "It's not good for the lad."

Later on, when my health broke down, they were certain that it was books that were to blame.

But my Uncle Bill seemed to take an almost grandfatherly pleasure in the company of the little boy, and every Saturday night he would go out to Bailiff's shop at the corner and buy me a chocolate fish or what we called a jelly-belly-baby. And he fashioned a boolie for me, at the Ironworks forge – an iron hoop, of about a foot in diameter, smaller than most, which you did not strike with a stick, like a girl's wooden hoop, but guided from behind with a little iron crook, held a few inches above the ground. That boolie was almost a vehicle to me, a means of transport, and I took my first expeditions into the country, as on a one-wheeled bicycle, running beside it to Haverigg or the Old Church or round The Knott.

The second brother, my Uncle Tom, was a silent, secretive, slow-moving gnome of a man, half-hiding behind his own moustache. He and my Uncle Jim had started work together, many years before, in the Boot and Shoe Department of the Millom Co-operative Society, but while Tom had been taken on as an apprentice cobbler, Jim had joined as a junior shop assistant, so that he had risen to be manager, though Tom was still a cobbler. Whenever I went into the Shoe Shop, it was my Uncle Jim who received me, chose the shoes for me to try on and ordered the assistants to take special care of this young man, now. I would sit with my foot on a stool – having made sure to put on clean socks before I went – and stare up at lofty walls, lined with shoe boxes and looking as if they were built of cardboard bricks. When my Grandma Cornthwaite had paid for the shoes – for it was she who, up till then, used to take me there – my uncle would put the money into a little wooden collecting box, suspended from a horizontal wire, like a cabin on a funicular railway. Then he'd draw back a kind of elastic catapult and send the box skimming along its wire, through a hole in the wall, away to the out-of-sight check-box. A minute later it would skim back again with the change, and all the time other little boxes were skimming through, backwards and forwards, from the Butcher's Department next door. I was so fascinated by all this hither and thither – like Bede's swallows flying in from the darkness and out into the dark again – that I could scarcely be bothered to notice if the new shoes fitted or not.

Then, when Grandma Cornthwaite had left with the shoes, my Uncle Jim led me behind the shop into the workroom to see my Uncle Tom.

It was like walking into a dark wood. From the ceiling and from all the walls hung long swathes and curls and tendrons of leather. You walked ankle-deep through leather shavings, as if through beech-mast or dead leaves, and the workmen sat at the benches, like the Seven Dwarfs, hammering, slicing, sewing, shaping. On each bench there was an open gas jet, flapping away, and all round were lasts and awls and scissors and nails. I could hardly see my Uncle Tom among the gloom and the smother, yet I was comfortably aware of his genial teasing.

When, a year or two later, we read *Julius Caesar* at school, I re-cognised the scene immediately:

"*Flavius:* Thou art a cobbler, art thou?
Second Citizen: Truly, sir, all that I live by is with the awl; I meddle with no tradesman's matters, nor women's matters, but with awl. I am, indeed, sir, a surgeon to old shoes; when they are in great danger, I re-cover them."

I did not find it very funny, but I recognised its authenticity. Shake-speare knew what he was talking about: he had met people like my Uncle Tom.

I doubt if he had met anyone like my Uncle Bob. Dickens might have met him, but not Shakespeare, for he was a shrunken, stunted product of an era much later than the sixteenth century. He was by far the smallest of the family; in fact, the skin of his head seemed too tight for his skull, so that the flesh was stretched to bursting point over the bones, which stuck out from his cheeks and his forehead, making him look rather like a monkey. He was agile as a monkey, too, and I never knew him to be ill. – He was killed, in the end, by being thrown off the pillion of a motor cycle, when he was visiting Uncle George in County Durham. – He had the sharpest temper of all the brothers, was continually pushing me out of his way, and could not bear to see me with a book. I sometimes wonder if his irritation with me may have been due partly to a certain jealousy towards my father. For, just as Tom and Jim had both been apprenticed to the shoe trade, so Bob and my father were apprenticed to the tailoring. And, again, while Tom had stuck to his last, Bob had stuck to his needle, working in Elias-My-Tailor's back room, with little hope of ever getting anywhere else. My grandmother told me that tailors sat cross-legged as they worked, perched on a thimble.

I looked doubtful.

"He had to have an extra big one specially made for him," she explained.

The baby of the family was Arnold, who, indeed, seemed not to be quite grown up, even when he was an old-age pensioner. He had served his time as a painter and paper-hanger, but, after the War, found a job at the Ironworks beside Bill. None of the brothers was out of work in 1921, for the post-War slump had not yet reached Millom, but soon afterwards the Ironworks went on short time, and Bill and Arnold were working only one week in two, or even three. As for Bob, his kind of rough, made-to-measure tailoring belonged to an age that was already dead, and soon Elias-My-Tailor closed down, and Bob found himself signing on at the Labour Exchange until the motor bike finally signed him off. Only my Uncle Tom kept his job until old age handed him his cards.

Arnold outlived all the brothers in Millom, including my father – Jim held out a bit longer, but spent his last years with my Cousin Donald, at Cleator Moor. So that I cannot really separate Arnold as I must have known him from the Arnold I knew much later. He was then and always like a big, clumsy lad, forever bumping into things, forever getting in other people's way, forever saying the wrong thing.

"When he opens his mouth, he puts his foot in it," said my grandmother.

But Arnold did not need to open his mouth. In fact, when he grew excited, which happened very easily, he became indistinct in his speech – "spluttering and splattering", my father used to call it – and then he would argue and contradict and blunder about, always getting the story wrong, always muddling his facts.

One night, just when I was beginning to get my work into print, he came up to the house with the news that he had got a job for me – £3 a week in the insurance. He had heard this chap in the pub saying that they wanted someone to take on a book – it was during the War, and all the usual agents were called up.

"And I told him that if he wanted a scholar, there wasn't nobody in Millom to touch you, and Stuart S. will bear me out" – mentioning an old school-teacher of mine.

"'Well, if he wants the job,' he says, 'I'll take him on,' he says. 'If he's like you tell me,' he says, 'he's what I'm looking for.' So all you've got to do is to go and ask for it and it's yours – three bloody pounds a week."

He bounced around the room, too excited to sit down, knocking papers off the table with the swing of his coat tails, and shouting and stammering as if he were cheering on a rioting mob. My stepmother, who never knew whether to laugh at him or be scared of him, cringed in the corner and looked apprehensively at the vases rocking on the mantelpiece. And when, finally, I managed to convince him that, It's very good of you, Arnold, but really I don't want to take on an insurance job just now, he went away as disappointed as if Yorkshire had been beaten by an innings.

For one of the most endearing things about him, so far as I was concerned, was his love of cricket, and his passionate support of the Millom team and Yorkshire. I remember how, after burying my Uncle Tom, the brothers walked down from St. George's churchyard to St. George's Terrace, and listened to the test match commentary on our wireless. It was the match in which Verity took fifteen Australian wickets in one day, and when the last wicket fell, Arnold leapt up from his chair, nearly knocking his head on the ceiling.

"HE'S OUT!" he shouted. "HE'S OUT."

And then, suddenly sobering:

"I wish poor old Tom could have lived to know about it. I wish he could."

His devotion to Yorkshire was well known, so that, on a Bank Holiday, if Lancashire were on top in the Roses Match, people would keep on slyly asking him if he knew how Yorkshire were doing. I once saw him come into the Millom field at the beginning of the second half of the match, and walk along the boundary, and, at every twenty yards or so, somebody would ask about Yorkshire. At last he could stand it no longer. He stopped and turned on the spectator.

"You bloody well know how the buggers are doing," he said, his voice squeaking with exasperation. "You don't bloody well need to ask me."

I cannot clearly remember the sleeping arrangements in the Albert Street house, but two, or maybe three, of the brothers shared the front bedroom, and the other one or two, as the case may be, must have slept in the attic with my father and me. It was a largish room, if you go by the square footage of the floor, but its roof sloped down like a tent, on either side, almost to skirting-board level, and the narrow, twisting stairs came right up in the middle, so that the floor had, as it were, a hole in it, railed off on each side by the banisters.

I slept in that room, sharing a double bed with my father, for six months, but I can remember little about it. The only room, apart from the kitchen, which stays clearly in my mind is the front parlour, which was rarely used except at funerals, rarely entered, indeed, except for dusting and polishing, and was dedicated to the memory of my Uncle Jack. Jack had been a cricketer. His picture hung on the wall, an enlarged tinted photograph. He stood in white flannels and black boots, with a cricket cap on his head and a cricket bat in his hand, posed in a firm and aggressive stance, and standing at a spot where – since I already had some knowledge of Millom cricket field – I knew no batsman ever would stand. He was a great hitter, my grandmother told me, and had once knocked a ball clean out of the field, across the railway sidings up against the wall of St. George's churchyard – the biggest hit, she said, ever made on the Millom ground.

He was even better known as a footballer, playing for the almost legendary Millom rugby team of the 1890s – "Triple winners of the Cumberland RUGBY UNION CUP, four times Champions of the NORTH WESTERN LEAGUE, and three times Runners Up: represented in the Cumberland County XV by twenty-nine players; in Internationals by two, in the North v South by three" – I quote from an article in the local paper, headed "Millom the Mighty". At one time Jack led the Millom Junior side, and the club distributed his photograph, printed on a cardboard shield, with the motto in an heraldic scroll:

> "PLAY UP   MILLOM A
>   NICHOLSON
>   CAPTAIN"

He was a member, too, of the team which was drawn at home to play one of the leading Yorkshire clubs in the earlier stages of the Rugby Cup. The story of this match was handed down in our family like a saga. With about three minutes to go in the second half, the visiting team was leading three-nil, when Sam Bucket, a famous Millom player of the time, took the ball about ten yards from the line and went over for a try. But the referee disallowed the try and ordered a scrum down.

My father's glasses used to sparkle with indignation as he told the story.

"It was a try," he said. "It was a clear try. And the score should have been at least a three-three draw, and, if he'd kicked the goal, we might have won."

The game was as vivid to him as if he could still see it – though, in fact, he had never seen it at all, for he had been busy in the shop, as always on a Saturday afternoon, on the day of the match. So that I did not take the story very seriously. Then, one day, when the match was already fifty years in the past, I was walking along the little village street of Holme in Westmorland, when an old man called to me over a garden wall.

"I hear you come from Millom," he said.

"Yes."

"And do you remember Sam Bucket?"

I did, for, remarried and bent with sciatica, he had brought himself into public notice by being confirmed into the Catholic Church at the age of over seventy.

Then the man in the garden began to talk of Millom rugby, and soon he was describing the same match which my father had so often told me about.

"It should have been at least a draw," he said. "The referee made a mistake. He thought it was a knock-on, but it should have been a try."

"But were you there?" I asked, wondering if this was somebody else who had not seen it. "Were you a spectator?"

"No, lad," he said. "I was the referee."

Much of this might have been forgotten had not my Uncle Jack enshrined himself for ever in my grandmother's memory by getting killed in an accident at the Hodbarrow Mines. It made him into a kind of war hero, a casualty on the Iron Front, the man who had given his life for his town. His body was brought up from below ground and taken to the old Hodbarrow Hospital at Steel Green, and a boy was sent to break the news to my grandmother. She did not see the corpse; I am not sure that she even attended the funeral. For there was one thing about my Uncle Jack that my grandmother had not told me. I knew that he had been a cricketer and a footballer and a miner, but I did not know that he had also been a husband, and that my grandmother had quarrelled with his wife. And this is how I found out about it.

Sometime in the late 'forties, I had a letter from Graham Sutton, a popular Cumberland novelist of that time, author of *Shepherd's Warning* and *Smoke Across the Fell*. Sutton, who was Cumbrian by birth and ancestry, always took great care over the background and historical details of his books, and he wrote, saying that he was at work on a story to be set in the early nineteenth century, in which a Cumberland young man was to join a troupe of strolling players and travel round the north of England. – It was eventually to be published as *North Star*.– Could I, he asked me, tell him of an inn in Millom where his troupe could have put up for the night and perhaps have practised in a barn.

Now there were two inns at the time in Millom – or in Holborn Hill, as it was then called: The Ship, which still stands today, and The Pilot, where the innkeeper provided the services of a boy to lead travellers across the Duddon Estuary by that same route over which my grandmother was to come to Millom fifty years later. In fact, instead of a painted sign, the inn carried a stone carved with a rhyme:

"William and Ann
    Barren live here
Who also sell
    Good Ale and Beer

1745

All ye who wish
    To cross ye Sand
Call here a Gide
    To your command"

The Pilot was pulled down in the 1890s, but the carved stone had been set in the wall of one of the terraced houses built on the same site, and I thought it might be a good idea to copy down the words and send them to Graham in case he might like to use them in his story. And, as I stood opposite the house with my notebook in my hand, one of the doors opened and an old man, his legs bent like a safety-pin, shambled across the road and began to talk to me.

After a while, he said:

"Are you coming in to see your auntie?"

"What auntie?" I asked.

"Your Auntie Annie."

"I haven't got an Auntie Annie," I said, thinking he was pulling my leg.

"My sister Annie is your auntie," he said. "She's your Uncle Jack's widow."

Knock at the door of any house in Millom, and the person who answers is quite likely to be your aunt.

So, towards the end of 1921, the winter and the dark began to close in on me. Yet everyone in the house tried hard to give me some kind of Christmas. The identity of Santa Claus had already been obligingly disclosed to me by my cousins, Billy and Donald, so there was no need to go through that farce, but my Christmas tree – a contraption of wire and green raffia, which folded up after use like an umbrella, to be stored away until the next year – was taken down to Albert Street, and, on Christmas Eve, my future stepmother called and presented me with a box of crackers like huge, over-dressed dolls, decked out in tinsel and crêpe paper. Now I hated crackers, though I was too polite to say so. I disliked the bang and, anyway, I wanted books. I grieved inwardly, too, that someone I admired so much should have so little understanding. After Miss Sobey had gone, my grandmother tried to console me.

"You should be right set up with them crackers," she said. "You're a proper lucky lad."

But I was not deceived. I knew quite well that she thought them a silly present and a waste of money, and for the first time, I began to sense something of what she thought about my father's second choice of a wife.

The disappointment did not last long, for, half an hour later, Christmas sprang up in the house like a cork popping out of a bottle, when the gas spluttered and went out, and we found a leak in the gas pipe, and no-one could come to mend it until the day after Boxing Day. The supply had to be turned off at the mains, and we spent the whole of Christmas by candle-light. Then my Christmas tree took pride of place. Instead of being lit only for a mere half hour while the gas was turned low during Christmas Day tea, it had now become the main illumination of the kitchen, the light shining in darkness. The dozen or so tiny candles sent a glimmer glissading along the bars of the bird cage and the knobs and grating of the big kitchen range. Elsewhere in the house, we stuck tallow candles in bottles, and groped our way along the lobby or down to the lavatory at the bottom of the black and menacing yard. On Christmas Day, they cooked a goose on the big range, and the smell of it made me sick

In the months round Christmas I scarcely ventured out of the house except to go to school, but, in February, the snow came, and on Saturday morning, I was pushed like a duckling into a pond and left to learn to swim.

Our yard door opened on the lane made by the backs of Albert Street and Market Street, the latter being a rather superior residential road wide as the town square, built at the turn of the century, with the fronts of the houses faced in buff-coloured freestone – they were known as the "khaki houses" during the Boer War. Albert Street, of course, was the longest in Millom, but our part of it was cut off from the main stretch by the intersecting Crown Street. Beyond this, you began to feel that you were among strangers. Moreover, my grand-mother's house was at the end of a block of eight or ten, above which there was a gap or "entry" as we called it, of about twenty feet in width, before the next block of completely similar houses. This entry, together with the back street running down to Crown Street, was to become my particular playground for the next eight or ten months. During February, however, the street was no longer a street, but a long, narrow gill or gully, with white screes of snow slithering down on either side from the height of the back-yard walls. Right along the centre, like a sheep trod, was a teetering path, picked out by feet, and, in front of each yard door, a little scooped-out Cheddar Gorge to give access to the yard. The shovelled-away snow lay by the door-steps in sooty dumps, dry as flour. Snow was piled high on walls and closet roofs, and balanced in long, upright ribbons on telegraph poles and clothes lines, while the slag banks, half a mile away, were as misty and blurred and distant as the Westmorland fells. In the strange, muffled silence, the sound of the scraping of spades seemed to linger and hover, as in an echo-chamber, and the clump, slosh and creak of the milkman's horse and cart came slowly towards me, as from a very long way. I remember looking with gentle curiosity at the horse manure, smoking warmly on the snow until, a few minutes later, it was hard, white and frozen, like everything else.

I did not know the Albert Street children very well, since most of them attended the Lapstone Road Schools, though a few of them were old enough to have started at the Secondary School. Now Lapstone Road scholars were believed, by those who went to Holborn Hill, to be savages, who swore, spat, threw stones, fired marbles and catapults, threw boys' caps into the gutter and pulled down little girls' knickers. But there was an orderliness in the back street which I had not expected. The snow, as it happened, had been lying for several days before the Saturday, and the snowballing phase had worked itself out – and snowballing, so far as I was concerned, merely meant broad-shots of thick, packed cannon-balls of ice in the face or behind the ear. So, instead of snow-fighting, a band of boys and girls, most of them two to five years older than me, were at work with shovels and trowels, building a snow house. It was an open-roofed fort really, a rectangle of solid ice walls, entered through a gap, over a block or threshold, about six inches high. This was a time of dead-still weather – no wind, no sun, just a perpetual calm, grey, freezing sky. There was no warmth in the day to melt the snow, and every night froze it harder till it was tough as concrete. Soon the little fort looked as if it had been there for as long as we could remember. It accumulated the dust and grime and mildew of old buildings, like the black slate of the walls that pushed through wherever the snow had flaked off. It was hard to think what the place had looked like before the snow came.

I soon began to realise that our back street was ruled by a matri-archal society. Though the boys had shovelled and dug and hauled up supplies of snow in orange-box sledges, it was a small group of eleven-or twelve-year-old girls who were in command. They set up an igloo community which stayed in being – or so it seems in memory – for at least a month. We guarded the fort as if it were an outpost on the Khyber Pass. During days away from school, it was never left unattended, except during the black of the night. Children from other streets might come and look, but were not allowed to enter except on invitation. The first thing each morning, before breakfast, we went out and inspected the premises, and swept away any dustings of snow that might have fallen during the night. On school days, we rushed home at four o'clock to make the most of what little daylight was left, and on Saturdays, we began to assemble at about ten o'clock in the morning. We had a piece of old carpet laid on the floor, and chairs and table made out of crates and boxes. Sometimes one of the girls would bring us bread and jam or a jug of tea, which we drank from the tin cups of a doll's tea set. There was an odd understanding among us. We argued and squabbled, and every now and then someone would go running back home in a huff". But no-one stayed away for long, and no-one ever dared to raise a boot or even a finger against the snow walls. Our hands were cold as frozen fish, our noses dribbled little icicles, yet, in many ways, that February was the high summer of my early childhood. The thaw came eventually; the snow house was swilled down the drains; the days began to lengthen. Lent brought out the boolies and whip and top to commemorate, as we are now told, the scourging of Christ, though I certainly knew nothing of this at the time. I doubt if I even knew it was Lent.

Then, with the lengthening nights, our little Eskimo community gathered together again in the after-tea twilight. This time the boys took control, and play became noisier and more active and began to range over a wider territory. The favourite game was a form of Prisoner's Base. First of all we counted:

"Nebuchadnezzar, the King of the Jews,
Sold his wife for a pair of shoes,
When the shoes began to wear
Nebuchadnezzar began to swear,
When the swear began to stop
Nebuchadnezzar bought a shop,
When the shop began to sell
Nebuchadnezzar bought a bell,
When the bell began to ring
Nebuchadnezzar began to sing:
Doh Ray Me Fah Soh Lah Te Doh OUT."

The player counted out was "It". "It" stood with his eyes closed and his head against the wall, and counted up to a hundred, while the rest of us scattered among nearby streets and alleys. "It" then searched for us, and, on seeing and recognising any one of us, he called out the name and raced back to Base. If he reached Base before the boy or girl who had been spotted, the latter was temporarily out of the game, and, in one version, had to become a kind of assistant to "It" and help him to search for the others. If, on the other hand, the player got back first, he just ran off and the game continued as before. Obviously – and especially if "It" was one of the younger and slower players – this was a game that could go on a very long time.

I had not the slightest chance of being able to run back to Base quicker than anyone else, so my only hope of staying in the game lay in keeping myself out of sight. Not for me to go tempting and taunting "It" by jumping suddenly into view from a shop doorway or running races across the gap at the end of the streets. My plan was to find some cleft or cranny where nobody could discover me, unless they came within half a dozen yards.

Now, to the back of our side of Albert Street, the other streets ran in strict parallels – Market Street, Lonsdale Road, Lonsdale Terrace – right down to the marshes of the estuary. And even on the other side, in the lower stretches, the streets marched off in the same pattern, for this was part of the nineteenth-century gridiron plan for working-class housing for the new town. But, at the top end of Albert Street, on the opposite side to us, the gridiron came raggedly to an end, and the next street, Lapstone Road, followed the line of a pre-urban cart track leading to the old farm of Lapstone Lodge, the outbuildings of which were – and still are – built into the present street. So that Crown Street, Albert Street and Lapstone Road formed a kind of triangle – the first two dead straight and at right-angles to one another, the third curving round in a wavery course. The end houses of the broken-off-terraces were all joggled in like pieces of a jigsaw, to make use of every available square yard of land – with triangular rooms or rooms of five sides, and with doors shoved in at unexpected places, and immensely long back yards, or little alleys bent like a hen's leg. And behind these streets was an irregular rhomboid of what had once been waste land, but was now walled-in or roofed-over as allotments, stables, workshops and tool-sheds.

It was here that I used to hide, skulking in the crack between Mr. Illingworth's, bookseller's, wooden warehouse and the high slate wall of the next building. We would go on playing till it was almost dark, and I would stand there, shrinking and shivering with excitement, the thrushes shouting in the dying green above the chimney tops, the darkness beginning to clot round me in black curds, and the silence drumming in my ears. It was not often that anyone came to look for me, though I fancy that they knew very well where I was. Most of the players preferred the fast run in the open streets, or the busy dodging round the corner of Crown Street, where the fish and chip shop was. Some even enjoyed a quick, daring skirmish into the No Man's Land of Katherine Street and Queen Street, where there was always the danger of being barged into the gutter, or pelted with gravel by the rough and ready bottom-end boys of the Slagbank Rovers. But I stayed quiet: tense, scared, until sometimes my nerves seemed to be strung so tight that they sang out like the telegraph wires at the top of the high poles. And when, at last, I heard the long "All-in-all-in-all-in-all-in" ululating like a falsetto curlew call over the black closet roofs, I was often so relieved at the thought of home and supper that I sobbed silently to myself all the way back to Base.

As the year shifted into spring, the afternoons grew quieter. The older boys moved away from the back street, played football on the Banking beside the estuary, or rambled off into the country. The older girls now began to take charge of me, pleased to find a bright, clean, gentle-mannered boy whom they could adopt as a little brother. There was one girl, about five years older than me, who made herself into a kind of aunt and school teacher combined – in later life, in fact, she became headmistress of a local school. Her parents were Cornish

Methodists in origin, and there was about her home a sobriety, a modest, neat, but quite determined respectability, which gave it a tone, even in a street where people prided themselves on the fact that no-one ever got drunk there. In the warming-up sun of early April, the two of us would put a step-ladder against the back-yard wall, and climb up to the level where a topping of smooth, flat flagstones made a cat-walk from one end of the street to the other. Here, sitting above the back-yard door, Judith would show me pictures in her books, and let me colour some of them with crayons. Here she taught me a few words of French, and showed me how to make coloured transfers on a sheet of paper. I suppose that, as with almost any female who had reached the age of puberty, I saw in her a substitute mother. Certainly there were times when there was an ache in my feeling for her, which I could neither understand nor express. I remember that once, in a queer little pang of longing, I rubbed my face against her shoulder.

"Don't wipe your nose on my dress," she said.

My grandmother was inclined to be rather caustic about my new friendship.

"You'll be turning Cornish next," she said, "like your father."

She meant that he was going to marry a Methodist.

CHAPTER FOUR

Preparations for the wedding went on during the early months of 1922 without my being greatly aware of them. For, while I was living with my grandma, Miss Sobey and the piano shop were no longer much in my mind. Albert Street was now my home, and I neither looked forward to, nor wondered about, my return to St. George's Terrace.

But hints and little advance notices began to come my way: the wedding was to be in April, and it would be held in the Wesleyan Methodist Church in Queen Street. The thought of it made my grandmother's face crack like an old chestnut into a hard, black-gapped grin.

"They'll be making a proper Cousin Jack of you," she warned me. "It'll be Cornish pasties for dinner every day."

She leaned back on her sofa, quacking like a self-satisfied duck.

"You'll have to be getting yourself Saved, lad," she said, "or there'll be no pasty. And you'll have to stand up and say Grace before you get even that."

"What God gives, and what we take,

'Tis a gift for Christ His Sake," – I said, for we sang those lines of Herrick's every morning at five to twelve, before school broke up for dinner:

"Be the meal of Beans and Peas,

God be thanked for those, and these –"

"Beans and peas," said my grandmother, "that's about it. That's what you'll be coming down to – unless you get yourself Saved."

"What's Saved?"

"You ought to have lived with me down in Lord Street where I

68

brought your father up, and you wouldn't have had to ask what being Saved was."

She paused for a moment, going back in her mind to the old house in the lower part of the town, opposite the railings of the Wesleyan Sunday School.

"It's going to Prayer Meetings and pulling a long face and thinking you're better than other people and telling everybody they're going to Hell-that's what being Saved is."

She stamped on the floor with the ferrule of the crutch, and began scratching away at the fire as if she were hoeing a row of carrots. She was well aware, of course, that Miss Sobey looked down on the family she was marrying into, and thought my Albert Street uncles rather coarse, and that, when she had brought me the crackers at Christmas, she had dressed up to impress. But my grandmother was not easily impressed. With her memories of the old Norman parish church at Beetham and the Dallam Tower family pew, she had only a poor opinion of Methodists. And, whatever Miss Sobey might think, she would always remain, so far as my grandmother was concerned, "nobbut one of them Wezleens".

April came into the town like a fussy old matron. Carpets and rag-mats were hung on the lines across the back streets and thumped and drummed. The old men who had not died during the winter began to shuffle out with one scarf less bandaging their throats, and those who *had* died were already losing interest in their jam-pots of field daffodils.

Tactfully guided by my father, I went to Sheward, the Jeweller, and bought a bedroom clock, enscrolled, like a Victorian photograph, in a twisting of brass wire, to give to Miss Sobey as a wedding present. (Like so much else that is hideous and completely useless, it has survived fifty spring cleans, and is in front of me at this moment – scratched, tarnished, the fly-wheel broken and one leg knocked off, unable to keep time or even to stand up, yet still sullenly defying me to throw it away.) Next, I was measured for a sailor suit, my dress for the wedding, which, I was told, was also to be the dress of my new cousin, Maurice Hughes. When the day arrived, I was sent round to the Sobey house in Wellington Street to collect a button-hole for my father – a rose, of course, because, as my father explained, "Miss Sobey's name is Rose." I was met at the door by Maurice's mother.

"They're in a tight comer now," I said, repeating a phrase I had heard used by my Auntie Tot, wife of Uncle Jim.

(I learned later that Mrs. Hughes felt that it was not a nice thing for a little boy to have said, and showed the bad influence of Grandma Cornthwaite on my infant years!)

Of the wedding, I can remember nothing at all, except that they did not sing "The voice that breathed o'er Eden", because my stepmother thought that the reference to Adam and Eve was in bad taste.

"Everybody knows what *they* were doing," she used to say, meaning that they ought to keep that sort of thing out of the hymn books.

The wedding breakfast, however, remains clearly in my mind. It was held in Miss Danson's Café, in St. George's Terrace, still there to this day, almost opposite our own front window, and still a café. I sat at the head table with the Bride and Bridegroom, the Bridesmaid (Dorothy Hughes, Maurice's sister), the Bride's father and mother, the Best Man and his wife (my Uncle Jim and my Auntie Tot), the Bridesmaid's father and mother (Mr. and Mrs. George Hughes), and the Methodist Minister and his wife (the Reverend Mr. and Mrs. Brewer). They all loomed up above my head, while I remained completely still, shut in a cube of silence. I was too embarrassed to eat, and did not much care for the cold ham and tongue, the veal pie, the bread and butter which were set before me – Miss Danson's cream cakes and chocolate éclairs, which Maurice and Billy and Donald were guzzling at the other end of the room, did not seem to reach our separate and superior table. Then, when the food was almost finished, a drop of port wine was poured into my glass, and I heard the Minister call loudly for a glass of water. The toasts – as even I could tell – were dull and painfully hesitant. Most of the speakers began by saying that they had known the Bridegroom for many years, though, so far as I can remember, no-one claimed to have known the Bride for a similar time.

First, there was my Uncle Jim; then Mr. Hughes, Mr. Sobey, Mr. Brewer. They had all known the Bridegroom for many years, and each of them led up to my having to take another sip of the wine that I did not much like. I could have done with an extra slice of wedding cake to take the taste away.

After a while the chapel-like silence began to thaw. Captain and Mrs. Fritz Elwell (son-in-law and daughter of old Mr. Walmsley) made it their job to try to jolly things along, throwing out remarks as if they were bidding at an auction. And the Minister felt it incumbent upon him to show that, in spite of the glass of water, he could enjoy a joke as well as any man. He had seen, he said, Miss Sobey – he begged her pardon, *Mrs. Nicholson*. To continue: he had seen *Mrs. Joe* seated one day at the organ, looking for the Lost Chord – and now she seemed to have found it. It was "Mrs. Joe this" and "Mrs. Joe that". Mrs. Jim began to look as if she were not called Nicholson at all.

Then, from nowhere in particular, a small parcel appeared, was pushed along the table to the Bride, and was found, on unwrapping, to contain a small, naked, celluloid baby doll. Shrieks of laughter, which left me wondering what on earth a doll had to do with a wedding, and why it was supposed to be funny in any case. I don't think Mrs. Joe thought it funny either, though she managed to squeeze out a thin, pink, peppermint smile.

Fortunately, the breakfast was not allowed to drag on, and soon the Bride and Bridegroom went off to Sammy Lamb's studio to be photographed, and afterwards called at Albert Street to let my grandmother see the wedding dress. Half an hour later, we all gathered at the railway station to see the couple off on their honeymoon – they were going to London because, as my father explained to me, he wanted to see Preston North End play in the F.A. Cup Final at Stamford Bridge. I expect there was confetti, but I can't remember. Later that afternoon, Mr. and Mrs. Sobey sent my grandmother a large basketful of tarts and trifle and cakes and so on, the left-overs from the feast. And that is how I came to have my share of the wedding breakfast.

During the week when my father was in London, I called on my new grandparents to see the wedding presents. Wellington Street, like Albert Street, to which it ran parallel, had lengthened westward as the town spread out from the Ironworks, but it was altogether more consequential, and, by the 1890s, the top end had become one of the main business centres of the town, with the Co-operative stores, the Co-operative Hall and many of the larger shops. Number Sixteen, where the Sobeys lived, was one of only ten or twelve dwelling houses not yet converted into shops. It was no bigger than my Grandma Nicholson's house in Albert Street, yet it was clearly a house of some modest substance. In an age when two pound ten a week was a good wage, this house spoke of steady employment, careful housekeeping and not too many children. "Wellington House" was painted in gold letters on the fanlight above the front door, which opened into a yard-square

vestibule, and somehow the grandeur of the name did not seem dispro-
portionate to the size of the house.

For it took its scale, as it were, from my grandmother. She was a
tiny, brown mouse of a woman – neat, bright, sleek, no longer quick
in her movements, but still sharp of eye – a Beatrix Potter mouse-wife,
who had lined her nest with the very cleanest and best quality straw she
could possibly find. Because she was so small, the house seemed far
bigger than it really was. She enlarged it with her language. The
narrow lobby was "The Hall"; the single attic room with its skylight
was "The Roof Garden"; the greenhouse, which my grandfather
had made by glazing over the top end of the yard, was "The Con-
servatory"; the yard itself was "The Garden". And the yard seemed
to understand that it was a garden, for it spread itself to the afternoon sun and grew what seemed to me to be the biggest lilac tree in
Millom. I was given two or three sprigs of the blossom to take home to
my Grandma Nicholson, who wondered what on earth to do with them.

What most impressed me, however, was the front room, where the
presents were on display on a table by the window, with my own brass
clock tactfully, though not too obviously, placed where I could not
miss it. For, unlike my Grandma Nicholson's front room, this was a
room that was used and lived in. The piano stood against one wall,
the piano-stool piled high with music, and the window, low and wide and
divided into two lights by a freestone upright, was not blocked off with
heavy curtains but left lightly veiled in lace, a viewpoint on the world.
For here, as I was later to learn, my grandparents would sit on a summer
evening, watching the people go by. They believed that their house had
one of the best situations in Millom, simply because so many people
did go by. On a Saturday, especially, Wellington Street was thronged
with shoppers, many of them from Haverigg or outlying villages, and
my grandparents would look out, silently and intently, as from a
grandstand. Those who knew that habit of theirs – and there were many
who did – would peep in at the window and wave as they passed;
others, more favoured, would call in for a minute. On Saturday
evenings in winter, my grandfather, who loved brass bands, would sit
there in the dark and listen to the Salvation Army holding its service
at the corner of Katherine Street, almost opposite, while my grandmother kept a penny in her hand, ready for the collector when he called.

Now that her younger daughter had left home – the only other surviving child, Laura, had married George Hughes about fifteen years
earlier – this window was to become more than ever important to

Grandma Sobey. Her husband, who was then over seventy, worked at Hodbarrow. He had started there as a joiner, and still carried on with his woodwork in a shed at the back of the house, having made, among other things, the greenhouse and all the wooden fittings in the bathroom – Number Sixteen was one of the few houses in Newtown which could claim to have a bathroom – and a solid wardrobe, which still holds my own clothes to this day. But, when he was in his late sixties, he had tripped over a stile, on the way from one job to another, and had badly injured his leg. The management at Hodbarrow were not very fond of the Unions, and there were rumours that Union men were always the first to be laid off when trade was slack. But my grandfather would never join a Union: it seemed to him to lower his dignity as a workman. "My work", he would say, "is a matter between Major Barrett and me, and nobody else." Hodbarrow had a kindly feeling towards men like that – they went on employing one such faithful servant, Jehu Date, until he was ninety. So, after his accident, they found my grandfather a job in the engine room, which controlled the power that drove the bogies underground. I know nothing of the mechanics of this, only that my grandfather's part was to work a huge switch-lever of the kind once used to drive a tram. Instructions came from a bell set in the wall above him: one ring for "Slow"; two for "Full Speed"; three for "Stop" – or some similar code. All day he would wait patiently, and switch on or off, according to the orders from sixty fathoms below. Often the bell was silent for a considerable spell, and he had time to oil the machinery, to keep the room swept and tidy and even to plant a few flowers and make a little garden outside the door. The whole of the above-ground workings have now been torn down, but there is still a thicket of tansy, which I like to think my grandfather may have planted, and, until recently, there was a bush of berberis growing up a broken wall. About twice a week, before she was married, my stepmother would cycle down to Hodbarrow during her lunch hour, and take her father a hot dinner, usually a Cornish pasty, carefully wrapped up in a white cloth. Sometimes, in school holidays, Maurice Hughes and I would go on the same errand. We would stand outside the engine room and look up at the twirling pithead wheels, the bogies coming up the shaft, the continual tipping of freshly-raised ore, the lovely, dusty, gorse-and-cinder bustle of what was still one of the great iron mines of the world. Ore-rouged faces greeted and chaffed us:

"Is that your Granda's dinner?"

"Mind you don't eat it 'fore he gets it."

"I bet you had your finger in it. I bet you helped yourself to a tatie, you little devil."

Afterwards, the mile walk home to my own dinner seemed a very long way, but my grandfather did that walk twice a day in all weathers at the age of seventy, without giving it a thought. I know of some miners who lived at The Hill, and walked the four miles each way, every shift, for twenty or thirty years.

In 1922, James T. Sobey was the only survivor of four brothers who had come to Cumberland in 1869 from Devonshire. Hodbarrow, in its early days, recruited many skilled men from the tin and copper mines of Cornwall and Devon, and John Barrett, the pioneer and prime mover in the mine, was himself a Cornishman, whose father had managed a mine on Dartmoor. (Recently, on a visit to Tavistock on the Cornwall-Devon border, I was delighted to see so many familiar Millom names painted above the shops – Doidge, Spry, Boase, Barrett.) The four brothers settled not in Millom but in the nearby village of Haverigg, where two of them lived for the rest of their lives. The third, Richard, quarrelled with the mine-captain, threw in his job and went off to Mexico. A year later, when his eldest son, also Richard, left the village school at the age of thirteen, he went to Hodbarrow seeking work.

"Are you Dick Sobey's son?" asked the mine-captain.

"Yes."

"Then you can get off home. There's nowtfor Dick Sobey's son here."

So young Dick went off to Mexico to join his father and, later on, the rest of the family followed. For years they worked hard and rough. At one time, Dick, still very young, was in charge of Indian labour at the building of a reservoir, and here he was befriended by another family from Millom, called Harris, whose children and grandchildren are friends of mine today. "Befriended" meant, chiefly, seeing that he kept off the drink, which, to a Sobey, was not much of a temptation in any case. So, after years of sober work, the family saved up a few hundred pounds, and were persuaded to invest them in a lead mine, and, almost immediately, the miners struck silver. A few years later, they were able to withdraw their capital and return to England, where cousin Dick, the boy who could not get a job at Hodbarrow, found himself moving up into the world of the Forsytes. Their story need not concern me now but for one thing – they decided to settle in Bournemouth, and that decision changed, and probably saved, my life. But that will be explained hereafter.

The Sobeys, like all the Cornish and Devonshire men, were Methodists, and attended the Haverigg Chapel of the Bible Christians, a sect
which, in my day, had amalgamated with another body to form the
United Methodists – or the "U.Ms.", as my stepmother called them.
In fact, when I was a boy, the Haverigg United Methodist Chapel was
run by Frances Sobey – "Auntie Frances" to me – daughter of one of
the four brothers, who managed its affairs with a devoted, pious and
fiercely autocratic rule, with which no superintendent minister ever
dared interfere.

My stepmother was born in a little house only a few yards from the
chapel and close beside the waters of Haverigg Pool, which, at high
tides, flooded both house and chapel. She could remember her father
baling sea-water out of the piano after one of the highest tides, and
there were stories of flukes or flounders left stranded on the kitchen
floor. My stepmother did not live long at Haverigg, for, when she
was five, her parents moved to Millom, and, unlike her cousin Dick,
who retained great affection for Haverigg, she soon learned to look
down on her humble beginnings – "Haverigg" in her vocabulary
meant "common".

"Proper Haverigg!" she would say, when she saw something of
which she disapproved, such as jam-pots on the tea table, or someone
washing clothes on a Sunday.

For, when they came to Millom, my grandparents took what they
clearly regarded as a step up the ladder by leaving the Bible Christian
congregation and joining that of the Wesleyans. Now that Methodist
Union has been achieved for many years, it may seem rather mean-
minded to speak of former interdenominational jealousies, yet the
Wesleyans, in all parts of England, tended to think of themselves as
socially a cut above their fellow Methodists. My stepmother would
sometimes refer to a visiting minister or chapel-goer as "ex-U.M."
or "ex-Prim", adding: "but we're all one now", with a laugh that
showed her disbelief. There is an historical explanation. The early
Methodists under John Wesley drew their first ministers from the
ordained clergy of the Church of England, men of education and gentle
upbringing, who brought with them much of the traditional Anglican
regard for order and propriety. The seceding sects, such as the Primitive Methodists, were founded mostly by the lay preachers, men
of the working classes, who were more radical, more determinedly
evangelical, more fundamentalist and often more Calvinist.

The Sobeys, then, became Wesleyans, and settled down to forty years of quiet respectability. I write that without a sneer or a giggle, trying to hear the words as they would have been understood by my grandfather's neighbours and contemporaries. When they said of him that "he was a real gentleman", when *The Millom Gazette* wrote in its obituary column:

"One of Millom's most esteemed and respected residents passed away on Friday morning last"

– they were not just conniving at a petty snobbery. Obviously, as a matter of social classification, my grandfather remained working class all his life. He reached no very high position, and he and his wife finished their lives on the old age pension, hardly ever moving outside their own yard or front door. But he had a dignity of carriage and behaviour which would not have disgraced a duke. On Bank Holiday mornings or after Sunday Evening Chapel in summer, my grandmother and he would walk very quietly round the streets, or over the railway bridge, and as far as the end of the houses. Both of them were nearly always dressed entirely in black, though I remember my grandmother sometimes in grey silk. Usually, she wore a black silk or satin dress, pulled tight across her flat little chest, like a parson's vest, and often she had a white lace choker wrapped round her throat. My grandfather carried a bone-handled walking cane, slender as a pencil. His white, pointed, carefully-trimmed beard resembled that of King Edward VII, though I now think his model was, in fact, Cedric Vaughan, managing director of Hodbarrow, of whose character he would have approved more than that of the King's.

These Sunday walks were no more than constitutionals, taken after a little conversation with the other members of the chapel congregation. But on Easter and Whit and August Monday, their walk became a Bank Holiday parade. They would saunter slowly round the streets, meeting friends whom they probably hadn't seen for six months, or even a year. Every few yards, they would stop and talk. There was raising of hats and shaking of hands, and a sober formality not, I imagine, unlike that with which Samuel Pepys greeted his acquaintances in St. James's Park. I can clearly remember how I was impressed, as a boy of eight, by the quiet and entirely serious courtesy which the old man showed to me as much as to anybody else.

My grandmother lacked my grandfather's patient self-assurance but she had a sharper awareness of the shades and half-shades of class. I have an idea that she may once have been a lady's maid at Chagford or Grediton in Devon, and it was perhaps because of this that she was determined to bring up her younger daughter "like a young lady". For Rosetta, or Rosie, as they always called her, had been her parents' favourite from birth. She had come to them rather late in life and had delighted them with her skill at the piano. She was equally devoted to them. If her new home in St. George's Terrace had not been within two hundred yards of the old one in Wellington Street, I am sure that her parents would never have countenanced the wedding at all.

As it was, she came to my father and me completely uninstructed in anything to do with running a house. For my grandmother believed that young ladies did not soil their hands with house-work, and she insisted that she herself did everything for her daughter – cooking, sewing, washing and so on. But, though my stepmother was unin-structed, she was conscientious –

(But I must stop calling her "stepmother".

"What are you going to call your new mother?" asked my father, a day or so before the wedding.

"Miss Sobey," I replied, with some surprise at the question.

"You can't call her Miss Sobey after she's married," he said. The thought had not occurred to me.

There was a silence.

"How about 'Mother'?" said my father.

I agreed readily enough, since the word had no previous associations for me, my own mother – like all the other mothers I knew – having always been called "Mammy".

So, from that moment, Miss Sobey became "Mother", and remained so for nearly fifty years, and that is what I will call her in the rest of this book.)

Mother, as I have said, was conscientious, so she tackled the job of house-keeping as well as she could. But the lesson her mother had taught her was one she did not forget, and she always felt rather ashamed of having to do any house-work at all. She would not let herself be seen in an apron or overall. She dressed at breakfast as if she were about to take a stroll in the park. Any house-work had to be rushed through early in the morning before anyone – such, for instance, as the milkman – called to see her doing it. "I was born for better things than washing up," she used to say, or again, with a sigh, "The trivial round, the common task." She thought it rather common to be seen carrying a shopping basket, and would trot backward and forward between house and shops, carrying a packet of sugar or a bag of tomatoes, and then returning for more. On the rare occasions when we entertained anyone to tea, she would apologise as she laid the table-cloth:

"It's the maid's day off."

She must have made the same joke to the same people many times over, but they always responded with the expected laugh, for I think they were aware of her unease as much as she was herself. And the cause for it was not, I think, her gentle snobbery but a feeling that house-work was old-fashioned. For my mother, in the years before 1914, had belonged to the new generation of young women who were beginning to look beyond the bounds of home and family. She herself was not able to cross those bounds, but she believed that her scorn for the household chores was a clear sign that she might have done, had she chosen to.

It was because of this that she looked down on all the old house crafts of her mother's day – jam-making, pickling, laundering, dress-making and the like. She despised home baking, too, bringing me up on a diet of Miss Danson's bread and scones and mixed fancy cakes – maids-of-honour, vanilla slices, cream buns, little sponge cakes in paper cups, all at eight for the shilling. She was convinced that these were of a far better quality than anything you could bake at home.

"Don't you eat any of that old home-made stuff," she would say to me, whenever I went to a children's party. "You never know what's in it."

When, sometimes, friends made her a present of little home-baked cakes or biscuits, she would accept them politely, and afterwards throw them out into the yard for the birds.

"They may look all right," she would say to me, "but I'm not going to risk giving them to you or your Dad."

In the early days of the marriage, my grandmother would often come to our house to see "how we were getting on", but my mother did not easily take advice – certainly not on the subject of house-work – even from her own much-loved mother. She hated cookery books and magazines of household hints, and when she opened a tin or a packet of foodstuff, she hadn't the patience to read the printed instructions.

"They have to say something," she would blithely reply when, in my prim manner, I pointed this out.

When she was among friends and the conversation turned to what she called "the domestic", she would sit silent, looking rather offended.

Once, an acquaintance, who had just moved into a new house, made the mistake of showing her the kitchen. She came home short-tempered and righteously indignant.

"I didn't call on her to see her kitchen," she said. "That sort of thing is of no interest to me."

Gradually, however, she adjusted herself to the job of feeding my father and me. Feeding herself was no problem, for I think the only food she really enjoyed was bread and butter.

"Lovely bread and butter," she would say, after a meal in a restaurant or even, in later life, a holiday at a hotel. "Brown bread and white bread and lovely, fresh butter."

And lovely bread and butter was almost our only food for breakfast – though, about once a week, my mother would ask my father if he felt like an egg, and then wonder why I laughed. It was our main course at tea, too, and often took the place of vegetables at mid-day dinner. My mother would have been shocked at the suggestion that she might have offered me margarine, but it did not occur to her that she was digging my grave with a bread-knife.

As the oven in the back kitchen could only be stoked up on a Sunday, and as my father would not have a gas oven in the house, my mother's first experiments in cooking were restricted to stews, boilings and fries on a single gas ring. The pasties my grandmother threatened me with did not often come my way, except the meat-and-potato pasties bought from local confectioners of Cornish ancestry.

"Shout when you find a piece of meat," my mother would say.

One shop, however – Harris's in Holborn Hill – used to make a special kind of pasty to our own requirements, with turnip, as well as potato. In the morning, on my way to school, I would call at the shop and leave a small piece of turnip, wrapped in greaseproof paper. Then, at twelve o' clock, on my way back, I'd call for the pasties and bring them home hot. Pasties, meat pies from the baker's, cold boiled ham ("cut thin, please") from the grocer's, cold roast pork from the butcher's (you could have a hot knuckle of pork, if you ordered it the day before), and, occasionally, fish and chips – these made up our mid-day meal three or four times a week. But I had not the slightest suspicion that I was not being adequately fed. Roast and stewed meat had little attraction for me, and I did not even see a steak until years later, when I didn't much care for what I saw. Moreover, my mother was quite good at providing the foods I really enjoyed – jellies, and such like, with next to no food value at all. In summer, we would sometimes order a crate of a dozen bottles of mineral water – 1/6d for the dozen – from Marmaduke Fawcett's "pop" factory, and I proudly believed we were dining in luxury and style.

My mother's attitude to the shop was quite different from her attitude to the house. She did not in the least mind being seen working in the shop. That was "business"; that was something a woman had no need to be ashamed of. She did not greatly like serving at the counter, since she did not know the prices – my father had a private letter code for prices, and my mother was never able to understand it. Indeed, she was only called on to serve when the shop was exceptionally busy, at Christmas, or when my father took his regular quarter-of-a-mile walk "round the block" – i.e. down Lapstone Road, and back by the High Road past the Park and the Library – as he did every weekday, except Wednesday, at one o' clock wet or fine, for fifty years. People living in Lapstone Road used to set their clocks by him.

My mother would spend hours polishing the counter, vacuuming the carpet, swilling the shop window and brushing the pavement. Years after my father's death, when she was over seventy, and the shop was let out, she would go down early in the morning and sweep out the doorway before our tenant arrived. Even with another name on the fascia board, she still thought of it as "her" shop, and worried if it were not as smart and clean and tidy as she felt it ought to be. It was as if the shop were part of her own self, the front she turned on the world – just as some men in the suburbs seem to lay out their gardens more for the eyes of passers-by than for their own.

I think the word "business" had a kind of aura for her. "He's in business," she would say, and it mattered little to her whether the man in question ran a small corner shop, or was the chairman of a ten-million-pound company. "Business", of course, meant either the retail or the wholesale – she would not have thought of, say, the Managing Director of British Leyland as being a businessman at all. The retail had its own hierarchy of assistant, head assistant, departmental manager, branch manager and that dimly understood, but much envied figure known as a "buyer". Of the wholesale, she had little knowledge. It was the in-between men, the commercial travellers, whom she really admired. She admired their dress, their manners, their way of life – travelling about the country and staying in "all the best hotels" – and to be married to one of them would have seemed to her the height of a woman's ambition. Being herself, in some ways, extremely naive, she was always completely taken in by a superficially ingratiating approach, and was correspondingly suspicious when she came up against a plain, blunt, unaffected, honest man. Which, of course, is just what my father was. But the fact that he was "in business" and owned his own shop gave him a status in her eyes which made up for what she saw as his shortcomings in style and manners.

Nevertheless, as soon as she came to St. George's Terrace, she set about the job of raising my father and me up to what she regarded as her standard. There was the matter of table manners to begin with. I had to learn to say "Please "and "Thank you" more often than it had seemed necessary before. One day, when I was out for a walk, I met Mr. John Stoddart, keeper of the shoe-shop near us, who had just gone to live in a large house, built on the site of an old quarry. He gave me a lettuce from his garden.

"Did you thank him for it?" asked my mother.

"No," I said, with some surprise, "I didn't know I had to."

My mother was indignant.

"Haven't you got any manners at all?" she said. "A fine way he'll think I'm bringing you up."

"But the lettuce was for you," I protested. "It wasn't for me."

"You're going to eat some of it, aren't you?" she said.

I had to concede the point. And the next day, I was sent to call at Quarry House, and say: "Please, Mr. Stoddart, Mother thanks you for the nice lettuce you sent yesterday." He gave me a couple of apples for myself.

It was repeatedly drummed into me, moreover, that whatever I did outside the home reflected directly on my mother. If I was ill-mannered, she would be blamed for not teaching me better; if I was polite, the credit was hers. It brought its difficult moments. As a small boy, I happened to detest ice-cream – the cold hurt the roof of my mouth and made my teeth ache – and once, when I was with my mother and father, we met Captain Elwell just outside our house, and he bought me an ice-cream wafer from the shop at the corner.

"No, thank you," I said.

"Oh, come on, now," he said.

"But I don't like ice-cream, thank you."

"Of course you like ice-cream," said my mother, "and you'll thank the gentleman for it."

"I did thank him," I said. "But I don't like it, I really don't."

"You shut up and get it eaten," she said.

And I stood there, with tears dribbling down to the corners of my mouth, miserably gulping gobbets of frozen custard, until my throat and my chest were bruised with the pain.

There were similar lessons to be learned about "Ladies First" – which meant, in practice, "Mother First" – and about taking off my cap when I entered a house, and about always keeping to the outside of a lady when I walked beside her on the pavement – which was awkward when the lady was thirty years older and, in the case of some of my aunts, ten stone heavier. Even today, when I am laying the table for a meal, I feel slightly guilty if I accidentally lay my own place before that of my wife, or any, woman guest, and I feel so awkward about wearing a cap in, say, a shop or a post office, that I will frequently pull it off in the street and stuff it into my pocket before I pass through the door.

During the six months I spent at Grandma Nicholson's, the house at St. George's Terrace had been redecorated, and further alterations were soon to follow. Not long after we had returned, the small bedroom where I had slept until then was turned into a bathroom, and I had to move up to the back attic, so that, throughout my adolesence, I slept in a tiny, airless box of a room, lit only by a skylight that was always shut tight against the rain and the soot. We had taken another step up the social ladder, and I had taken a step down towards chronic ill-health.

After the bathroom came the piano. It was an upright Collard and Collard, not entirely new – in fact, my mother had sold it to a customer some six months before her marriage – but it was a bright-toned, lively instrument, which is still making music in one of the Lake District valleys, not more than ten miles from here.

The piano, in fact, was a sign of a great change that was to come over my life, since my mother was both a pianist and the assistant organist of the Wesleyan Methodist Chapel. From now on, the once-a-month Sundays on which she accompanied the service became the twelve pillars around which the rest of the year was built. My father and I did not attend chapel in the mornings, but, on the Sunday evening, we would go down and take our seats in the rented pew – "Mrs. J. Nicholson, 2", on the little ticket; they didn't rent a place for me!

My father explained that when I entered the pew, I was to sit down and lean forward for a few seconds, with my elbows on the hymn-book ledge and my head in my hands, and I did this at his side for several weeks, before I realised that we were supposed to be praying!

That was typical of my father's attitude to the chapel. He outwardly conformed to Non-Conformity, but was inwardly detached, even rather embarrassed about it. "We're all going to the same place," he would say, with an air of large magnanimity, but he secretly thought that the Methodists had chosen rather a poor route. Nevertheless, when my mother was at the organ, my father could feel that he had a real share in the worship, that he was no longer just an awkward visitor from St. George's who didn't know many of the hymns, and didn't altogether like the company. So, at the end of the service, the stewards would greet us as we stepped out through the main doors to where the congregation stood about in the street, raising hats and shaking hands, reluctant to disperse.

"Tell Mrs. Nicholson how much I enjoyed her playing," people would say.

And my father would nod in a complacent way, putting his pince-nez into one pocket, pulling his watch out of another, as if he had made a particularly gratifying sale.

"Very good," he would say, "I'll tell her. Very good. Much obliged."

As for me, I would sit through the service, dithering with pride, looking up from our pew, on the right-hand aisle, under the horseshoe gallery, to the big pulpit of stained wood and the raised choir-stalls, running right across the front of the chapel; and looking beyond all this to the spiked and pinnacled organ, which stretched up its iron fistful of pipes to grasp at the whole end wall and diminish everyone and everything to creaturely size. When the Lord spoke in that chapel, it was never in a still, small voice.

Oddly enough, though we must often have attended chapel on Sunday evenings in summer, I remember it almost entirely in winter. From our pew, I seem always to have looked onto a gas-lit and winterly cave, with the incandescent mantles glowing in their white globes and the windows black against the outside night. We were boxed tightly into our pew, the gallery roof low above our heads, and Grandma and Grandpa Sobey in the seat behind. The chapel, if not packed, was respectably full; there was rarely an empty seat in the choir, and the boys of the congregation nudged and squinted over the gallery rail. As the service wore on and the temperature rose, the gaslight turned mistily green, the tremolo of the organ became almost visible, and the moisture oozed down the painted walls and the iron pillars that carried the gallery. The sermon lasted twenty-thirty-forty minutes – too long, often, even for the addicts – and we all settled into a hot, furtive, greenhouse doze, until the last hymn. Then suddenly, the organ sang out, the best basses and contraltos of the Millom Mixed Voice Choir tromboned into four-part chording, and every member of the congregation opened wide his mouth, until the whole baffle-board of pews and panels boomed and echoed with all the fervour of Charles Wesley's thousand tongues.

If my father had married five or ten years later, I would have missed some of the voices and much of the fervour, but, in 1922, though the high tornado of the Evangelical Revival had been dying away for at least half a century, there was still a following wind that blew through these services. Conversion, the changed life, "the heart strangely warmed" were still at the centre of Methodist theology, even if, for many, they were now something of a formality. Indeed, few of the congregation were converts in Wesley's sense – they were children of converts, or grandchildren, or, more likely, great-grandchildren. They came from families in which, for generations, life after conversion had been the norm. Some of the preachers – more particularly, the lay preachers, or "local preachers", as we called them – made a direct "Come to Jesus" appeal to the congregation, but my mother found this rather embarrassing. That sort of thing, she implied, was better left to the U.Ms.

All the same, there was a formal Mission every five years or so, when a visiting Evangelist or team took over the running of the chapel, and services were held every night of the week. There were Moody and Sankey hymns, with the choir augmented by singers from other chapels, and the thumping, hand-slapping, heart-prodding tunes banged and bounced about the galleries, till the pillars shook and twanged:

> "At the Cross, at the Cross, where I first saw the light,
> And the burden of my heart rolled away –
>> *Rolled away*
> It was there by Faith I received my sight
> And now I am *happy* all the day –
>> *All the day.*"

As the mission moved on towards its climax, and the Evangelist began to make his appeal, there was a tension and expectancy about the congregation. I think it was almost as much a sporting instinct as a religious response. They were like farmers with whippets, gathered round the last grass in a nine-tenths-mown hay-field, waiting to see which way the hares would run.

You could usually bet on who would be the first two or three to come forward – the old stagers, who could be relied on to start the pot boiling.

"It's the same crowd that gets Saved every blessed time," my father would say, in an aggrieved voice. "You'd wonder how they ever found time to get lost."

And after them came the few younger people, to whom this was their first Mission. But what the congregation was waiting for was the real convert, the unexpected and unpredictable, the man to whom the decision would mean a spectacular break with his old life. For such breaks did happen, however the psychologists may choose to explain them, and there are men and women walking about Millom today whose upbringing would have been quite different, if their father or grandfather had not suddenly given up drinking, or gambling, or knocking his wife about, and turned on the snap of a response into a sober, hard-working, hard-saving, hard-praying chapel man.

To the children of the ninety and nine who felt no need of repentance, the whole event was exciting, but rather unreal. We all signed a little ticket, saying that we accepted Jesus as our Saviour, rather as if we were applying for membership at the public library. Once or twice I would have liked to have gone forward with the others in answer to the appeal, but I knew that, if I did so, my mother would accuse me of showing her up in public.

"It only makes people start wondering what you've been up to," she would say, "if you go traipsing out there."

But I do not think people really wondered what the old stagers had been up to. We might laugh at them, but they were too much of a piece for us to doubt their genuineness. Even old Mr. Allen, who was so troubled by the draught that he wore a boy's school cap throughout the service, managed to maintain his dignity in our eyes, though we sniggered behind his back.

There were others I came to know better: Seth Slater, who, now that he had found my father in the same congregation as himself, had begun to acknowledge him again, though there always remained a stiffness between the two men. Relations had been made easier, however, by the fact that Mr. Slater had sold his premises in St. George's Terrace to the Post Office, and had shifted his business into a smaller shop, on the corner of Lapstone Road, so that the two rival traders were no longer forever staring at one another across the street. At the same time, the Slater family had moved to a dark, Victorian house on the slopes of Holborn Hill, among what the elder son called "the aristocracy of the

Mine Owner, the Bank Manager and the Rate Collector". It was from there that they all marched the hilly mile, there and back, twice a Sunday, to the Wesleyan Chapel, though the pretty little Primitive Methodist Chapel stood next door to where they now lived. Once the Slaters reached the Chapel, they would arrange themselves in order, side by side, in their pew, almost opposite to ours, the whole seven or eight of them – there were two sons, but I forget how many daughters – with the father at the end, so that he could step easily to the aisle, when the time came to take up the collection. He invariably held himself, whether in pew or in shop, bolt upright, stiff as a bed-post, with his bald head polished like a brass knob, and he spoke always in a piping counter-tenor, which, in various ways, was inherited by his children.

"I'm not going to be converted," John Slater would say, in his father's voice. "I'm going to be one of those who cry out on the last day."

We replied with a shocked and rather guilty giggle.

Chris Walmsley was another of the older Methodists whom I had known before I joined the Wesleyan congregation. He had come to Millom, many years before, from Yorkshire, as manager of a grocery store called "Cheap and Best", and later had set up his own shop in Lapstone Road, with a back door that opened opposite to our own. It was a shop that perpetually simmered and fumed with the aromas – I must not call them smells: the Walmsleys did not deal in smells – of spices, pickles, currants, cheese and bacon. Sackfuls of flour and sugar and dried peas were stacked about the floor, waiting to be shovelled into blue paper bags. Pepper and cloves and cinnamon were sifted into little ice-cream-cone-shaped bags, fashioned by Mrs. Walmsley, who must have weighed at least eighteen stone, with one delicate twist of her finger. Cheese was bisected with a long piece of string, anchored at one end to the cheese board. Coffee came to the shop in beans and when, every few weeks, these were ground in the hand-turned grinder, in the little store room behind the shop, all of us in the houses round about breathed and savoured fresh coffee for the next two hours.

Chris Walmsley was a little man, who wore a King Teddy beard, like Grandpa Sobey, but was altogether quicker, livelier, more nervous and more agile. Like many other small men, he was given to the big gesture:

"WALMSLEY'S TEAS, 1/2 AND 1/6 PER LB, ARE SPECIALLY BLENDED TO SUIT THE WATERS OF THE DISTRICT" –

he proclaimed in large whitewash letters on his shop window, on the printed programmes of concert and carnival parade, and in many issues *of the millom gazette.* And again:

"WALMSLEY'S DELICIOUS MILD CURED HAMS & BACON
CANNOT BE BEATEN",

or:

"WALMSLEY'S CUSTOMERS DECLARE THAT THEY SAVE FULLY 5/-
IN THE £, AND GET BETTER VALUE."

That he would put punctuation into even an advertising slogan was typical of the man.

At one time he ran a weekly Junior Bible Class, which I attended regularly when I was eleven or twelve, and on one occasion, he asked me to "give a paper". God knows what I found to say, but, in the end, he thanked me warmly, and added:

"I'd like to have a copy of that paper."

I was flattered and pleased for, at that time, it was my secret ambition to become a Local Preacher, and I toiled for several evenings, making a neat and careful copy. Two or three weeks later, the Minister's son, Henry Foss, was also asked to give a paper, and did so on what I thought was the very odd subject of "Prayer".

"And I'd like to have a copy of that paper," said Mr. Walmsley, afterwards.

I suddenly found myself begrudging the time I had spent copying mine!

Chris Walmsley had one special interest which particularly endeared him to me: poetry, or, at least, two poets. He did not seem to read them – he did not have to; they were locked away in his head. One of them was Pope. Over and over again, in his little addresses to the boys of his Bible Class, he would suddenly break out into the urbane humanism of the *Essay on Man,* often in complete contradiction to his text and pretext:

"Know thou thyself, presume not God to scan;
The proper study of mankind is man."

The other poet was Edgar Allan Poe, and the contrast between the two is so great that I sometimes wonder if, in his youth, Chris Walmsley had failed to notice the omission of the "p", and thought that the two were one and the same. He was well aware, however, that Poe was not proper material for the Bible Class, and kept him, primarily, for

Henry Foss and me. I think he knew the whole of "The Bells" by heart, but his most passionate love was given up, totally, head over ears and tongue, to "Annabel Lee".

I remember how, one evening after the Bible Class, he walked home with Henry Foss and me, and we stopped for a minute or two, outside the door of his shop in Lapstone Road. It was mid-April, just before Easter. The days were lengthening, the new green light was dawdling about over the chimney pots, the thrushes were whistling from the allotments – there seemed to be no blackbirds in those days – and the year's new hatching of adolescent girls was taking its first flutterings through the streets. Mr. Walmsley started to recite, side-stepping from one foot to the other, as people dodged past him on the pavement. Even in the greening twilight, I could see his eyes shining, and his sharp, little beard forking this way and that, as he jerked his head with the rhythm:

> "I was a child and she was a child
>   In this kingdom by the sea;
> But we loved with a love that was more than love –
>   I and my ANNABEL LEE;
> With a love that the winged seraphs of Heaven
>   Coveted her and me."

One hand held me gripped by the wrist, trapped me like the Ancient Mariner's wedding guest, the other suddenly skewered upwards, as his voice squeaked on the word "coveted", emphasising its daring.

Then the potent, sexy, heavy-seasoned witch-brew of the words began to go to his head, like the alcohol he never touched. He tipped back his neck, staring up at the roof tops, and his voice shrilled up, like a bagpipe. Passers-by, now almost unrecognisable in the congealing dusk, turned their heads, paused, sniggered. He took no notice.

> "For the moon never beams without bringing me dreams
>   Of the beautiful ANNABEL LEE;
> And the stars never rise but I see the bright eyes
>   Of the beautiful ANNABEL LEE;
> And so, all the night-tide, I lie down by the side
>   Of my darling – my darling – my life and my bride,"

It was, to a boy of thirteen, embarrassing stuff. I squirmed as far away from him as the grip of his hand would let me. I felt that everybody in the street was laughing, jeering, "skitting", as we used to say. But the words cut their groove deep in my memory and, as he went into the darkened shop and closed the door, the last lines echoed after him, across the black gap of the back street:

"In her sepulchre there by the sea–
In her tomb by the sounding sea."

Marmaduke Fawcett was the third of the old Methodists who towered over my boyhood. I fancy he was stricter with his children than either Seth Slater or Chris Walmsley, but, to me, he was more endearingly human than either. His odd Christian name also singled him out, though, at times, it gave rise to confusion – one Dutch Bulb firm regularly addressed its catalogue to:

"His Grace, the Marmaduke Fawcett."

I am not sure exactly what office he held in the chapel, but I remember that he taught in the Sunday School, for I was in his class, and now and then, he would offer sixpence to any boy who could learn a set psalm by the next Sunday. It was as easy as spitting for me and I collected quite a few sixpences, and, when he died, his daughter found the name "Norman" written in pencil, on the margin of his Bible. It was not, so far as I can tell, against one of the psalms I had learned by heart.

Like most of the Methodists of his generation, Marmaduke was an off-comer; from a farming family near Hawkshead. I had no romantic image of the farmer. I regarded farms as places of barking dogs and cow muck, while my mother had taught me that to become a "farm yocker" was the lowest any lad could fall to. Yet about Marmaduke there was something of the strange strength that I was already beginning to sense in the mountains. He was like one of the Old Testament shepherd-prophets, striding out from the hills of Judaea.

What is more, as a manufacturer of mineral water, he was part of the hagiography of youth, far better known to us than men of greater standing in the town. "Fawcett's Pop" was as essential as sunshine to summer galas, picnics and Cricket Club teas. It was manufactured in premises situated opposite the old shop where my father had been apprenticed to Seth Slater. They were ramshackle and haphazard as an old farm – maybe they once *had* been a farm – for there were stables and lofts and out-houses and roofed, open-sided structures, like Dutch barns, where they piled the empty crates. The stables were still used by the horses which pulled the pop wagons, and, on the empty patch of land between the factory and the Wesleyan Methodist Minister's manse, Mr. Fawcett kept hens.

When I was about twelve, I used to go there once a fortnight to collect our regular order of a dozen eggs, and sometimes he would give me an egg for myself, which seemed an odd sort of present, since all I could do with it was to hand it over to my mother. But, after a while, he began to give me a bottle of pop. I was often accompanied on those visits by a friend, and we would share the bottle between us. Usually, it was dandelion and burdock, which is what Mr. Fawcett thought boys preferred. It was not, however, what *I* preferred. So once, as we drank our dandelion and burdock, I let my eyes roam over the other bottles, stacked ready for the crates.

"American Ice Cream Soda", I read aloud, from one of the labels, my voice as studiously casual as if I had scarcely taken in what the words meant. But, sure enough, next time we went round for the eggs, we were given a bottle of American Ice Cream Soda. I expressed great surprise.

"You asked for it last time," said Mr. Fawcett, who was as down-to-earth as Elijah.

There was, indeed, an extraordinary matter-of-factness about these old Methodists. To call them "fundamentalists" is to underestimate them. They did not just take the Bible literally; they took God literally. One can imagine them arguing back with God.

"But Thou said'st so-and-so," they would point out, quoting chapter and verse of the Bible.

I remember that once Henry Foss and I met Marmaduke Fawcett in the street. He was beginning to be rather bent by that time, his legs bowed by sciatica, but he still had the leanness of a dalesman, and his sharp, little, gingery beard jabbed up and down as he walked. He was wearing a black coat and hat, so maybe he was on his way to some mid-week service. We talked for a minute and said good-bye.

"I'll see you again," he said, and began walking away.

Suddenly, he stopped and turned and stared, his hoary, leathery face slowly taking on a new brightness, as when the sun strikes a lichened stone.

"I'll see you again up there," he said, raising his stick towards the chimney pots.

It was as if, for a moment, the whole street stopped dead-still, listening.

"Both of you," he went on. "I'll be going there before you, but I'll be waiting for you. Think on. I'll be expecting you."

It was not just a promise: it was a pact between him and us and God. I felt that, if I failed to keep it, I should have let Mr. Fawcett down.

CHAPTER FIVE

I MUST not pretend that I was a particularly religious-minded child. I have only one clear memory of any experience which might be called religious, and I am not sure that I would call it so now. And even this was only indirectly connected with the chapel. It was at a time when there had been some Special Weekend, a Church Anniversary, or the like. For the Methodists, having discarded the church calendar, often made themselves a kind of non-liturgical calendar of church events. On the Weekend in question, there was a visiting preacher, who stayed on to give a talk to the Women's Meeting on the Monday afternoon, and a lecture-sermon in the chapel in the evening. His subject was *The Pilgrims Progress*. I can remember nothing of the lecture, which, however, impressed me enough to make me seek out my father's copy of the book when I got home. It was a green, cardboard-bound volume in The Harmsworth Library, Price One Shilling, with gilt lettering on the spine, and the pages rather neatly printed with paragraph headings in larger type: "THE SLOUGH OF DESPOND" or "WORLDLY WISEMAN MEETS CHRISTIAN". The style did not deter me, for I was used to that of the Bible; the homely talk, the rugged, urgent, romantic story caught my fancy. I sat on my stool, beside the fire, reading it as if I were hypnotised, until I came to the passage where Christian calls at the Interpreter's house – maybe I had skipped a bit to reach this so soon, or maybe the lecturer had given it particular mention. Then I read how Christian was taken to see the PARLOUR FULL OF DUST and the FIRE BURNING AGAINST A WALL and A MAN IN AN IRON CAGE. At last, I came to the man who shook and trembled as he tried to put on his clothes:

"This night, as I was in my sleep, I dreamed; and behold, the heavens grew exceeding black; also it thundered and lightened in most fearful wise, that it put me into an agony. So I looked up in my dream, and saw the clouds rack at an unusual rate; upon which I heard a great sound of a trumpet, and saw also a man sit upon a cloud, attended with the thousands of heaven; they were all in flaming fire, also the heavens were on a burning flame. I heard then a voice saying, 'Arise, ye dead, and come to judgement;' and with that the rocks rent, the graves opened, and the dead that were therein came forth: some of them were exceeding glad, and looked upward; and some sought to hide themselves under the mountains. . . ."

No words I have read since then have drilled so deeply into my mind. I trembled like the man rising out of bed, until I nearly fell off my stool. It was not a thing I could talk about to my father and mother. I shut the book almost furtively, and went off to bed as soon as I was told, and, in my cold attic – it never occurred to either of my parents that "a young boy like you" could possibly need a hot-water bottle – I shook and trembled and muttered smatterings of prayers, until sleep anaesthetised my fears.

But that was quite unlike my usual experience of chapel. For the Methodists, in my youth, contrary to what was often said of them, rarely preached, or even thought, about hell-fire. Theirs was not a religion of fear, but one of an extraordinarily reassuring warmth and comfort. It was, in fact, a social religion. I suspect that, for many members of the congregation, as for my mother and certainly for me, the dogma, the theology, the sectarian tenets hardly mattered at all. In my argumentative, near atheist early twenties, I once challenged my mother to say what she meant by "Christianity".

"We believe that God is Love," she said, confident that she had summed up all she had been taught.

What people find so hard to understand today is that most Methodists went to chapel because they enjoyed it. The chapel was not only their Place of Worship – it was their place of entertainment, their ancestral home, their music hall, assembly room, meeting house, club and gossip-shop. It came to me as a complete surprise, in my teenage years, to find that the Methodists were considered to be kill-joys, who got little pleasure out of life. For, at least up to the age of thirteen, the chapel seemed to me to be one of the happiest places in the town. I rather pitied the Church of England children, who seemed to have little going on in their communion; as for the Catholics – I had been led to believe that they went about in continual fear that the priest would turn them into a nanny-goat if they missed Mass.

When I say "chapel", I mean all the activities which took place in the chapel itself, in the two schools, in the Men's Institute and in the charmingly-named Church Parlour, where the Wesley Guild held its weekly meetings. But, of course, it was in the chapel building that the bonding process began, the welding together of the congregation into a group, a tribe, a family, a religious Trade Union or Friendly Society, all in one.

To begin with, we all belonged to the same country. And that country was the Holy Land. The landscape of the Bible was far more familiar to us than the geography of England. We had news of it twice every service in the lessons; the preachers preached about it; the hymns depicted and extolled it. Jerusalem, Jericho, Bethlehem, Canaan, the Sea of Galilee, Mount Carmel, Mount Ararat, Gilead, Moab, the Brook Cherith and cool Siloam's shady rill – all these seemed no further away from home than, say, the Duddon Valley. They were like a private estate to which all chapel people had a key, a secret but accessible region, where they could call in and visit and rest for a while at any time of the day. It was not only that the Bible lands seemed near to home: in some ways they *were* home. And they looked like home. To me the shepherds keeping watch over their flocks were men like the Watsons of Millom Castle, or the Tysons of Beck Farm, or the Falconers of Water Blean. I have heard that right up to the time of the eighteenth century, you could find country people who still believed that Jesus spoke in English, and, so far as I was concerned, the shepherds who found him in the stable spoke in the Cumberland dialect. There is a Yorkshire version of the first Book of Genesis, which begins:

"First on, there were nobbut God."

It seems to me far better than the *New English Bible*. And once, I remember, a Sunday School teacher gave us a lesson on the Good Samaritan – oddly enough, it was not at the Methodist, but at the Church of England Sunday School, and the teacher was my Uncle Jim!

"Now there was a man", he said, "sent out on a walk from Jerusalem to Jericho, just as he might have been going from Foxfield to Brough-ton" – mentioning two villages eight or nine miles from Millom, just over the Lancashire side of the old County boundary. And even today,

I cannot walk or drive along those two miles of highway, without seeing the man left half-dead, lying in the dyke bottom at the roadside.

But more important even than this sense of a shared country was the act of singing. It was the hymns which made the congregation one. The hymns were our liturgy, our initiation ceremony, our war chant. It happened that many of the best singers in the town belonged to the Wesleyan choir. There was Jack Woodruff, with a voice as wholesome as cider, who, for twenty or thirty years, took the lead for the Millom Amateur Operatic Society. His parents were both Welsh-speaking Welsh, but he sang "The Floral Dance" with such proprietorial pride that you would think the Bristol Channel had been done away with. All his life, he was proud of the fact that he had never had a music – as distinct from a *singing* – lesson, and could not read a note. Once, as a very young man, he had been persuaded to enter for the Baritone Solo at the Blackpool Festival, and the adjudicator, awarding him First Prize, commended him for his "nasal resonance".

"I had never heard of nasal resonance," he told me, when he was well over eighty. "And I don't know even yet what he meant."

And there was Sam Sheldon, then one of the leading undertakers of the town, who buried the Non-Conformists and the Catholics, while Lawrence Fairclough, Churchwarden at St. George's, buried the Anglicans. Sam had less of a voice than Jack Woodruff, but he was a more versatile performer, partly because, as a tenor, he was rarely given the lead in the amateur opera, and had to adapt himself to comic or character parts. He was a shortish man, jerky as a jack-in-a-box, who would hop and glide at the head of a funeral cortège and give his orders to the bearers with baton-like flourishes of his silk hat. He buried you as if it were a pleasure. He would hop and glide through his music, too, sometimes condensing a long phrase into a little rush of quavers; sometimes missing out several bars altogether. My mother used to say that accompanying him on the piano was like trying to swat a fly – she would slam hastily down chord after chord just where he had been a fraction of a second earlier.

Among the women in the choir, I remember two in particular. Violet Barnes took the lead opposite Jack Woodruff in the opera, singing such things as *The Country Girl* with the same serious concentration as if she were singing Handel or Mendelssohn. When I knew her, she was already dying of consumption, and from her dead-pale and emaciated face, with its pathetically trembling lower jaw, she produced tone of heart-breaking beauty. Nelly Gendle, on the other hand, was a completely different type – a robust, red-faced, middle-aged tomboy of a spinster, who went on singing year after year, until she had no voice left. I remember best one moment, round about 1927, when at a chapel concert, with a shawl over her shoulders, she astonished us by singing:

"In Millom's fair city
Where the girls are so pretty. . ."

(Pause, while she teased the audience with her eyes, over the top of the shawl.)

"'Twas there I first set eyes on. . ."

(Long pause: the audience holding back its giggle like a sneeze.)

"Sweet Mabel James."

But it is not yet quite time to tell who Mabel James was.

The hymn book from which we sang was not John Wesley's original "Large Hymn Book" of 1780, which he arranged with all the method of Methodism, as a manual and refresher course in conversion:

"For Persons Convinced of Back Sliding
For Back Sliders Recovered
For Believers Rejoicing
* * * * * * * *   Fighting
* * * * * * * *   Praying
* * * * * * * *   Watching
* * * * * * * *   Working
* * * * * * * *   Suffering
* * * * * * * *   Seeking for Full Redemption
* * * * * * * *   Saved
* * * * * * * *   Interceding for the World."

We used what my mother still called "The New Hymn Book", compiled in the early years of the century, and since succeeded by a more recent collection, if not more than one. With each revision, the book has moved further away from the eighteenth century, and the uncompromisingly evangelical theology has been watered down. So, too, has much of the uncompromisingly strong and precise diction. Congregations may still be asked to sing words like Doddridge's

"'Tis done, the great transaction's done!
I am my Lord's and He is mine" –

but not very often.

Nevertheless, the *Methodist Hymn Book* of 1904 still contained enough of Charles Wesley at his most exuberantly confident to hammer its way into my mind for ever. When I wrote my first poem at Holborn Hill School, at the age of ten, I added the metre, "7 7 7 7", at the bottom of the page:

"So in September" (I wrote)
"Summer slowly sinks to rest
Of all the seasons, the best."

I did not yet know how to scan – as you can see from that last line – but I knew how to count my syllables. In fact, I was writing syllabic verse nearly as early as Marianne Moore!

Those hymns went on sounding in the back of my mind like an organ pedal-point long after I had moved out of the orbit of the chapel. My first love poem, written when I was fourteen, began:

"Ineffable, infinite, true" –

for by then, alas, I was under the influence of a very different hymn book. I presented the poem, with some pride, to the fifteen-year-old girl for whom I had written it.

"It isn't true," she said, with what, I suppose, was becoming modesty.

I regarded this as an inadequate response. So far as I was concerned, it was "Love me, love my poem."

Yet, splendid as the words of the old hymns often were, the tune mattered far more to us. We sometimes sang those elaborate, chorus-like hymns, said to be specially favoured by the Primitive Methodists, the best known of which is probably the Welsh "Guide me, O Thou great Jehovah", with its massive bass-line banking up a one-in-three slope on the dominant seventh. And many of the congregation loved the more intense Welsh tunes, such as "Aberystwyth", or the cloying minor harmonies of "Angelus", set to "At Even, when the sun was set".

Our best tunes, however, were the straightforward ones: "The Old Hundredth", or "Miles Lane", set to "All hail the power of Jesu's name", or "Remington", sung to Isaac Watts's "Praise ye the Lord" or "Jesus shall reign where'er the sun". "Remington" was overwhelmingly the most popular hit of the time, and we sang it almost every other Sunday. It had, for me, one almost intoxicating moment, at the end of the third line, when the tenors soared high above the tune, as if they were singing a descant. Often, I would join with them, leaving the treble line just for that one note, until my cousin, Dorothy, kindly pointed out that I always made the same silly mistake at the same place!

"Remington", in fact, has a certain monotony of shape, but it also has a fine, steady, deliberate drumming in the first line, which gets the congregation off on the right foot, and keeps them at full stride all through the verses. We stood up together, straightened our backs, lifted up our heads, held the books well in front of us to catch the light, and flung the tune full in the Devil's face.

Nor did we stop singing when we left chapel, for, after the service, we would gather at my grandparents' house in Wellington Street, and my mother would sit down at the piano she had learned to play on as a girl. And, though she might begin with what my grandfather called "those pieces with the twiddly bits" – meaning Dvořák's "Humoresque" or the "Barcarole" from *The Tales of Hoffmann* – yet she always came back to the hymns in the end. My grandparents had loved these plain, wearable tunes for sixty years, and *their* parents had sung them, in their little Devonshire chapels or at Society Meetings in cottage parlours. Few tunes, few verses of any kind have stood up so long to such hard, continuous use. They became, in fact, the folk songs of industrial nineteenth-century England, and lasted well into our own century. After all, the tune of "Ilkley Moor Baht'at" began life as the setting of "While shepherds watch".

Methodism, however, was not just a Sunday religion: in fact, it was what happened between Sundays that meant most to us. There were a good many mid-week groups and gatherings, which were not much in my line – the Band of Hope, the Christian Endeavour, the Prayer Meetings, the Wesley Guild, the Sisterhood, called by the United Methodists the Women's Bright Hour. But there was much else that I could take my share in. Practically every important Sunday in the chapel calender spilled over into a concert, or some other festivity, on the Monday – Sunday School Anniversary, Chapel Anniversary, Harvest Festival, Men's Sunday. Then there were choir concerts, children's concerts and concerts with refreshments served by the members of the Young Ladies' Committee, of whom my mother was still one of the youngest. There was a marvellously-named Married

Women's Effort, of which, unfortunately, I have no memory at all. There were little operettas and musical sketches performed by the Sunday School children, and once there was a pantomime, in which my mother, then turned forty, played Prince Charming to a rather less youthful Cinderella. There were innumerable Bazaars, Sales of Work, Special Efforts and Faith Teas – so called because the food was not ordered in advance, and you had to trust that people would bring enough to share round. The bazaars often went on for seven or eight hours, with an Official Opening at three o'clock, a sale of work and produce in the afternoon, public tea at five o'clock, and a concert to follow. On Boxing Day, there was the Annual Effort, with the big Christmas tree hung all over with little collection envelopes, like oblong, bleached-white cones. The Guest of the day plucked them off one by one, and a steward read out the contents to an audience, intent as a modern bingo crowd:

"Mr. and Mrs. A: Ten shillings
Mrs. B and family: Five shillings
God Send You Back To Me: Twopence."

I can still see one Superintendent Minister, a busy, fussy little man, fizzing like a bottle of soda water with the unstaled enthusiasm of an Edwardian youth, as he introduced the Guest of that year:

"When we arranged this Bazaar," he said, "we decided to invite Mrs. D of Ulverston to do us the honour of performing the Opening Ceremony. She was, unfortunately, not able to accept, but she sent us a cheque for ten guineas."

He bent forward, like a short-legged heron about to strike, and triggered off a loud round of applause.

"Then we thought again, and invited Mrs. E of Barrow, and she, too, could not come, but she sent us a generous gift of five pounds."

He paused again, waiting for the – this time – more subdued applause.

"And, finally, we said to ourselves, who could we possibly choose better than our own Mrs. G, who I'm delighted to welcome here tonight, and who has kindly donated two pounds."

The indignant woman turned red as a pickle cabbage, from her feather boa to her toque hat, and stalked out of the hall, when the ceremony was over, without spending so much as sixpence at any of the stalls.

And spending sixpences, of course, was what these bazaars were for. For these were the lean days in Millom, with thirty or forty per cent of the men unemployed, and the shopkeepers barely holding their heads above bankruptcy. In those times, even loyal chapel-goers like my grandparents were content if they could put a silver threepenny-bit in the collection, and it was a very successful bazaar that raised as much as twenty, or even ten, pounds. As it was, the money side of the chapel sometimes puzzled me.

"The collection this evening is in aid of the Circuit Fund," said Henry Foss's father, sifting the air through the dark, hairy over-hang of his upper lip, as if he were drinking from a moustache-cup.

"Why did they take a collection for the circus?" I asked, after the service.

But whatever they were in aid of, I enjoyed these weekday evenings more than almost anything that came my way. I enjoyed the bustle, the buzz, the excitement, the jingle of music – often with my mother at the piano – and above all, the lovely scrimmage and mixing together of so many people of so many types and ages. For, as a young boy, I always preferred the company of adults to that of children my own age – except, of course, that of my own particular friends – and here, in the merry-making and money-making of the chapel society, I felt thoroughly at home, thoroughly accepted. I had no sense whatever of being too young to take my proper part. I would go down with my mother in the morning of the event, and help to decorate the stall. I would run errands or carry messages, and sometimes I would be put temporarily in charge of the bran tub or the darts board. No child has ever had a more comfortable feeling of belonging than I had in the Methodist schoolroom or, indeed, anywhere in Millom, for I was Joe Nicholson's lad in the streets, just as I was Rose Sobey's stepson at the chapel, recognised and greeted everywhere. And before long, I was to make myself, of my own right, one of the best-known boys of my age in the town.

Which brings me to Mabel James. Miss James was one of a score or more of young ladies, in their late twenties or middle thirties, who were, I suppose, really casualties of the War, widowed before they were married. My mother had escaped that fate only at the last possible moment. Without their help – to make tea and sew curtains and decorate the pews at harvest and sell tickets for concerts and keep the children in order at the Anniversary Walk – I do not know how the chapel could have kept going. Mabel James was a "worker", as Nelly Gendle had called her in that valedictory song:

> "But now she's going to leave us
> And I'm sure it will grieve us
> To lose such a worker
>   As sweet Mabel James –
> As she wheeled her wheelbarrow
> Through streets broad and narrow,
> Crying: Cockles and mussels,
>   Alive, alive-o."

(She was, in fact, at the time of the song, about to leave Millom to join, I think, a missionary brother in South Africa or India. Henry Foss and I went to see her at her home, the day before she departed. We shook hands across the little iron gate of her table-cloth-sized garden.

"Good-bye," I said.

"God speed," said Henry.

I gawped at him as if he had used bad language.)

Among Miss James's many works for the chapel was the running of a Junior Wesley Guild, or social evening, for the younger Sunday Scholars up to the age of eleven or twelve. I can remember little about it, except that it was held in the Church Parlour. I expect we sang a children's hymn, said the Lord's Prayer and played games. I don't suppose they were my sort of games, and, probably, my interest would soon have died away, had we not been told, after a week or two, that we were to give a children's concert during the course of the winter. We practised a few songs together, singing as a choir, but, for the most part, the concert was to be made up of individual items – vocal solos, recitations, a piano solo, there may even have been a four-hands piano duet. Nearly everyone was asked to do something, and since I had shown no musical talent to speak of, I was asked to recite. I accepted without much excitement, for, though I had always found it easy enough "to learn a poetry", I did not particularly look forward to making what seemed to me rather an undistinguished contribution to the evening.

Then, one afternoon, just before tea-time, my father came in from the shop and announced that "two ladies" had called to see me. Both he and my mother put on such an elaborate parade of having not the least idea of why the two had come, that I guessed that something must have been talked over beforehand. Miss James and Miss Spry – I forget now whether it was Maggie, or her sister, Ada – entered the room. My father went back into the shop; my mother busied herself in the little back kitchen, leaving me alone with the two ladies.

"You know about the children's concert?"

"Yes."

(Of course I did!)

"We have come to ask you to be the Chairman."

Now, in the concerts of those days, the Chairman was the most conspicuous figure on the stage. His name was printed on the posters larger than that of the artists. At devotional or Sunday afternoon concerts, the Chair was often taken by the Minister, but on more ambitious occasions – price 1/6d, instead of sixpence or ninepence – the organisers would invite the Managing Director of the Ironworks, or a Bank Manager, or some such notable to carry out the duty. He would sit on the stage at a small, round table, covered, like a parrot's cage at night-time, with green plush, and tastefully decorated with flowers by the ladies of the congregation. From here, he announced each artist, led the applause, and made his "Chairman's Remarks" after the second or third item. "The Chairman is expected to do three things" – I heard more than one of them say – "Stand up; speak up; and shut up." One might add: "Pay up", since, if he did not make a donation at the end, he was not likely to be invited again. Paying up, of course, was not yet expected of me. For the rest, it was what I was quite sure I would be able to do. I gulped down the invitation, like a dog swallowing a chocolate.

"Now, can we ask you one other thing?" said Miss James. (She could have asked me anything she liked!)

"Do you mind not telling anybody that you are going to be Chairman? We want to keep it a secret until the night."

I approved of secrets, and agreed willingly enough.

"And I've written out your speech for you, so that you'll have plenty of time to learn it," said Miss James.

The little bubble of soapy complacency that had been floating and gleaming in my mind suddenly burst. I looked at Miss James with sharp, almost petulant, suspicion.

"But a Chairman dosen't learn his speech," I protested. "He speaks *ex tempo*. I want to be a proper Chairman. I don't want to learn any speech."

"It's better than not knowing what to say," said Miss Spry.

"I'll know what to say," I said.

It is to Mabel James's eternal credit that she understood:

"All right then," she said. "But there are one or two things we specially want you to mention – a few people we have to thank, and so on. So I'll just write out a few notes on a card, to make sure you won't forget them."

My mother came rushing in.

"Well, are you going to do it?" she asked, forgetting that she was supposed to know nothing about it.

"Yes, and I'm not going to learn my speech," I said. She swung round, ready to put me in my place.

"Of course you're going to learn it, when Miss James has gone to the trouble to write it out for you."

"Never mind about that," said Mabel James. "He wants to be a proper Chairman. Let him do it his own way."

The secret was well kept. I went down to the Hall with Henry Foss and met Miss James just inside the door.

"Who is to be the Chairman?" asked Henry, probably wondering if he himself might not be chosen at the last moment. There was a pause, like the indrawing of a breath. Then Miss James seized hold of Henry's hand, and pushed it across to mine.

"Shake hands with our Chairman," she said.

He shook, very handsomely, I thought, in the circumstances.

Apart from the Co-operative Hall and the two cinemas, the Wesleyan Methodist Sunday School was then the largest public hall in the town. Outside, it was typical of the end of the last century – a gaunt building of black slate and red freestone, a cross between a warehouse and a rather unecclesiastical monastery. Inside, it was plain and ugly, with high square windows, set so deep in the walls that half the boys in the audience could sit in the window sills. There was a short, steep gallery at the back, boxed off like a medieval choir, under which were two small classrooms. Other small rooms opened off the main hall, and there was a lesser schoolroom at the side, which could be used as the gathering and changing-room for the performers. The stage, which I was to come to know almost as well as my own home, was just a raised wooden platform, approached by steps at either side. But, for a concert, the sides and back were screened off, so that you could enter from the lesser schoolroom without being seen by the audience, while across the front, were two green draw-curtains, worked by a cat's-cradle of string and pulleys. At a signal, the two curtain men, hidden on either side, hauled on their ropes like sailors, and the two curtains would jerk and slither slowly apart, though more often than not, one of them would stick half-way, until a hand appeared from behind and dragged it, screeching, into place.

With the curtains still closed, we were herded onto the stage, thirty or forty of us, and sat on benches along the back and sides, the girls in black stockings, the boys with bare knees, and all of them scared and goggle-eyed as waxworks. I had a little table on the left of the stage – audience's right – with a proper chair to sit on.

At last, someone rapped the table for silence. The murmur of the room shushed down, and the curtains zipped and puckered slowly open. There were no footlights, for electricity had not yet reached Millom, and the gas burners in the Hall were not turned down, so that we stared straight at the audience, as they stared at us. The Hall was packed, floor and gallery, extra chairs in the aisles, children on the window ledges. Miss James, who was standing in the wings, gave me a nod. I stood up, finding to my surprise, for I had not been told about stage fright, that my legs were joggling as if I were walking the cake-walk. I picked up my programme, opened my mouth and – thank God – the words creaked out.

"Ladies and gentlemen," I said, "we will commence our concert by singing the opening chorus."

By the time I had announced the first two or three items, my legs had steadied themselves, my voice sounded as it ought to sound, and I was ready for what, to me, seemed the focal point of the evening.

"Ladies and gentlemen," I began again –

Mr. Foss, sitting in the audience, kindly led the applause.

I have no idea of what I said, but I do know that I was listened to.

"Remember to speak up," my father had said to me, before I left home – it was the only advice he ever gave me on such matters.

And I did remember to speak up. I had a good voice at that time – a boy mezzo, rather than a boy treble – and I could see from the cocked heads and intent eyebrows that I was making myself heard, even at the back of the Hall. This, in itself, was quite a feat in a concert where the majority of the performers breathed prettily in tones that barely floated beyond the first three or four rows of seats. When I walked among the audience at the interval, I knew that I had made a success of the job. People kept shaking me by the hand.

"We're enjoying the Chairman more than the concert," said old Mrs. Walmsley.

Then Mr. Slater came to me with a request: would I return to the stage and make an announcement, saying that Mr. Huggins, Rate Collector for the Parish of Millom Without and Superintendent of our Sunday School, had arranged a museum of missionary curios in one of the classrooms at the back of the Hall, on show to the public, price 2d. I pushed my way through the gap between the curtains, waited while the stewards called for silence, and said that I would be very pleased if as many people as possible would go to see the museum. I think I made them feel – as, indeed, I probably felt myself – that I would take it as a personal favour.

When the second half of the concert began, there was no shaking of the legs, no quaking of the voice, and the evening moved on towards the moment but for which I might not have written this book at all. The little singer or pianist, whoever he or she was, finished his piece, bobbed, and went back to his place. I glanced down at my programme, as if I did not know what was there.

"The next item", I said, "is a recitation by myself."

I walked from my table out to the centre-point of the platform, hearing first of all a suppressed titter and then a burst of applause. (My mother, though she was very proud of my performance, seemed to find this announcement of mine very funny, and laughed over it for days.)

"BIG STEAMERS," I said, "by Rudyard Kipling:
'Oh where are you going to, all you Big Steamers
With England's own coal, up and down the salt seas?'"

I write entirely from memory. The words were copied out for me by Miss James, and I do not think I have ever seen them in print. If Kipling's version is different from mine, then I do not want to know about it. As the bouncy, sailor's-horn-pipe rhythm, the jingo rhetoric, the far-flung imperialist place names ("Address us at Hobart, Hong Kong and Bombay") rippled out, I felt, for the first time, the lovely, dangerous, electric power of verse to excite and communicate. The audience were not just listening to the poem – they were saying the poem with me; they were inventing their own poems in their own heads. The verse rounded to its final grand bombast with the sound of an organ. This was the "Christianity and Commerce" that Livingstone had preached about; this was Empire and Foreign Missions rolled into one. So far as I was concerned – and so far, I suspect, as most of the audience were concerned – Kipling's sentiments were indistinguishable from those of "Greenland's icy mountains":

> "'Then what can I do for all you Big Steamers,
>   Oh what can I do for your comfort and good?' –
> 'Send out your big warships to watch your wide waters
>   That no-one may stop us from bringing you food.'

>   *

> 'For the bread that you eat and the biscuits you nibble,
>   The sweets that you suck and the joints that you carve,
> They are brought to you daily by all us Big Steamers,
>   And if anyone hinders our coming – *you ll starve*.'"

At the last words, I raised my hand in a rehearsed gesture, and pointed directly at the people. In a way, I have been pointing at them ever since. I cannot pretend that I walked back to my chair with my mind made up to be a poet, but, from that time onwards, the idea that I might be a poet was persistently in the back of my thoughts. And always, when I thought of the poetry I might one day write, it was as if I raised my hand and pointed. I did not want to be a solitary poet, talking to myself in an attic or beside a lake. I wanted an audience; I wanted to make people listen. Forty-five years later, when I gave a reading of my own poems in, I think, Accrington, a man came up and told me that he had been in the audience at the Methodist School Room for that first concert in 1924.

"I heard you make your début," he said.

It was still some time, however, before people outside the Wesleyan persuasion became aware of that début. My first appearance after the concert was on Whit Sunday, at the Sunday School Anniversary, when, from the pulpit, I recited some moral verses, which I have mercifully been allowed to forget. I enjoyed Whit Sunday well enough, with its Anniversary Hymns, the packed congregations, and my own little moment of glory in the evening; but Whit Monday, the day of the Sunday School Treat, was a complete bore. It began with a procession "round the principal streets of the town", then tea in the Sunday

School, followed by sports and games in a field "kindly loaned by a member of the congregation". The sports I detested from the start, and, after the first year, came to an agreement with my parents that as long as I attended the procession and the tea, I might leave at five o'clock, and go to the Cricket Field for the second half of the Millom and Haverigg match. I tried to get out of the tea, also, but my mother insisted that this was an essential part of my religious obligations and I could not be allowed to shirk it. One memory remains. I had fulfilled, as I thought, my duty, and was waiting for the moment to rush off to the cricket match, when one of the stewards walked behind the trestle table with an enormous enamel can, slopping out tea as if he were watering an herbaceous border. He looked at me queryingly, having noticed that I was no longer eating.

"Finished," I said, peremptorily.

To my surprise, he began to pour tea into my cup. I put up a hand to stop him.

"I said: Finished," I repeated.

"Oh! I thought you said: Fill it."

I blushed with shame. That he should have thought I hadn't the manners to say Please!

It was some months after Whitsuntide when my mother told me I ought to enter for the Elocution Class on the Children's Day of the Millom Musical Festival. We were much aware of the Musical Festival in our house. My father was on the committee – not that he could tell one note from another! – and my mother often accompanied singers in the Solo Classes. Once, she presented the Prizes at the Children's Day – a ceremony which was dropped in subsequent years. I remember that my cousin, Bill, won Third Prize for the Boys' Solo, and I thought it odd that my mother should shake hands with him when she handed over the prize, as if she did not know who he was.

The Musical Festival of those days was one of the favourite winter sports in our part of the world. Ours was not one of those enormous Festivals, where you've got to sit through one hundred and twenty consecutive Merry Peasants. We usually had ten to twelve entries in each class – more in the children's classes — and the audience would back their fancies, like a crowd at a hound trail, waiting, tense and excited, at the winning post for the Adjudicator's verdict. Then out would come programmes and pencils, and down would go the marks, and everybody would start arguing and whispering and buzzing. I've seen a male voice choir scrum down like a rugby pack to tackle a difficult test piece. I've known a baritone from Barrow, who had missed the Rose Bowl by one point, raise his fists angrily to the Adjudicator until Herbert Thomas, of whom I will have more to tell, threatened to throw him down the stairs.

The Adjudicator – I think it was Armstrong Gibbs – came on to the platform, vibrating like a violin string with justified indignation.

"I give my judgements without fear or favour," he declared, righteous as a martyr.

We applauded thunderously. After all, it was a Millom man who had won the Rose Bowl.

On the Children's Day, there was much less animosity, except, perhaps, among the mothers. I already had some slight experience as a competitor, having sung for two years in the choir of Holborn Hill Boys' School, conducted by the same Herbert Thomas. We entered by a door marked *Competitors Only*, and climbed to the top of a three-storey building, up stairs so steep that some of the older competitors in the adult classes had no breath to sing for the first quarter of an hour of the session, and had to go early, if they were due to sing first.

The test piece for the Elocution was a long, picturesque, narrative poem by R. L. Stevenson, called "Christmas at Sea":

"The sheets were frozen hard and they cut the naked hand;
The decks were like a slide where the seamen scarce could stand;
The wind was a Nor'wester blowing squally off the sea,
And cliffs and spouting breakers were the only things a-lee."

It tells how a ship in a storm is driven dangerously close to a rocky coast, and how one of the sailors recognises his old home, the place he had run away from, years before:

"And they heaved a mighty breath every soul on board –
    but me,
As they saw her nose again pointing handsome out to sea.
But all that I could think of, in the darkness and the cold,
Was just that I was leaving home, and my folks were growing
    old."

It was obviously a boy's piece, and as the twenty or so competitors ploughed their way through it in the afternoon's Preliminary Round, it soon became clear that the girls were not going to get much of a look in. The winner of the class for several years previous was an extremely pretty girl, a few years older than me, who, having already taken her turn, was sitting near her mother and looking rather downcast. Suddenly, at her mother's suggestion, she sidled up to me on the bench.

"How old are you, Norman?" she asked.

I was terrified. Any nervousness I may have felt in facing the audience was nothing to what I felt then.

"Eleven," I hiccupped out. "Just."

I was, in fact, precisely eleven years and ten months, which is more a matter of "twelve – nearly" than "eleven – just". I still do not understand the reason for that "just". Maybe it was a kind of apology.

At the Final, in the evening, the stage was stacked high with children, the body of the hall with parents. I sat with my mother in the fourth or fifth row, and went up to the stage only when my class number was called. No smoking was allowed, but the air was smoky-blue with breath, and the damp trickled down the green-painted walls, as if they had just been swilled. I walked out onto the stage, and waited for the tinkle of the bell which was the signal to start. Then I gave the piece all I was capable of. It was, to begin with, my own version. My mother had helped me to learn it by "hearing me say the words"; and once I recited it to Mr. Foss, who made one or two sensible suggestions. Apart from this, I was left to myself, which, I think, gave a kind of authenticity, even to my so blatant melodramatics, as compared with those who had been taught, line by line, to say the piece.

I imitated the voice of the Captain and the Mate with the ventriloquial gusto of a Punch-and-Judy man. I took about a quarter of a minute over the final line, wringing out the last drop of sentiment like a girl wringing out a wet hanky. The audience clapped like mad. The Adjudicator – it was Henry Coward, an ageing choral conductor from Sheffield – commended my handling of the parenthesis in one of the stanzas, and gave me ninety-four marks out of a hundred.

From then onwards, I began to receive invitations to recite at concerts, but, for a while, my mother turned them all down. She had her own plan for me. About once a year, she used to arrange in the Wesleyan School Room what she herself considered to be *the* Concert of the Year. There were reserved tickets – price 2/6d, equivalent to the top seats at the Millom Opera; refreshments were catered for by Miss Danson – "None of your home-made stuff at *my* concerts," my mother would say; and the artists were very select. This year, she had invited, as a special guest, a singer from Barrow, whom she had made friends with on her earlier visits as a pianist – she had a pre-1914 visiting card, inscribed:

The other artists were either First Prize Winners at the Festival or people considered to be of some local standing, such as the wife of the Underground Manager at Hodbarrow (soprano), or an Assistant Bank Manager (bass), and it was in company with such as these that the name of Master Norman Nicholson first appeared on a concert poster.

We had found, in an anthology of popular recitations, a long, humorous ballad by Sir Arthur Conan Doyle, entitled "The Groom's Story" – I find myself slipping unintentionally into the language of the Chairman's announcement. It told a ridiculous tale of a broken-down racehorse which was harnessed to a motor car to drag it out of the mud, and it was intended to be spoken in a kind of sub-Cockney or ostler-ese by a man who hadn't an "H" to his name. My mother, however, disapproved of dialect, and thought that the dropping of "H"s was common, so that I had to learn to say the lines in my better-end-of-the-town Millom accent, with every "H" neatly in its place.

For two or three years, "The Groom's Story" made me better known in Millom than I have ever been since. I recited it to the Wesleyan Methodists, the United Methodists, the Primitive Methodists, the Baptists, and in St. George's Hall and the Plough Room. After a while, I began to enlarge my repertoire. There were a number of verses from a book of "More Recitations for Boys and Girls". There was a piece called "The Minister to Tea", which was unfailingly successful at Methodist Socials. I appeared at concerts arranged by every religious body in the town, except the Catholics and the Salvation Army. I took part in a Harvest Festival at the Haverigg United Methodists, arranged by my Auntie Frances; I recited at the Haverigg Primitive Methodists, where the pews were steeply raked round a central space, like the seats in a circus tent. I spoke and sang my way through the lead in a children's operetta, and I appeared as Corner Boy in a Nigger Minstrel Show, in which we sang "We're coming back again", without the faintest suspicion that we were singing about reincarnation:

"A monkey you may be,
Climbing up a tree,
    Or a poor little worm out in the rain –
But cheer up and say: 'Here goes,'
As you're turning up your toes,
    For we're all coming back again."

And once I helped to open a Bazaar.

It was in 1926 or '27, when the Wesleyans, like all the other religious bodies in the town, were desperately struggling to reduce a heavy load of debt. This time, they were to make an all-out effort, and hired the Co-operative Hall for a week, for a Grand Japanese Bazaar. The stage rocked and twinkled with Japanese lanterns and Japanese bells. Pagoda-like wooden stalls lined the sides of the hall, and everything was titivated and tinselled into a gaudy Willow Pattern plate, with Japanese jugs, Fujiyama biscuit tins, paper chrysanthemums, cotton-wool mimosa, tassels and streamers and silvered greenery and miles of crêpe paper. All the Bazaar helpers looked as if they had just stepped out of a dress rehearsal of *The Mikado*. Poo-Bah ordered the day's procedure; Nanki-Poo sold shreds and patches; and I took charge of the dart board as a Japanese page, in a chintz kimono, trimmed with yellow ribbon.

The Bazaar went on for three or four nights, for there seemed to be an apparently unending supply of all that the people for many weeks had been sewing, knitting, crocheting, baking, bottling, painting, cutting-out, stitching-together and begging – jams, pickles, cakes, knick-knacks, children's clothes, embroidered tea-cosies and teapot stands, and home-made calendars with photos of Coniston Lake. There were concerts every hour in a side room, given by a different concert party each night. There were continuous musical selections from Ketelbey and Gilbert and Sullivan, played by my mother, among others. There were side-shows, and exhibitions and games – darts, quoits, hoop-la, and the like. It was my job, along with three other boys, to look after the darts. We gave pencils as prizes, and our customers seemed to be such notably bad darts players that we ended up by having to sell the pencils at three a penny.

Each evening had its separate Official Opening, which, on one of the days, was to be carried out by the children of the Sunday School. This was where I came in; I was to take the Chair, while the actual Opening was to be performed by Marjorie Elwell, daughter of Captain and Mrs. F. Elwell, and granddaughter of Chris Walmsley.

Once again, the question of the Chairman's Remarks cropped up, but this time I found myself in something of an embarrassment, for one of the organisers of the event had been in touch with the members of a Methodist chapel in another part of the country, where, at a similar Children's Opening, the speeches of both Chairman and Opener and, indeed, the entire ceremony, had been written out in rhyme. It was proposed now to use the same rhymes, modified to suit the place and the occasion. I protested as before, but my mother pleaded with me, and called in Mrs. Elwell, who told me that Marjorie had already learned *her* speech. I found the combined feminine pressure too strong for me and agreed to learn my speech, on condition that I was allowed to make my own modifications to the lines. This was, in fact, the first time I ever spoke my own verse in public!

The two of us – Marjorie, looking like a very pretty chrysanthemum, and me, in sober blue serge – sat at a table on the stage, with Mr. Foss between us. I was not surprised at this, for, on such occasions, it was taken for granted that the Minister would offer a word of prayer: "O Lord, Thou knowest that Thy servants are now in debt to the sum of over two hundred pounds." What I did not realise then, and what, in fact, I did not realise until this very moment of writing, is that he was present as a kind of insurance, in case the boy and girl Openers forgot their lines, or muddled things up. It has taken nearly forty years for that penny to drop.

Of the rest of the ceremony, I remember nothing. Indeed, as my public appearances became more frequent, so the memory of them becomes less clear. Older people sometimes claim to have heard me recite in places where I have no recollection of ever having been. But one memory remains with strange, almost foreboding clarity. It is of a concert when I found myself sharing the bill with an off-comer to the town, a Scotsman called – if I remember rightly – Mr. Me Waters, who was something of an oddity, and also something of a mystery. He wore his white hair down to his shoulders, like Lloyd George, and I think he may have been lame. He was an ardent Labour Party man, and was rumoured to have been divorced, which, in each case, made him seem almost as strange as a Chinaman. He was also a great writer of topical verses, which were printed in *The Millom Gazette*, and, round about this time, he had begun to make yet another reputation for himself as a light entertainer, singing or half-speaking humorous monologues to his own accompaniment at the piano. My mother, of course, would never have invited him to one of her concerts, but the United Methodists *had* invited him, and I was able to listen to him for the first time. On the day of the concert, unfortunately, he was suffering from an attack of catarrh, which struck him stone deaf, so that he could not hear the piano he was playing or the pitch of the note he was supposed to be singing. The result was ludicrous – pathetic, rather than comic – and when, during the interval, he pushed his way purposefully through the crowd towards me, I began to feel apprehensive.

He caught hold of my hand and shook it as if he were waving the Red Flag.

"I enjoyed your reciteetion verra much indeed," he said, gripping my hand in both of his, and staring intently into my face. "But I never haird a warrud."

I must have looked blank.

"It was your feecial expression," he explained, "and the wee you went aboot it."

My mother shrieked with laughter when I told her, but I still think it was one of the most understanding compliments I ever received.

Of the other kind of compliment, I had had about enough. For one thing, by the time I was thirteen, I had begun to realise that most of the pieces I recited were little better than rubbish. For another, I was more critical of my own performance. This was brought home to me when I entered a second time for the Musical Festival, and the test piece was Walter de la Mare's "Off the Ground", with its lovely polka-rhythm:

> "Three jolly farmers
> Once bet a pound,
> Each dance the other would
> Off the ground."

Now, like most children of those days, I had been taught at school that you should not stop at the end of a line if the sense ran on into the next, so, in common with all the other competitors, I recited the poem as if it were written in four-stress lines:

"Three jolly farmers once bet a pound,
Each dance the other would off the ground."

The Adjudicator – a woman, for a change – came straight to the point.

"Has none of you children noticed that this poem is written in short lines?" she asked.

My mother said, afterwards, that she couldn't see what she was getting at. But I could, and though I had been awarded the First Prize, I knew I did not deserve it.

For all this, I should probably have gone on reciting until the audiences were completely sick of me, as, indeed, the boys and girls of my own age already were, had not Mr. Sharp, Headmaster of the Secondary School, called one day to see my father. I was getting on for fourteen, by now, and had just started on the two years' run-up for Matric.

My father reported his interview with Mr. Sharp.

"'All this reciting and acting and going on the stage,' he said to me. 'It's all very well in its way,' he said, 'but the boy needs his evenings for his homework now,' he said. 'So cut it out,' he said."

My father sliced the air with his hand, almost ferociously.

"'Cut it out', he said."

He sliced the air again.

"For a year or two," said my mother, with a slight note of alarm. "Just for a year or two."

"He said, 'Cut it out,'" my father repeated, using, I suspect, this moment of reinforced authority to put the whole Non-Conformist social scheme just where he thought it ought to be.

He need not have worried. I cut it out all right. And it was not to be just two years, but forty-two, before I made my next recitation in Millom.

CHAPTER SIX

THE tale of my small-town stardom has bounced me on to my fourteenth year, leap-frogging over the bumps and blanks in between. I must now return to the early days of my father's second marriage, when I was no more than nine and already half-way through my four years at Holborn Hill Boys' School.

The School, as I have said, was built round a quadrangle, with the Boys' section laid out in the shape of a large L on two sides of the inner square. You came up from the Infants' into the quadrangle, and then worked your way, year by year, along the arms of the L – with Standards II and III, divided by a partition, in one of the arms, and, in the other, Standards V, VI and VII, divided only by a gap between the desks. We lived perpetually within the murmur and scuffle and smother and smell of the classes round about. When any teacher lost his temper, anywhere in the School, we pricked up our ears, like nosy-parker neighbours; when any class spluttered into laughter, we were as startled as if a brass band had struck up in the playground.

In the quadrangle, we were entirely imprisoned in the School, completely isolated from the outer world. Our windows, when they were not blocked up with cardboard, looked only into other classrooms. Light reached us through a white-washed glass roof and air entered only when the skylight could be propped open. In winter, the rain rumbled its drum-roll on the roof and the coke stove fumed in the down-draught, until our eyes were bloodshot from the smirch. We rubbed them with inky fists and went home with lids streaked red and blue, like a freak tulip.

We were all of us pretty cowed in those first months in the quad-rangle. From being among the bigger children of the Infants', we now found ourselves to be the smallest of the Boys', surrounded by enormous, noisy, rough fourteen-year-olds, some of whom were even bigger than the teachers. We huddled together in the playground, or hid in the lavatories, keeping out of their way, as they charged around, banging a sorbo ball, kicking up the gravel, or hounding and bullocking about in chaotic rough-and-tumble tig.

Our teacher, Mr. Benjamin, who had taught my father in the days before Queen Victoria's Diamond Jubilee, was a short, stout, ovoid old man, mildewed with, age, and rockily balanced on his bottom tip, like a very large egg in a very small egg-cup. The bulged-out tweed of his waistcoat and trousers was grained and flecked with chalk, ink, glue and all the snotty hazards of his profession. Older boys said that he used to retire behind the blackboard to chew tobacco, but this, so far as I could tell, was a libel. He taught with the stick on the hand, the knuckles on the back of the head, and the voice that snapped down hard and heavy as either.

We had said good-bye to the tiles, the crayons and the coloured paper of the Infants' School, and began by scratching "Holborn Hill Boys'" and our own names on slates that skidded and squeaked hideously under the pressure of the slate pencils. A quick spit and a rub with our nose-rag put right a mistake before old Benji spotted it. But soon we had to take grasp of stubby, wooden pens, stabbing the nibs in the ink-well as if we were skewering live bait, and forcing our often stinging fingers to – "Careful now, dot the 'i's, cross the 't's, what did I tell you?" – trace the impossible copperplate in our Cumberland County Education Committee Exercise Books. Every blot meant "Hold out your hand", making it even harder not to throw more blots next time.

We learned like parrots: the multiplication tables, the months of the year, the Ten Commandments. The almost meaningless words were recorded in some part of the brain as on wax. Even today, when the needle drops unaccountably in the right groove, I can hear them creak out in the same monotonous whine, and the same up-and-down sing-song:

> "Thou shalt not cuft thy neighbour's ouse
> Thou shalt not cuft thy neighbour's wife
> Nor is manservant
> Nor is maidservant
> Nor is ox
> Nor is ass
> Nor enthing that is is."

The metronome click of the stick keeps coming down, again and again, driving us on, like a child bowling a boolie.

I was so numbed in Standard I, that I do not know whether I was there for a year or only six months, and I cannot remember the face or the name of a single one of my class-mates. Except for the parrotings, I have no recollection of having learned anything at all, of acquiring anything, discovering anything, finding anything out, or of growing even a day older in all those months. Yet I must have learned something, for at the end of the School Year, when we were shifted into Standard II, under Sid Mudge, I had scarcely time to settle into my new classroom before I was moved next door, into Standard III. This, for me, was where school really began.

First of all, our new classroom looked out on to the world. I say "looked out", though school windows were not built to be looked out of, and, in any case, we sat with our backs to them. But the windows, nevertheless, opened south-west, across the playground, which dropped steeply away on this side to the cricket-field wall. Through the summer afternoons, a great blueness opened behind us, as if a shutter had been lifted; and the shadows and shafts of light slowly cartwheeled across the opposite wall, telling the time like a sundial. I remember that, a year or so earlier, when I was still in the Infants' School, we were told to write a sentence on "Today". This was a regular exercise. And we usually wrote "It is raining today" or "It is sunshining", and were satisfied with that, but this time I looked through the classroom windows on to that same blue, and wrote:

"It is fine today. There are clouds in the sky, but they are not rain clouds."

I was surprised to be commended. I had only written down what my grandmother had said at dinner-time.

From then on, school began to come into a new focus. The faces of the boys who were to be my companions, on and off, for the next six or seven years, push themselves sharply into view, as if a mist had been blown away – John Slater, Dudley, Harry, George, Jacker, Pasty Jackson. I fancy that, because I started school half a year late, it had taken all this time for me to catch up with the others. I took to learning as a healthy boy takes to running about. It didn't matter much what I was learning, so long as the little slide-rule in the brain could keep on clicking and connecting. When the visiting parson came round to inspect us in Scripture, I thrust up my hand at every question, straining to attract attention. It did not seem strange to me, when the inspection was over, to be given an atlas as a reward for answering well. (I still have the atlas, with about a quarter of the world coloured red.) Yet I had no great sense of competition. I was spurred on less by a wish to do better than the others than by the only child's inbred desire to please, and this desire was increased by the fact that my two teachers in Standard III were both of them women – Miss Mackereth and Miss Hurst. Miss Mackereth was married, round about this time, and resigned from her job, since Education Authorities would not have dared to employ a married woman. I remember still the look of surprise on Herbert Thomas's face when I handed him a two-shilling piece for the collection for the wedding present. Two shillings was a lot of money, but Miss Mackereth was marrying a tailor, and my father knew the respect that was due to a fellow tradesman, even if he was a competitor.

With Miss Hurst, however, there began to develop the kind of personal relationship which, from then onwards, existed between me and nearly all my teachers. It was partly, no doubt, that, at that age, any reasonably kind woman teacher became a substitute for my dead mother. Indeed, one incident belongs more to the kitchen than the classroom. It happened when Dudley – who, being clean, neat, healthy and very bright, was a natural favourite – was having some kind of playful mock-struggle with Miss Hurst in front of the classroom, and I suddenly jumped up, and slapped her loudly on the bottom. The class screeched with laughter and I was not reproved, but when the door suddenly opened, and Mr. Brunskill, the Headmaster, walked in, boys and teacher alike sank into a sheepish silence.

Standard IV differed from every other class in the School in that it had a room to itself – a room built as a kind of after-thought, in the angle made by the main wall and the School porch, from which the bell-turret jutted up like the spike on a Hun officer's helmet. Here, for the first time, I was taught by a man under the age of sixty – the few days with Sid Mudge had not been long enough to count. Stuart S. belonged to the kind of old-fashioned Methodist family whose sons almost inevitably went to Training College or Theological College, and became either teachers or Methodist ministers. Today, he would have gone straight into university, but, fifty years ago, he was a vigorous, inventive, infinitely curious animal, confined in too small a cage. He had just married a beautiful young woman from Haverigg, and her early death, some years afterwards, so troubled him that his later career was clouded, and his natural gifts went partly to waste. Once, in those later days, he agreed to "give a paper" to the Wesley Guild. When the time came, he failed to turn up. The gathered members sang a few hymns, and remained chatting round the Church Parlour fire until, about an hour later, Mr. S. knocked quietly on the door, and asked if he could speak to the Secretary. She went outside into the corridor, to find him in a state of nervous anxiety, not much clarified by whisky. He apologised with enormous sincerity, saying that he had forgotten about the meeting until that very minute.

"But I was not unprepared," he said. "I was going to talk about the Immortality of the Soul."

Then, suddenly, he began to prove his assertion by favouring her with an only slightly shortened version of the whole talk.

"It's a pity," he said. "It's a pity, but I can't do it like this, can I?"

The assembly waited in the Church Parlour, tense with curiosity, until, at last, they heard Stuart's voice lifted exultantly in Wordsworth's "Immortality Ode":

> "Our birth is but a sleep and a forgetting:
> The Soul that rises with us, our life's Star,
>   Hath had elsewhere its setting,
>   And cometh from afar."

"It's a pity," he kept on saying. "It would have made a good paper."

And, to give him his due, I think it would.

At this earlier time at Holborn Hill, he was still vital and alert, capable of electrifying us into attention, or making us cringe with guilt. At times, he would take it into his head to entertain us, often with no reference at all to the lesson we were supposed to be having. Once, when we were struggling with some poem or other, he began to give us a set of variations on "The Charge of the Light Brigade", mimicking it as it might have been rendered by a Scotsman, an Irishman and a Welshman:

> "Into the jawss of Hell, bach
> Right down into the bucket, look you!"

We laughed till the little room nearly broke off from the main building.

"He got it from a Turn at The Palace last night," said one of the more knowing boys. "My brother told me."

At other times, Stuart S. became suddenly the sharpest disciplinarian in the School. He did not have to shout. He would walk up to a boy and take hold of his cheek between finger and thumb, smiling all the time. It was a pretty frightening experience, even when he was in no more than a warning mood and did not grip tightly. You stared up at him, your neck angled back, your head slowly wagging from side to side, while he pretended to talk to you as kindly as a grandfather. But, when he was really angry, his fingers clamped hard on the flesh, till you felt as if your mouth was one whole bursting gumboil, while your head was nearly snapped off your spine, as he shook it back and forward. For half an hour afterwards, you sat with eyes glassy from tears and one cheek as red as a geranium.

It was in Standard IV that we first came up against the Scholarship, and those of us who passed the Preliminary were given extra tuition by Mr. Brunskill. We did a little homework and stood around his desk each morning, while it was marked. He was then in his last year before retirement – stiff, tall, grey-flecked at the temples and almost completely bald on the crown. Parents were as much in awe of him as we were. To them, as to us, he was still "the Gaffer", distant, silent, but with an authority no-one ever thought of questioning. Once, as we stood round his desk with our homework in his hands, he emitted one long, serene, almost musical fart. We dared not look at one another, and not one of us sniggered, not one of us admitted, even by so much as a flicker, that we had heard anything at all.

To those of us who were only ten the Scholarship gave no great anxiety in Standard IV, since we knew that we would get a second chance in Standard V, under Mr. Thomas, the Senior Master, who conducted the School Choir. Herbert Thomas was a genial, fifteen-stone tenor, shaped like one bubble balanced on another. He was a man who kept his strength and his temper seemingly hidden, but ready and tight as a catapult. A thrown book or ball hit its target with the speed of a bullet. In spite of his size, he was agile as a jockey. There was the time in the annual Amateur Opera, when he was cast as Oberon, King of the Fairies.

"I do ride upon a swallow," he sang, bouncing across the stage as lightly as a rubber ball.

"Oh, my God, you must be hollow," sang someone from the back of the balcony.

Herbert Thomas was a gifted musician, who later moved to Barrow, and helped to make the Barrow Male Voice into one of the best choirs in the North West. At Millom, he was organist and choir master of St. George's Church, and one day he called me to the classroom.

"Do you go to the Wesleyan Chapel now?" he asked.

"Yes."

"Does your father go?"

"Yes," I said, not following his drift. "Not every week," I added.

Mr. Thomas smirked.

I was puzzled, and repeated the conversation at home.

"He wanted you to join the Church Choir," said my father, seeing the point at once.

There is one thing more about Herbert Thomas, which I have so far left untold. And about Sid Mudge and Stuart S. They were all of them cricketers. Thomas and Mudge played for Millom First XI, in the North Lancashire League; Stuart S. played for Haverigg; while Miss Hurst was engaged to yet another Haverigg player. Cricket lay close to Holborn Hill School in every way. There was an arrangement with the Club for the boys to use the field in the morning, for what we still called Drill. We would "line up" on the edge of the boundary and number off from the left, while the shouts and whistles of the thrushes were blown across the ground in the often chilly wind of early spring, and, later, we would sub-divide into four separate elevens, and play two matches under the hazardous control of one umpire.

I was hopeless at all this, of course. I could neither catch a ball nor swing a bat, and, when there was any scrimmaging to be done, I was always the first to be knocked down. I did not worry much about it, for I took it for granted that, if you were good at games, you would have no brains. "*Mens sana in corpore sano*" struck me, when I first came upon it, as utter bosh. So, with John Slater, I formed a member-ship-of-two club of complacent non-competitors. It applied not only to games, but to almost all manual pursuits, such as woodwork and draw-ing. When John tried to draw a ship, the result looked like a blackboard in full sail, and, as I did not see myself as playing second to John, I presumed that my drawing must be equally bad. That was the way I continued to remember it until very recently, when I happened to look through my Term Test reports for the first two years at the Secondary School and found that my marks for drawing averaged forty-four out of fifty and were always rated either "Very Good" or "Excellent"!

But about games no such mistake is possible. I was not just bad, I was terrible; I was an embarrassment to any team. And, in the case of cricket – and of cricket only – I was an embarrassment to myself. When we were in Standard IV, Stuart S. arranged for a team from our class to go out to Haverigg, one evening, to play the boys of the Haverigg Club. There were only thirteen of us who were available, so that, as one of the thirteen was John, who held a bat like a vacuum cleaner, there seemed a good chance that I might be among those selected. But I was the one to be left out and my eyes spurted tears. Stuart, who could be witheringly sarcastic at times, was surprisingly sympathetic, and appointed me official scorer. So, for the next few weeks, I attended the Millom Club matches with a notebook and pencil, and scored every single run!

The Cricket Field lay beside the railway, below the clay drumlin which hoists St. George's Church seventy feet nearer heaven. In fact, the railway sidings had cut deeply into the slopes of the clay, and a footpath ran – and still runs – along the edge of the cutting, in a kind of elevated promenade or grandstand, giving a fine, free view of the Field. When there was an important match, the footpath was crowded with men who could see all of the play except the score-board, and managed without that by ticking off each wicket and run. They were out, too, for value for the money they didn't pay, and would barrack loudly over the noise of the shunting wagons, whenever the game became too slow. There even was one supporter who paid his Vice-President's subscription every year, and watched the matches from the free grandstand. And once, when Dudley and I were sitting for the George Moore Scholarship – Five Pounds per Annum for Two Years – in the Vicarage Room, close to the church, we slipped out on to the footpath, during the afternoon break, to watch ten minutes of the game, between Scripture and Composition.

On the Holborn Hill side of the Field, the land rose steeply in orchards, from which we were chased out whenever we climbed over the wall to look for a lost ball, while the fourth side, opposite the School, opened into meadows, hay fields and farm land. The boundary hedge was, in fact, the old hedge of the eighteenth-century enclosure – huge, unlopped hawthorns, trying to look like elms, with ungainly sticks of elder shoved in here and there to patch up the gaps. At midsummer, a six-hit dropped plumb into a yellow cream of buttercup and sorrel, and the dyke-bottoms were awash with red, white and blue flowers, campion and stitchwort and germander speedwell, the names of which I knew, if I knew them at all, only from cigarette cards. All the green of Ireland blew up in the west wind, dropping like manna on the bread-and-cheese of the young hawthorns, while in the heavy, anticyclonic days of July, the smoke from the railway engines smirched across the

Field into the batsmen's eyes, or mingled with the sickly, choking scent of may blossom and elder and meadow-sweet, till we sat on the boundary, sneezing and sneezing.

It was round about this time that Herbert Thomas suggested that we ought to become Bob Members – membership open to boys under fourteen, who, for one shilling, could attend every League Match of the season, First and Second XI, and use part of the Field for their own cricket practice any evening of the week, except Saturday and Sunday. It is doubtful, however, whether I would have joined, since I did not like going over to the Field on my own, and very few of my Holborn Hill friends lived on our side of the railway bridge, but, sometime in 1924, I had found a new friend. I was walking up the back street, when a boy, about a year younger than me, but decidedly sturdier, came out of the back-yard door of one of the houses. I knew who lived there — it was old Mrs. Norton with her daughter and son-in-law, who were all vaguely related to the Sobeys. Albert, it turned out, was her grandson. His mother – Mrs. Norton's other daughter – had married and emigrated to America, where she died, her epitaph being carved below the "Ever Loving Memory" on the family tombstone in St. George's Churchyard.

"Also ALTHEA,
Their Beloved Daughter,
Who Fell Asleep at CRYSTAL FALLS, USA,
July 26th 1915, aged 28 years."

I used to take this to mean that she had fallen into the water when she was sleeping and been swept away, but I realise now that she must have died in giving birth to Albert. He, at any rate, was brought back to England as a baby, and reared by an aunt in Lancashire, and had now come to Millom to live with his grandmother, who, it was explained to me, was a sister of the girl who had married the Sobey brother who had gone off to Mexico so many years ago. Albert's mother, therefore, like my stepmother, was a cousin of Dick Sobey, and we both of us rejoiced to think that we had a millionaire for an uncle – neither the uncle-ship nor the millionaire-dom was strictly true, of course, but it was near enough for us.

Apart from our joint claim on Uncle Dick, our family relationship mattered very little to either of us. It did mean, however, that each was immediately welcome in the other's home, but for which we might have taken some time to get to know one another, for Mrs. Norton –

incomprehensibly, as it seemed to me – had chosen to enrol Albert at Lapstone Road School, rather than at Holborn Hill. It was over two years, in fact, before we found ourselves at the same school – the Secondary – and his arrival there roused in me a certain slight resentment. Until then, I had been able to say that I was the boy who lived closest to the School, having to walk only about sixty yards from our back door to the School's side gate. But Albert only had to cross the back street.

He and I now began to go over to the Cricket Field nearly every evening of summer, carrying our bats and ball and wickets. My father was delighted. For the first time in my life, I seemed to be interested in a boy's game, and had not to be chased out of the house into the fresh air. He even bought me a new bat, with which I was so obsessed that once, when I was sent to Dixon, the chemist, for a packet of bicarbonate of soda, I came back from Dixon, the ironmonger, with a bottle of linseed oil. Luckily, though Albert was an active lad, he could play cricket little better than me – a failing which I attributed to his having been born in America. So we rarely joined in with the other Bob Members, but played our own one-a-side matches in a rough corner of the Field, where the rushes stuck up out of the grass like the bristles from a worn-out hairbrush. We would carefully pace out our pitch, hammer the wickets into the ground with the bat-handles, and devote three or four preliminary minutes to taking a centre, or, as we grew more knowledgeable, leg-and-middle. Then one of us would start to bowl, and, if we managed to keep half the deliveries within two yards of the wicket on either side, we judged that we were in good form. When either of us hit the ball, he insisted on running between the wickets, and, as the bowler-cum-fielder invariably shied at the wicket, trying for a run-out, we scored more from over-throws than from hits. More than once, Albert ran up to ten on one shot.

Before long – usually after my third consecutive duck – our patience ebbed, and we began to argue and squabble. If the ball hit the batsman anywhere below the neck, the bowler claimed he was plumb l.b.w. while neither of us would ever admit that he was run out. In the end, Albert, who owned the stumps, would pull them out of the ground, and throw them disgustedly under the boundary seats. Yet this was only the beginning of by far the most rewarding part of the evening, when we fielded – we always said "fielded out" – for the men practising at the nets; retrieved cricket balls from the railway line; searched for lost balls in the meadow; rode on the horse-drawn roller, in the belief that our extra weight would help to prepare a good pitch for Herbert Thomas's fast off-breaks; and generally made ourselves useful by lifting, pushing or turning over anything that could be lifted or pushed or turned.

"Hey," shouted John Kidd, the lightning-fast bowler of the First XI – "leave them sods alone."

I looked up, startled.

"You little sod," he added.

I could not understand why the bigger lads laughed.

There was one time, however, when we really were able to help. It was in 1925 or '26, when the Club, which was always acutely in need of money, held a Grand Midsummer Fête on a non-fixture Saturday. There were to be stalls, side-shows, sports et cetera, and the Bob Members were to be responsible for a Produce Stall. Mr. Thomas called a meeting in the Cricket Pavilion, when he divided the town into a number of zones or wards, in each of which every house was to be visited by one pair of Bob Members. Albert and I were allotted to St. George's Terrace and the Market Square, a small area, but a promising one, as it included the town's three banks – one of the Bank Managers was Chairman at the Club – the Vicarage, the town's largest hotel and several of the principal shops. We called on the householders about a week before the event, carrying a notebook, inscribed:

"MILLOM CRICKET CLUB MIDSUMMER FETE
AUTHORISED COLLECTOR
(Signed) H. H. THOMAS."

Each householder wrote his name and address in the book, followed by whatever he proposed to give. We had no refusals. Miss Danson gave us a large cake; Mrs. Hornsby, who still lives in the house where we called on her, gave us a pound of biscuits. We collected eggs, butter, tea, jam, bananas, tinned fruit. It was no good anyone saying that they could not think of what to give, for I was ready with my list of suggestions. Later on, people told my parents how impressed they were with the two polite young boys who seemed to know exactly what they wanted. Whether the other boys were equally polite, I do not know: but they were equally successful. We collected the goods on the Friday evening before the Fête, and, if Albert and I had to carry two basketfuls, other lads had to call in the help of prams and bogies to bring in their gatherings. At a time when at least half the mothers in the town had scarcely enough money coming in to feed their own families, few had been able to reject the appeal of the Bob Members. Herbert Thomas was overjoyed and had to arrange for an enlargement of the stall, and Sid Mudge came over to help him, leaving, for a while, his preparations for the Special Midsummer Show: "The Holy Friar amid Summer Swallows".

Saturday was brilliant.

("Nice morning for the Feet," said a woman in one of the shops. "Why, are they troubling you?" asked my mother, and kept on laughing at the joke all day.)

The Cricket Field was crowded; the Bob Members' stall besieged. Albert and I each distributed our sixpences as carefully as we could, over six well-chosen penny attractions. "The Holy Friar" was left to the last. We were a bit suspicious of it, for it did not sound quite in Sid Mudge's line, and he seemed to be having some joke with himself, as he rang the hand-bell at the door, announcing each show as it was about to begin, but we were completely unprepared for the battered frying pan and the empty bottles of Fawcett's Pop, which we found on display inside the Pavilion. Nevertheless, we thought it well worth the admission, and urged our friends not to miss it.

For, by this time, I had attached myself to the Millom Cricket Team with the fierce faith of the born-again Evangelical. County Cricket I was scarcely aware of, but the Saturday afternoon matches of the North Lancashire and District League were quite another matter. On Saturday morning, I could scarcely keep my eyes away from the sky, wondering about the weather; and all Sunday, if we had lost, I would go round, as my father said, "like a bear with a sore head".

But we did not often lose.

"Whitehaven is famous for coal" – said our handicraft teacher, who travelled from Barrow each day to take woodwork in a hut at Lapstone Road – "Haverigg for flooks and Barrow for men."

"And Millom for cricketers," I broke in.

For, in those days, Millom had what now seems to be an heroic team, the like of which no-one will ever see again. At one time, at the annual Cumberland-versus-North Lancashire League Match, for which Cumberland had the first pick, five Millom players were chosen for the Cumberland team and four for the League. The players of those days seemed to walk about the Field two foot taller than ordinary men.

Our own Herbert Thomas opened the bowling with the great pro of the time, Maurice Gill, who was expected, every week, to take five wickets or score fifty runs, or both. Sid Mudge, in the years when I was at Holborn Hill, was the wicket-keeper – a good keeper, but still, in our eyes, only a keeper – and went in number nine or ten. But one day, in some desperate time-saving game, he stayed in for nearly an hour, and scored ten runs, and after that, he and the team began to take his batting seriously. Soon he was opening with Maurice Gill, and made himself into the best wicket-keeper-batsman in the League. Alec Rigg, the Captain, had been a telegraph boy at the time when my father had been a tailor's apprentice, each, in a different way, employed under the same roof by Seth Slater. He was in his middle age as a cricketer when I knew him, creaky in the shoulders, slow in the Field, and as rigid in his batting stance as if he were posing for an old-fashioned photograph. Yet, when he walked out to the pitch, he raised the game to an almost liturgical dignity. "The gentleman postman", some people called him. Then there was Billy Allen, left-handed, tubby as a teddy bear, a batsman with only one stroke – the left-hander's pull or sweep to leg – but with the power also of hypnotising bowlers into sending him repeated long-hops, which he promptly flicked on to the railway line – "Like feeding an elephant with a strawberry", my father used to say. There was John Kidd, who walked back so far for his run that we reckoned he could not see the stumps and had to bowl from memory. And there were the Doidges, brothers and cousins, Alf, Charlie and W. G., who came on the Field, one after another, like a series of reinforcements – get one of them out, and the next was already walking to the wicket.

I recite their names like a Roll of Honour, for they brought the ring of the Sagas, once a week, into the life of what I was already beginning to realise was a small and not particularly distinguished town. We did not dare to be familiar with them, treating them with the respect we had been taught to show to schoolmasters and ministers of religion. It was always "Mr. Thomas", "Mr. Rigg", "Mr. Doidge". Most of them are dead, and the few who are not are now "Alf" and "Bill", when I meet them in the street. But the respect remains. They gave a boy a glimpse of glory; they helped a whole community to hold its head up.

It was, of course, the Slump which accounted for Millom's cricketing greatness, for, in the long, workless summers, it was better to practise at the nets than to stand, hour after hour, at the church gates or the street corners. There was always a chance, too, of a collection for a Fifty, or even, for the specially talented player, of a season's engagement as Saturday afternoon professional for some other club – one of Chris Walmsley's sons, who learned his cricket in our back street, played for years as pro for Haverigg.

But far more important was the fact that the Club stood for the town, for every single one of us. When I referred to the team, I said simply "Millom": "Millom won," "Millom drew," "Where are Millom playing this week?" The crowds which filled the Field at a First Team match came from every age and class. If the Unemployed found their places in the First XI, so, too, did the Manager of Hodbarrow Mine, and I do not think that, as a player, he was treated differently from anybody else. The very old men who had known the Club in the 1890s, when my Uncle Jack came in second wicket, sat and smoked under the orchard wall; the little boys cheered every run for ten minutes, and then set up their own games on seat tops, with a marble for a ball and used matches for wickets. A surprising number of women were among the regular team supporters in those days, giving a bright inflorescence of prints and art silks to the privet and thorn hedges behind the boundary. Even my mother would occasionally attend, in the company of Mrs. Elwell, though she was never quite sure whether the two men who were batting belonged both to the same side, or one from each.

"Who's winning?" she would say, when I rushed home for my tea, at half-time, and I became more and more exasperated as the years went on, trying to explain that nobody at all was winning at half-time.

Nobody was winning quite often at End of Play, for those were the days before over-limited cricket. The match began at two-thirty and ended at seven-fifteen, and the first team to bat was usually bowled out, or had declared, by four-thirty or five o'clock, but if they were not All Out, they could bat as long as they chose. Two points for a win; one for a draw. So the saving of the match often became more important than trying to win. It was then – rather than when one side was romping away – that true tension came into the game.

I can remember many a time when the crowd sat menacingly silent, watches in hand, elbows on knees, crouching forward, concentrating on the game so hard that you half expected the ball to explode by force of mind over matter. An unnecessary risk, or a near run-out, would bring a warning yelp: "Steady on, there"; a disputable umpiring decision would rouse a low, threatening growl: "Get away!", "Play the game."

"It's no good asking that bugger," said a voice from the railway grandstand. "He can't bloody well see."

But it was only a visitor from Lancashire. We did not approve of such language on the Millom Field.

The hands of the Market Clock – just visible from where I sat on the Field – would move on past seven o'clock, as the sun sloped down over the meadows, and the shadows of the old bedsteads in the hedge lunged out, till they touched the shadows of the players. The sightscreen – made of old iron-ore-stained sleepers from Hodbarrow, that turned pinker and pinker as the season advanced and the whitewash wore off – glowed and gleamed like the Holborn Hill orchards in full blossom.

It was then that Original Sin went in to bat. Every possible excuse for hindrance and delay was tricked up and tried – asking for the sight-boards to be moved, shielding eyes against the sun, looking round at the fielders, testing the bat as if it were damaged, and demanding a new one from the Pavilion. Slogger Doidge, who seemed to take a curious pleasure in the times when he was required to do the opposite of slogging, knew them all. And he had one more trick of his own. At times of greatest tension, his kneecap would suddenly go out of joint, and he would have to be helped slowly back to the pavilion, to return again, if necessary, with the aid of a runner. The weakness in the joint was, of course, quite genuine, and often his kneecap really did give out. But nobody ever believed it.

"The crowd nearly lynched me," he said, with justifiable pride, speaking of a match when Millom batted out time, on a Lancashire ground.

I remember one of those rare Wednesday afternoons when my father was able to attend. The match was against Whitehaven, and Millom, batting second, collapsed to four or five wickets down for under twenty. Then Alec Rigg set himself to the task of stemming the game like a leak in a tank. For nearly an hour, the ball was rarely driven more than a couple yards, and the fieldsmen crowded in as close as a male voice choir round a conductor. It was fifty-five minutes of agonising stagnation, but when the last ball went down, with Millom still two wickets in hand, my father leapt up with the rest of the crowd and applauded the two batsmen all the way to the boundary.

At times like this, Millom was everywhere that mattered, and we were Millom.

Yet, by the age of eleven, I was beginning to be at least aware of a world outside Millom. I had spent one holiday with Sobey cousins at Birmingham and another with Nicholson cousins at Wheatley Hill in County Durham, and, when I was nine, I went with a party of boys from Holborn Hill School to the British Empire Exhibition at Wembley. I recall the giraffes at the zoo; the fig-leaf-less, sculptured cherubs in St. Paul's, which sent us into a misery of embarrassed giggles; the steps, where a woman rushed up to me, saying: "Tell your mam and dad you've shaken hands with Mrs. Morgan at the Houses of Parliament." My parents heard that news with cries of astonishment. I could not see why. After all, people were always shaking hands with me on the streets of Millom.

Of the Exhibition, I can remember only the Prince of Wales in butter. Yet something more must have stayed in my mind, for I wrote a long letter on the subject, which was published in the Children's Corner of *The West Cumberland Times*, and won First Prize in the week's Essay Competition – my first published work, in fact.

The Lake District, too, began to loom up on the boundary of my notice. Two or three times a year, on August Bank Holiday or a Wednesday, my parents would take me to Broughton-in-Furness or Coniston, travelling by the old Foxfield-Coniston railway, and once, with my Uncle Jim and Auntie Tot, we sailed from Coniston to Nibthwaite, on the lake steamer *Lady of the Lake*.

One Saturday afternoon, my mother organised a family party – minus my father, of course – to climb Black Combe, which was as familiar to me as the steeple of St. George's Church. It was good to feel it under my feet for the first time, and to look down to Millom at the mouth of the Duddon; to Walney Island, bent like a barb round the shaft of the Furness Peninsula; and, beyond Furness, to Morecambe Bay. We strained our eyes through the sun-dazzle to catch sight of Blackpool Tower. West was the sea – the Isle of Man invisible; inland was Coniston Old Man, and lots and lots of hills we did not know the names of. It was still a country that seemed far away, not part of the world I belonged to. We ate our sandwiches, scratched our names on visiting cards of slate and added them to the summit cairn, and slithered down the grass path to the bilberry corries and the valley and Silecroft station.

I was already beginning to feel curiosity about the Lake District; but it was the kind of curiosity that I felt about the Mediterranean or

Africa. I thought of myself as a Millom boy, not as a Cumbrian. Any pictures that remain of Coniston, Eskdale or the Duddon Valley come to me from my middle teens. Before then, it was not the hills which etched their images on my memory, but the smirched and scruffy workland at the town's fraying edge.

For, every Sunday morning, my father and I went for a walk. In his own way, my father was quite a Sabbath Day Observer. He had long given up church-going and he rarely attended chapel after the first few years of his second marriage, but he dressed for the day as solemnly as a churchwarden and even kept a special walking stick for Sundays. He relished the silence which descended on a Sunday morning, and resented any breaking of it as a usurping of his prerogative as a shopkeeper. When, as sometimes happened, people came to the back door on a Sunday in urgent need of a shirt or a collar for some special occasion, he would "oblige" them, as he said, if they were friends of his, but he would accept no payment there and then. They were expected to come round to the shop, later in the week, and pay up what they owed, and if, as sometimes happened, they did not come, he was prepared to risk losing the money.

So, on Sunday morning, round about the time the church bells began to ring, my father and I set out. My mother used to try to persuade us to delay until ten-thirty.

"You don't want to meet all the people going to church," she would say.

"I don't question how they spend their Sundays," said my father. "I'm not having them question how I spend mine."

We went, first of all, to call on my Uncle Jim, who lived in Devonshire Road, on the way to the Ironworks. Uncle Jim had married the sister of my Uncle George's wife, so that my Auntie Tot was, as it were, married twice over into our family. My uncle and aunt had courted for nine years before they were married, and even then had lived with Tot's own Uncle and Aunt Curtis, who had brought her up from childhood. Yet, in spite of this, my Uncle Jim had stamped his personality on the household as my father never did on ours. This, as I understood even from the age of seven, was essentially a Nicholson house. My grandmother would have been at home there, though, even if her lameness had not prevented her visiting us, she would never have put up with my mother's edgy gentility. My cousins, Bill and Donald, were allowed to make ruder jokes than my mother would have permitted me.

"It's a good job it doesn't smell," they would say of the Millom Opera Society's double bass.

And my Auntie Tot, in spite of her kindness, her gentleness and her old-fashioned, almost Edwardian primness of dress, was far readier than my mother to take notice of the harsh world outside the parlour. My Uncle Jim's down-to-earthness would have pained my Grandpa Sobey, yet, when he so wished, he could call on a dignity of presence far greater than anything my father could aspire to. He walked about, as people said, as if he owned the place. Right up to the time of old age, he wore the high, stiff, starched collars which forced up his chin, so that his Adam's apple seemed to stare you straight in the face, and, on Sundays, he always carried a heavy, polished ebony walking stick, which he swung and jabbed down as deliberately and forcibly as if he were giving the earth a helpful push in its daily revolution.

He had the carriage of a millionaire, and used to tell how, when he and my Auntie Tot had gone to some country mansion in County Durham, finding it closed for the day, he had announced himself as Lord Muncaster, and been shown round by the butler.

"Of course, I gave him something for himself," he would add, magnanimously. "They expect that, you know, Joe."

In later life, he allowed his daily routine to take on almost the obligation of a ritual. For years, he would return home from the Co-operative Shoe Shop at about half-past six, go straight into the back kitchen, take off jacket, waistcoat and collar, and have a good wash, to freshen himself up for the evening. Now, every Boxing Day, my mother and father and I used to spend the afternoon and evening at Devonshire Road, arriving there at about four o'clock, or a little later if my mother and I had been to the Newton Street Methodist Boxing Day Effort. We would have a huge tea at first, and afterwards, sit down to play whist. My cousins sloped off at this point, but I was so keen to take my hand at the cards that my Auntie Tot would usually stand out. Then, round about six-twenty, my uncle would start glancing at his watch. Suddenly, he would push back his chair and stand up.

"Take my hand for the next round, Tot," he would say.

And then, with a kind of graciously condescending apology:

"I won't keep you more than a minute, Rose."

And the next moment, we would hear the cold tap running in the back kitchen.

My father and I used to enter my Uncle Jim's from the front, but we always left by the back. Devonshire Road back street was different from any other in Millom. It was as broad as the front street; it was metalled; it had a proper curb and pavement, running the whole length of the back doors. It even had a name, "Argyll Street", and to walk out of your back door onto a street with a name of its own seemed to me to be a kind of distinction worthy of my Uncle Jim.

Then, when we came out of the back door, we always turned left, towards the industrial outskirts of the town. We had the choice of two routes. We could walk down Devonshire Road to the Ironworks, with its great funnels and furnaces, smoking and blaring, like a battleship aground on the tidal banks of the Duddon. The town lived perpetually in the groan and hum of the furnaces, though custom had so dulled our ears that it was only in the still, small hours of the morning that we noticed the sound. But, when you were closer to the works, you were stunned by the insistent, menacing drumming, as if the whole iron hulk were a dynamo, alive with power. We would stop for a moment, beside the wall, and look over to the cooler reservoir, where hot water spurted out from a dozen pipes and fountains, filling even the winter air with little tornadoes of steaming spray. The ducks and moorhens paddled about as unconcernedly as if it were no more than a midsummer shower.

More often – and more, in fact, to my choice – we would set off by the allotments at the end of Argyll Street. Allotments have always been my favourite form of garden. I like the turned soil, the clumps of weed, the potato plants and the bean sticks; I like the little heaps of manure, the old buckets, the tool sheds, the ramshackle enclosures, where hens scratch and cluck behind rusty corrugated iron and wire netting. These allotments, however, had a special attraction: for the way through them was disputed, and the old man who rented the ground was continually ordering people off, and had even tried to board up the gap in the fence which we used as a gate. Now, my father had a horror of trespassing. It was not that he had an undue respect for private property, but he could not bear the thought of being caught out. My Uncle Jim had no such qualms. He would push the board out of the way with his foot and motion us to go through.

"It's all right, Joe," he'd say. "I've been going through here for twenty years. The old fellow knows me."

And the old fellow did know him. He would glare at us as we passed, but say nothing.

"Nice morning," said my uncle.

Then he'd gesture with his black walkingstick – "condescending as Chloe", as my father used to say.

"You want to get some horse muck on those roses, man," he'd go on. "Nothing better for roses than good horse muck."

From the allotments we passed on to a lane which led to the Secondary School playing field, where, later, I was to spend the most miserable hours of my schooldays; then to another lane, between marshy fields, with deep ditches on either side, from which ferns fronded out in great burst water-mains of green – some of the roots are growing in our back yard to this day. On through a farmyard, round the back of the quarried limestone of Red Hill, across a Clapham Junction of railway lines, out to the gorsy Mains and to Hodbarrow Point. Here, on one of the only three or four rocky headlands to come down to the sea between Scotland and Wales, we could look at the whole history of industrial Millom.

At our back, was the stump of the old windmill, older, indeed, than the town, which had been used for storing explosives in the early days of the mine. Close to the windmill was the very first shaft, Towsey Hole, sunk in the 1850s, and, until 1973, unsealed, its gap hidden only by a thicket of hawthorn, blackthorn and blackberry, which roofed it over like a thatch. One Sunday morning, our dog, Roy, chasing a rabbit, overshot the edge, and fell down the shaft. My father shouted and waited until he had almost given up hope.

"I'm afraid you've lost your dog, Joe," said my Uncle Jim.

But, at last, scratched, bruised and bleeding, Roy painfully crawled back over the rim, and my father half carried, half dragged him home.

I can see it all so clearly, yet I was not with my father that Sunday morning and remember it only from his words.

One thing that I must certainly have seen, though not until years later did I learn to understand what I saw, was the great ground-plan of the mine, stretching from Towsey Hole to Moor Bank, a mile and a half away, where, at that time, the last shaft of all had not yet been sunk. For, from Towsey Hole, one after another in the 1850s and '60s, new shafts were sunk, all around the curve of the old foreshore, with its porcelain-smooth limestone rippling down to the shingle. The high tide came galloping through the mouth of the Duddon, leaping and curveting right up to the red dunes of the pit-heaps. To protect the mine the company built, first of all, a wooden palisade, and, later, the old sandstone sea-wall of 1886. Then, in 1904, when enormous deposits of the highest grade haematite were discovered to lie out beyond the high-tide mark, they built the great new sea-wall – one and a quarter miles of superb engineering, strung like a bow, from Hodbarrow Point to Haverigg.

It was, and still is, the town's seaside promenade. But, by the time I was a boy, millions of tons of ore had been won from behind the new sea-wall, and the land collapsed and subsided into a huge hollow, like an enormous soup tureen, seventy feet below sea level in parts. One winter, when I was at school, the tide began to break through the barrier and threatened to flood the mine, but the breach was blocked up and the water pumped into a stone aqueduct, which ran, red as blood, right through the mines, till it emptied into a little bay, just below Hodbarrow Point, staining the high tide a deep cochineal. For years, I thought that this was what the Red Sea looked like.

What mattered most on those Sunday mornings was the sense of freedom I felt at Hodbarrow Point. The town was almost out of sight, and Black Combe no longer seemed to loom paternally above me. I was lifted up on my little headland, as on the deck of a ship, sailing straight out into the sea. And, all about me, in spite of the red dust and the cinders, the clanging of the pit-heads and the shunting of the engines, was, though I did not know it, one of the richest areas of plant-life in all Cumberland. Rock-rose, agrimony, greater mullein, ploughman's spikenard, teasels, and more than one species of spurge and orchid and St. John's-wort; on the shore, sea holly and the yellow horned poppy; on the sea-wall, sea spleenwort, figwort and the giant horsetail; and down in the Hollow, the bee orchid, the round-leaved wintergreen, the Grass of Parnassus, adder's tongue and moonwort. I list the names, knowing that few will recognise them. As a boy, I did not recognise them myself; for the most part, I did not even notice them.

Yet I noticed some. I was far too old, of course, to pick flowers, but, now and again, my Uncle Jim and my father and I would each put in his buttonhole one specimen of a frail, pink, chalice-shaped bloom, which grew on the very peak of the headland. It was always dead before we reached home. Now, as it happened, in the period after boyhood, I was prevented from returning to Hodbarrow for about ten years, yet, when I did go there again, memory took me straight to the spot where the flower grew. I knew, by this time, what it was: the bloody cranesbill, *Geraneum sanguineum*, common enough further north in the country, but rare in South Cumberland. Today, all above-ground remains of the mines have disappeared; acres have been bulldozed down to a grim, level waste, with every herb and shrub grubbed up and torn out. The

Hollow itself is flooded, making the newest lake of the Lake District –
as large as Rydal and very much deeper. The bee orchids, the wintergreen, the badgers' sets, and the meadow pipits' nests where the cuckoo
used to lay – all these are under the water. But the frail pink cranesbill
still blooms exactly where I first found it, over fifty years ago.

We returned home by a Right of Way that ran straight through the
mines. Hodbarrow was then just at the beginning of its long decline.
The annual output was down to about a quarter of the half a million
tons of the great years between 1880 and 1910, and Mainsgate Road
was no longer black with men when the morning shift knocked off.
Sunday, too, was a quiet day, but every now and then, the pit-head
wheels, at one shaft or another, would revolve against the sky, and
little locomotives would fuss along the lines which swooped and
hummocked along the broken ground like the Big Dipper at Blackpool.
Every now and then, one of the few surface workers on Sunday shift
would push a bogie along one of the high, wooden ramps, that looked
like viaducts on the Canadian Pacific, and one more load would be
added to the growing heaps of unsold ore. For the landscape at
Hodbarrow was continually changing: the new tips, like enormous
dark-red prehistoric barrows, steadily spread outwards; the older tips
were scooped into red gills and screes, as wagon loads of ore were
taken away; the original outcrops of silvery limestone were newly
dynamited into harsh, raw cliffs and crag-ends; and the great Hollow
slowly sank, hour by hour.

Everywhere nature was fighting back. The old rubble heaps were
already whiskered over with the green of barley-grass and horsetail; the
abandoned railway lines were bedded deep in yellow St. John's-wort
and Carline thistle; the little becks running up from the pump house
pulsated dark red along gully and aqueduct; and over the whole scarred
and fractured industrial battle-field, an army of willow and elder and
hawthorn scrub was gradually taking re-possession. Down in the
Hollow itself, re-colonisation had so far progressed that the Mine
Managers were able to organise an annual partridge shoot. They even
ploughed a patch of the sunken land, and grew a crop of kale, well below
sea level, to provide cover for the birds. All this area was placarded with
"Keep Out" and "Trespassers will be Prosecuted" notices, and patrol-
led by watchmen, who were mostly old miners, retired from underground service. More than once, when we had strayed from the path,
as we often did, one of the fiercest of the watchmen stumped up to us
on his wooden leg.

"Now then!" he said. "You've no business here, you know. Or are you the sort that can't read?"

"We're doing no harm," said my father, immediately on the defensive.

But my uncle was not demeaning himself into making excuses.

"Don't you worry, Joe," he said, and turned to the man with the tolerant air of one who could understand his position.

"Just mention my name to George Vaughan," he said, "and he'll make it right with you."

Then he calmly led us past the watchman and straight across the forbidden acres, casually prodding the pickle-cabbage lumps of ore with his ebony stick as if he were making a rough evaluation.

Mr. Vaughan was the Chairman of the Board of Directors. I doubt if my uncle had ever spoken to him in the whole of his life.

CHAPTER SEVEN

WHEN we returned to School, one Monday in 1923, we found a new Gaffer in charge. He was slightly built and not very tall. His wrists pushed out of his sleeves as if his jacket were too small, and he wore very large boots below trousers that were far too short. His voice, when he spoke, was blurred with the accent of West Cumberland which was not quite the same as ours. His name was Walter Wilson, and, at the side of the handsome, confident and well-fed Herbert Thomas, he looked rather an insignificant figure.

It took us only a minute or two to realise our mistake. We marched through the door of the porch into the main classroom, lined up for prayers, and waited, as usual, for the late-comers to hare across the playground on the last stroke of the bell and barge through to take their places in the line. But Mr. Wilson quietly held out one hand and detained them. The boys, not yet sure who he was, looked questioningly at Mr. Thomas, wondering if this new man had any authority. Mr. Thomas stared steadily out of the window, studying the clouds. He was waiting, like the rest of us, to see what would happen. The clogs of one of our most regular late-comers could be heard clattering across the gravel, and Mr. Wilson waited, in complete silence, until the boy arrived, his pullover on back to front, his socks down over his boot-tops, and snot oozing from his nose like resin from a pine tree. His face gaped with a query as he saw the stranger pointing to a place beside the other three boys in front of the class, but he took that place and said nothing. We none of us quite knew whether to be scared, apprehensive, curious or impertinent.

At last, Mr. Wilson spoke.

"This is not the way to make a good impression on a new Headmaster, is it?" he said.

"No, sir," the boys said, embarrassed into a humility which the stick would never have achieved.

"Then go to your seats, and don't let it happen again."

So far as I can remember, it rarely did happen again.

It was a beginning quite typical of the man. Outwardly, Walter Wilson was unimpressive. He shrank away from people in public. He did not catch the eye. He was not good at window-dressing. He seemed to be without the ambition which drives a career man from one appointment to another. I sometimes wonder if the Cumberland Education Authority ever realised what an exceptionally gifted teacher they had on their books. The boys realised it all right. And not just the brighter ones, like me, who, in any case, were going to leave for the Secondary School when they reached eleven. For among the boys who stayed on until the age of fourteen, there are many who still look back to their last three years at Holborn Hill with a kind of marvelling gratitude. Some, indeed, remained there beyond the school-leaving age, for, in the 'twenties, when few boys had much hope of finding a job, more than one reported at school after he was supposed to have left.

"I couldn't enter him in the register," Mr. Wilson said to me, "but if a boy wants to come to school, I'll never turn him away."

Walter Wilson was born at a time when education did not come easily to a child from the working class. To him, it was something you had to fight for. He had struggled for several years as a pupil-teacher in order to work his way into a Training College, and when he left, with a teaching certificate, he set out to acquire some, at least, of the knowledge that college had not given him. When he came to Millom, he was studying biology, and took a degree in that subject soon after he arrived, and when he died, at over eighty years of age, he was still teaching himself Spanish. He received no graduate allowance for his degree, he did not add the "B.Sc." to his name, and, of course, he had no chance to teach biology at Holborn Hill, but, fifteen years after I had left his school, his knowledge was of enormous help to me, when I first began to take an interest in botany. More than once, when I found some rare or, to me, unknown flower, I hurried back to the school for his confirmation or identification.

"I know where you've been," he'd usually say, as soon as I walked through the door, with the plant in my hand.

And when, to my great delight, I found the little fern called adder's tongue, he at once said:

"You've been to Hodbarrow."

But I hadn't. I had found the plant growing in the rough grass in the middle of Millom Pleasure Ground. There were hundreds of them, in fact, looking, at a first glance, no more distinguished than a dandelion or a sorrel leaf, and all scattered within a few yards of where people walked and the boys played football. Mr. Wilson could scarcely believe it.

"Just wait till the end of this lesson," he said, "and I'll come and have a look."

The boys have rarely had a quicker end-of-school dismissal.

Years later, when I dedicated my book on Cumberland and Westmorland to

"Walter Wilson,
Schoolmaster and Friend",

his first reaction was somewhat unexpected.

"I only once had to give him the cane," he said to a friend of mine.

That once was so odd that it needs to be told.

I was in Herbert Thomas's class at the time, and with me were one or two older boys of obvious ability, who had remained at Holborn Hill, as I now realise, not because they had failed to gain a Scholarship, but merely because their parents could not afford to keep them at school for the extra two or three years which the Scholarship entailed. And one of these, a sturdily built, serious-faced boy, named Casson, had a quiet composure, which I recognised and, perhaps, in a way, slightly begrudged him. We had been busy writing an essay on a country walk near Millom, and I, always glad to air my adjectives, had described a walk round The Old Church. Suddenly, Mr. Thomas, who was marking my exercise book, laughed to himself, and beckoned Casson over to him.

"What do you call the church you go to?" he asked.

"The Holy Trinity, sir."

Mr. Thomas pointed to the book. The boy looked and laughed. I was watching them enquiringly. Mr. Thomas handed me the book without a word, and I saw that I had written: "The Old Eternity".

I flushed with annoyance. I could see exactly what had happened. My father had explained to me, at some time or other, that the Old Church's proper name was "The 'Oly Trinity", and as "Trinity" and

140

"Eternity" meant much the same to me, the confusion was easily explained. But the implication of that dropped "h" stung me like a jibe.

It may be that a certain resentment hung on in my mind, and attached itself, in particular, to Casson, so that once, when he was away from the room, I noticed, with a slightly malicious eye, that he had left his School Library book lying open on his desk. Now, it happened that on my own desk there was a pot of paste – we must have been putting together our geography scrap books – and I had the sudden idea of pasting two pages of the book together, so that, when the boy turned the page, the story would not follow on! I carried out my plan, putting the book down in exactly the same place as before.

"That'll cod him," I said to myself.

Then, as I was not one who was easily distracted from my own work, I returned to my scrap book and forgot about what I had just done.

About ten minutes later, I looked up and saw Casson standing at Mr. Thomas's desk with the book in his hand. The two of them were turning a page backward and forward, with a look of puzzlement on their faces. And immediately, I realised that I had made a mistake. Not until that very moment had it occurred to me that I would be damaging the book. I raised my hand. Mr. Thomas nodded.

"Please, sir," I said, "are there two pages stuck together?"

"Yes."

"Please, sir, I did it."

"You pasted them together?"

"Yes, sir."

Mr. Thomas looked at me for a long time, too surprised, it would seem, even to make a comment.

"Why?" he said, at last, rather tense, but still very quiet.

"I don't know."

"You must have had some reason."

I hesitated.

"I thought it would be funny for him to turn over two pages at once, sir."

"Well, it isn't very funny, is it?"

"No, sir."

Mr. Thomas looked at me with pained, speechless incredulity, as if I were an umpire who had given a bad decision.

"This had better go to Mr. Wilson," he said, eventually.

Mr. Wilson seemed disappointed, rather than angry.

"I'm surprised at you, Nicholson," he said.

To tell the truth, I was surprised at myself.

"It's not the right way to treat a book."

"No, sir."

He looked away, wrinkling up his nose like a mouse sniffing at a piece of cheese.

"I'll have to give you the stick," he said. "But, since you've owned up, I'll only make it two."

I considered this quite fair. It was not that I was in the least stoical about corporal punishment. I hated being physically hurt, and bit my lips and wrung my hands and remained close to tears, if not actually in tears, for a long while after the caning. I had to admit, however, that he had been fair. I had no compunction about getting my own back on young Casson. But it was not, after all, the right way to treat a book.

For, what I learned, above all else, from Mr. Wilson was that a book was something you treated with respect. Until then, all the books I possessed had been children's annuals and the like. Except for *Robinson Crusoe*, very few of the children's classics had come my way. I had read no Kipling nor *The Wind in the Willows* nor *Alice*. And, though I was brought up within twenty miles or so of the place where Beatrix Potter was writing her thumbnail masterpieces, I do not remember having even heard her name until I first came across it in one of Auden's poems.

Mr. Wilson changed all this.

That he had the chance to do so was due, oddly enough, to my having failed the Scholarship examination, when I sat it in Standard IV, at the age of ten. "Failed" is not quite the right word; in fact, two of us, Dudley and I, were offered Free Places, which meant that we could have free tuition at the Secondary School but would have to buy our own books and equipment. Mr. Wilson advised our parents to reject the Free Place, and to let us stay on at Holborn Hill and aim for the full Scholarship next year. It was a wise decision. I was certainly not ready for the move, which, in any case, would have deprived me of one of the happiest years of all my schooling.

We must have had other lessons in that last year at Holborn Hill, but the only ones which remain in my mind are Mr. Wilson's twice-weekly readings. He did not waste time on the Blackmores, the Ballantynes and Stevensons; he took us straight to his favourite Dickens. We had met Dickens before, but only *The Old Curiosity Shop* and *The Chimes*, both of which, in their mean little school editions, were enough to sour a boy against the novels for the rest of his life. Mr. Wilson had no more patience than we had with Little Nell and the atrocious Trotty Veck. He shovelled the sentiment and the tushery behind him, and started straight off with *Pickwick Papers*. *Pickwick* is not very mature Dickens and not very mature humour, but it seemed to us quite the funniest book we had ever met. And not just to Dudley and John and Harry and me. It appealed to everyone, even the roughest and dimmest. I can see the class, sitting at their desks, bolt upright, eyes staring, ears alert: Marshall, with his round, red farmer's face, like a turnip, eyes and mouth cut out of the rind; Oz, with his Eton collar so stiff that it nicked his ears when he turned his head; Mitch, with steel-rimmed spectacles, looking like a crab's eyes on stalks; Wigan, gawky as a giraffe; Stan, Les, Porky, Pasty, Twinny. We stretched our necks forward and gaped with our mouths, like a nestful of fledglings, frantic to be fed.

"'Heads, heads – take care of your heads,'" read Mr. Wilson, as Mr. Jingle and the Pickwickians drove under a low archway in the Rochester coach.

"'Terrible place – dangerous work – other day – five children – mother – tall lady, eating sandwiches – forgot the arch – crash – knock – children look round – mother's head off – sandwich in her hand – no mouth to put it in.'"

We laughed till we choked and cried and nearly messed our pants.

I do not know whether Mr. Wilson read *Pickwick* right through, but *I* certainly did. My copy bears a plate inside the cover:

> "County Council of Cumberland
> Education
> Committee
> PRIZE
> Awarded to:

Name	Norman C. Nicholson
Class	VI
School	Holborn Hill Boys'
Date	31st March, 1925."

It was the first of a succession of Dickens volumes on Indian paper, in stiff blue covers, with the original Phiz and Seymour illustrations. In 1926, at the Secondary School, I received *Barnaby Rudge*; in 1927,

Dombey and Son; in 1928, *Nicholas Nickleby*. *Great Expectations*, which followed *Pickwick* in Mr. Wilson's scheme, I acquired in the red, cardboard-backed Nelson's Classics, price One Shilling and Sixpence – a series which became my regular source of Christmas and birthday presents from uncles and friends. I would be given the eighteenpence and sent across to Illingworth's, Booksellers, opposite the Post Office, to make my own choice.

These books were my winter reading between the ages of ten and fourteen. I took four or five weeks over each of them, reading avidly on my stool, under the gas lamp. I read for as long as I was allowed to – bed was never later than nine o'clock in those days; I read until my eyes were stinging from the strain and from the heat of the fire. Nor was it just the comic Dickens that caught my imagination, but the darker Dickens. Except for *Great Expectations*, I did not read any of the later novels, of course: nobody in my hearing ever mentioned *Bleak House* or *Little Dorrit*. But my mind roamed in a scared, but delighted, freedom through the flickering grotesqueries of *Barnaby Rudge* – Gashford on the roof-tops, waiting for a flame in the night sky; old John Willet, tied to his chair among the wreckage of the *Maypole bar*; Dennis, the Hangman, taunting the prisoners, while the gaol burned down – I must have read that book at least a dozen times. Once, I remember being asked why I liked Dickens.

"Because he's so real," I said.

It seems an odd answer, and yet, so far as I was concerned, it was an honest one. There is a Phiz drawing, in my edition of *Dombey and Son* – a book, which, by the way, my form teacher in the Secondary School tried hard to persuade me not to read! – which shows old Mrs. Pipchin, in her widow's weeds, sitting beside little Paul Dombey, and staring into the fire. I had never seen widow's weeds, of course, but everything else in that illustration, drawn in the 1840s, was as familiar to me, eighty years later, as the flags of my own back yard. The little, high, wooden chair, with rails like the rungs of a ladder, is the chair I sat in at meal-times when I was Paul Dombey's age. The fireplace itself, the bars across the grate, the kettle on the coals, the bellows hanging at the side, the brass shovel on the curb, the mirrored over-mantel, the mat, the table swathed in plush, the aspidistra on the wall-bracket – all these I had seen many times in my own house, or Grandpa Sobey's, or Grandma Nicholson's or Uncle Jim's. On a winter tea-time, before the gas was lit, the fitful firelight populated the room with fantasies as weird as any in Dickens. I would pick up my book sometimes and try to read by the glow from the coals, and the world I entered seemed not far removed from the world I left. It was no more than walking from one room into the next.

Mr. Wilson introduced us to another author – Victor Hugo. He said he wanted us to know that foreigners could write good books, too. I now find Hugo unreadable, though I shall go on reading Dickens until I can no longer read at all. But, in 1925, *Les Miserables* gripped us even more than *Pickwick*. Mr. Wilson must have abridged it ruthlessly, but he made everything in nineteenth-century France sound as if it were happening in the England of our own day. For one thing, his voice was our kind of voice; his vowels, now that we had got used to the slight tang of West Cumberland, were our vowels. He did not chop off his "u"s in the back of his throat, but gave them the full, plummy, front-of-the-mouth sound of the born Cumbrian. "Ooncle Poomblechook", he would say, when he read *Great Expectations* – I spell it in that way for the benefit of southern eyes, well knowing that, to northerners, it will look grotesque. Moreover, when he read *Les Miserables*, he pro-nounced all the proper names as if they were English – Jean Val Jean, Thenardier, Gavroche and Javert, all without any accents, acute or grave, and all sounding as if they might have been seen above the door-way of any Millom shop. It made it easy for those of us who went on to read the book itself, though it did seem rather strange that the proud, defiant, all-enduring and twice-life-size hero should have been given a girl's name.

The reading of *Les Miserables* bound us together in one common experience. There was one boy in our class – his father was a loyal non-commissioned officer in the Salvation Army – who used to deliver our evening milk. Milk came twice a day in the 'twenties, straight from the morning or afternoon milking, with no time wasted on bottling or cooling or pasteurising. The first time I saw a bottle of milk, in Birmingham, I burst out laughing. Now, on the principle that a trades-man ought to share out his custom among his fellows, we took our morning and evening milk from two different dealers, the evening supply coming direct from a farm, brought round by the farmer him-self, with two churns on a cart and my class-mate to help him. Just as we were having tea, the boy would walk up the back yard, give me a wave, and pour the milk from a tin into the jug we left waiting by the door. There was one occasion when a wave was not enough: I wanted to speak to him. My parents were dubious. I had been off school for a week, with mumps, and my swollen neck was still swathed in medicated cloths. But I was determined. I had missed two readings of *Les Miserables* and I wanted to know whether Jean Val Jean had escaped from the convent. My father insisted that the boy should stay in the yard, in case I was still infectious, but I stood by the door, and listened to his story of the coffin and the mock funeral as eagerly as the people of England, in 1815, had listened to the news of Waterloo. I don't know if the milk boy delivered my mumps to any of his customers, but that night, I went to bed, sweating, but content.

By now I had been caught up into the mill-race, for this year we were taking the Scholarship in earnest. I have no love for the examination system. I look back begrudgingly on the hours spent stuffing myself with unnutritious stodge, to regurgitate it on to the examination desk, in chemical formulæ, quadratic equations, meaningless dates. It would not be so bad if I could forget them, but many still clutter up my memory, like dust-piled boxes in an attic:

"1713. Treaty of Utrecht: the English gained the right to cut logwood in Honduras Bay."

At this stage, however, I thoroughly enjoyed exams. They were the sport at which I knew I could win. In any case, what was being examined was largely our ability to read, write and add up. We sat, first of all, what we called the Prelim, in autumn, and in our own school. Then the ten or twelve of us who had passed through this first sieve went on to take the main examination, held on a Saturday morning in March, in the Secondary School, above the Public Library.

By this time, I was beginning to learn the technique. I did not charge round the play-ground or shout my head off, as many of the others did – obvious failures from the start! There was no point, Mr. Wilson told us, in getting ourselves tired, getting out of breath, getting our hands dirty and sticky and in a tremble. I stood, very quietly, close to the wall, my hands in my trouser pockets to keep them warm, and a pen with a new nib and two freshly sharpened pencils in my breast pocket. From the side of my eye, I could see my father and mother watching me from our bathroom window, but I already had enough gumption to pretend not to notice them.

Of the examination itself, I can remember nothing, except the Dictation when a rather old man, who was a stranger to me, slowly rolled out the word: "Mel–an–co–ly". My spelling was my weakest point –

it still is! – and I doubt if I got it right, but I knew how to pronounce it, which was more than he did. A month or two later, those who had passed this second written test went forward to the Viva Voce examination, also held in the Secondary School, but on a week-day, when the rest of the School was at work. We were interviewed, one by one, in the big upstairs room, where I went when my name was called. There were three examiners, sitting at a table. One was the Headmaster, Mr. Sharp, who, through the kind instruction of my cousins, Donald and Bill, I had already learned to call "Jimmy"; the second was G. B. Brown, Director of Education for Cumberland; and the third was a very fat, very silent man, who was said to be headmaster of an elementary school in the north of the county.

They asked me to sit down, and Mr. Brown put some preparatory questions about Holborn Hill and our new Headmaster.

"Do you know where Mr. Wilson comes from?" he asked.

"Cockermouth, sir."

"And do you know why it's called Cockermouth?"

"Because it's at the mouth of the River Cocker where it flows into the River Derwent."

Mr. Sharp was surprised, but Mr. Brown pressed on with his local geography.

"Do you happen to know which lake the River Derwent flows out of?"

"Derwentwater," I guesssed.

"No," he said. "Bassenthwaite."

"I took it from the name," I said, being honest about it.

I need not have apologised. If G.B.Brown is allowed the use of maps in the heaven where he deserves to be, he will be able to see that the river which flows out of Derwentwater and into Bassenthwaite is, in fact, called the Derwent.

They tried me out with some trick questions: an Irishman wrote to his mother, and, at the end of the letter, he wrote: "P S. I've forgotten to put a stamp on the envelope", and what did I think about that? They asked me a lot of spellings, remarking at the end that I did not seem so bad, after all. At last, I was dismissed with the same kindly courtesy with which I had been received. I walked to the door, paused and turned:

"Who would you like to interview next?" I asked.

I was, as I thought, repaying courtesy with courtesy.

"Spell 'interview'," said Mr. Brown.

I managed the "inter" quite confidently, and then, slowly and hesitantly, tackled the "view". There was a burst of laughter when I finished, and Mr. Brown, with a kind of reassuring gesture, looked down at the list on the table.

"You may ask Marjorie Thompson to come in next," he said.

I went outside, closed the door, and saw a small, fair, pretty girl, standing at the foot of the stairs.

"Eh!" I yelled. "Are you Marjorie Thompson?"

"What's that got to do with you?"

"Well, you have to go in next."

It was my first encounter with one of the girls who were to be my school companions for the next five years.

I went back to Holborn Hill in an influenza of excitement. The unfamiliar lay-out of the Secondary School, the stairs, the notice board, the presence of the girls, the almost adult consideration with which I had been treated, all made me feel that I was changing into a new skin. Then, later in the afternoon, the fattest of the three examiners, who, so far as I can remember, had not spoken at all in the course of the interview, called at the School to see the Headmaster, and, as he was going away, he caught sight of me, sitting in the second row.

"I'd like to speak to that boy", he said.

Mr. Wilson called me out.

The man bent slowly toward me, like Humpty Dumpty taking care not to fall off the wall.

"We were very pleased with you this afternoon," he said. "You answered well."

He gradually disengaged an arm from the rest of his bulk, took hold of my hand and began to raise and lower it very slowly, as if he were beating time to the Dead March in *Saul*.

"I'm not promising anything, mind you," he went on. "But I hope you get a good result."

I went back to my seat, looking as if I had the measles.

"It's a good sign," said Mr. Wilson, after the visitor had gone.

So far as the Scholarship was concerned, it was.

CHAPTER EIGHT

On my first day at the Secondary School, in September 1925, I rushed home at the dinner hour and bolted down my meal so that I could find time to see Albert and tell him how I had got on.

"And put your new cap on," my mother said, as I was going out of the back door.

I was rather self-conscious about that cap. It was not that I objected, in general, to the wearing of caps, for every boy wore a cap in those days, but this particular cap was a uniform or livery. It marked me out, as I felt, for life. Even the buying of it had been a new experience.

For the agency for the Secondary School caps, ties and badges was held by Seth Slater, by now established on our side of The Terrace, and I had to push open his door and enter a place which, up to then, had seemed as mysterious and utterly out-of-bounds as a public house or the Catholic Church.

The school uniform – apart from the green and white ties, which were optional – consisted merely of a plain, dark-blue cap with badge at the front. Most boys bought this complete, as it were, but my father did not intend to spend more than he needed at another man's shop, so he provided the cap out of his own stock and sent me to Mr. Slater's to buy the badge which he then sewed on. I was always rather embarrassed by this procedure, though Mr. Slater seemed to take it quite for granted, and, indeed, it was probably what he himself would have done in the same circumstances. (The wheel took another turn when Mr. Slater died and the school outfitting agency passed to my father, who protested strongly at being expected to supply badges without the caps!)

The Slater family were now settled in their new house, next to the

Primitive Methodist Chapel, more than half-way up the slope of Holborn Hill. I could – and still can – see the chimneys of the house from our own attic window. Here, round about Christmas, our little society of schoolboys was invited to John's annual party. We each took a pair of slippers or pumps to change into so that we would not mark the carpets. Except for John's elder sisters, the parties were all-male affairs, as were my own: none of our parents would have dreamed of inviting a girl to the house, nor would we have expected it. But, one year, there was an extra member of the party – John's brother, Charlie, who was on vacation from Oxford. Our main entertainment was always charades, for which the Slater house was well suited, with its many rooms for changing in, and its long, dark corridors for queuing up and waiting your turn. Charlie at once showed himself a highly ingenious inventor and producer, and before long, he had us ransacking the wardrobes and cupboards for old clothes, table covers and curtains. In one scene, he dressed me up as a monk, in an old black coat and a hood, and with a huge string of wooden beads, dangling from my waist.

"You come in," he said, "damning and mountains. . . ."

It was the first time I had been so casually encouraged to use bad language and I was more than casually gratified.

Unfortunately, I was scarcely ever to meet Charlie Slater again, and, indeed, heard very little about him for quite a long time. Soon after he left Oxford, he published two novels, which aroused some notice in literary circles, though his father and mother kept so quiet about them that hardly anyone in Millom even knew of them. By this time, he had dropped the "Charlie" – which, in the Millom of his days, was the slang word for a hump – and used, instead, his middle name of "Montague", and it was as Montague Slater that he became known as a journalist, a writer of film scripts, and, above all, as the librettist of *Peter Grimes*. Britten's opera is a Suffolk opera, set on the East Anglian coast, in the late eighteenth or early nineteenth century. That is how the composer thought of it, and that is how the Co vent Garden audience saw it. But, to anyone who knew the background of Montague Slater's youth, it is obvious that *Peter Grimes* is also a Millom opera. His portraits of the narrow, uncharitable, maliciously gossiping church-goers is tinged by Slater's resentment of the strict chapel-going regime of his boyhood. His picture of The Borough, with half the population rotting away in idleness, at the edge of the foetid tidal marshes, continually recalls the Millom of the dole-days – broken boats mouldering in the salt mud, the almost worked-out mines, the men standing about in aimless clumps at the street corners and the churchyard gates. The scandal, the injustice, the waste, the muddle of it, made a deep mark on his soul.

It made no mark on mine – or not, at any rate, in those party-going years. I was aware of unemployment all round me, but it was something I took for granted, like bad weather in winter. It did not seem to be my concern.

"Are you working?" was then the usual greeting of men meeting one another in the street. And even if they *were* working, it was probably only one week in three. As for the General Strike of 1926, the one thing that I can remember is that the Train Pupils were not able to come to school.

At Holborn Hill, of course, there were boys whose elbows pushed through their worn-out sleeves; boys whose boots were bought from a fund, run by the local police; boys who, if they ever got to the Saturday afternoon film show at The Palace, had to pay a penny to go downstairs, while we paid tuppence to go in the balcony. Even at the Secondary School, there was one girl, the most brilliant of my year, who used to beg her mother in tears to let her stay away from the School Christmas Party, because she had nothing but an old cotton frock to go in. And, as late as 1929, the father of one of my friends was sacked from Hodbarrow, just three weeks before we sat for Matriculation. He kept the news from his son to save him from worry, until the examination was over, and every morning, for three weeks, he would get up at six o'clock, as if he were going to work, and walk the fields until after the hour that school had begun.

I was sheltered from such worries. My father, I felt contentedly sure, would never have to go on the Dole. The little shop would always be our stronghold and security. It was not until my father died, nearly thirty years later, that I realised how precarious that security had been. For, throughout those years, my father's annual profits – if you can call them profits, when they were no more than was due to him as wages – can never have been more than two hundred and fifty pounds; usually, they were nearer one hundred and fifty. One grim year, he barely averaged two pounds a week. Another year like that, and he might have been facing bankruptcy.

Yet not the slightest suspicion of this reached either my mother or me, at the time. I doubt if my father himself realised quite how vulnerable were the foundations on which he had built his life. He had what he regarded as a good little business. He relied on "the better class trade" – which meant the bank clerks, the local government officials, teachers and clergymen, who were the only people in the town who could be sure of keeping their jobs. He saw one shop after another go smash, and he survived them all with a quiet, untroubled confidence.

"How's business, Joe?" asked one of the visiting Sobeys.

"Mustn't grumble," he said.

"You're not feeling the pinch, then?"

He hesitated, having an intense dislike of discussing money matters.

"I might be," he admitted, "if I hadn't got a little bit coming in."

That little bit, as I discovered later, was less than five shillings a week.

Of course, he was always "careful". He smoked ten cheap Turkish cigarettes a week, and, though he went into the Conservative Club for an hour every evening after the shop was closed, he declared with pride that he had never once drunk a pint of beer there, nor staked sixpence on a game of cards. Our house was one where every penny had to be accounted for and not one was wasted. Nor was one owing either, for my father had a moral horror of debt. He was lenient to those of his own creditors, whom he knew to be genuinely hard up, but he had nothing but contempt for what he called the "high-ups" who ran up bills they could not afford to pay.

"Look at her," he would say to me, nodding at the wife of the manager of one of our local industries. "Walking about like Lady Muck, and she hasn't paid for the pyjamas she gave her husband last Christmas."

And when she greeted him effusively, smiling and nodding, he raised two fingers to the brim of his trilby, and stared accusingly through his spectacles.

Once he came rushing in from the shop, with a bill in his hand. My mother, it seemed, had ordered some article from Illingworth's and, by an oversight, had failed to call and pay for it.

"What's the meaning of this?"

My mother attempted to explain, but my father, who was usually cowed by the sharpness of her tongue, brushed her words aside, as if he were flicking a fly.

"A nice thing, this," he went on. "What will Jack Illingworth think?"

He stood with his weight back on his heels and his waistcoat pushed forward, holding out the bill like a summons.

"I've been in business for a good many years without giving tradesmen any call to send me bills," he said. "And I'm not starting now."

I did not, however, feel in any way deprived, in spite of what would today seem to be a cripppling shortage of money. Yet it must have been in sympathetic, or even conscience-stricken, response to one of my father's homilies on the need for "carefulness" that I invented *Ekky*. This came at a time when Albert and I were continually founding new clubs and sects and Secret Societies, with complicated rules, a private terminology and a membership restricted to two. Most of them I have completely forgotten, but *Ekky*, which was our code word for 'Economy", keeps its grip on my memory with a strange, mean-minded stubbornness. Its aim was: by care and ingenuity and due consideration, to reduce and curtail the expense incurred by our parents and guardians in feeding, clothing and bringing us up. I have a suspicion that Albert was rather less enthusiastic about this than about some other ideas of mine – less enthusiastic, for instance, than he was about the elaborate private language we constructed together.

("We'd better have *choc* for *shit*," he said, "in case I forget myself, and say 'Oh, shit' in company.")

In matters of invention and imagination, however, I was the leader, and Albert loyally plodded on behind for the week or ten days that the idea held my fancy.

I can recall only two of the economy measures I devised as part of the scheme, and neither of them, unfortunately, is of much practical use to me now. The first was that, whenever we went out into the country, we were to walk on the grass or soil, instead of the hard road or gravel, and so avoid wearing out the soles of our boots. It was, I think, of all my economy suggestions, the one which appealed most to Albert, and we went rampaging about the Old Church fields, saving boot leather at a high rate. It came as a complete surprise to me when my mother held up my boots – "all mud up", as she said.

"Why can't you walk in the middle of the road, like a boy with any sense?" she complained, angrily.

I realised it was useless trying to explain, and when I saw my father, struggling to scrape the mud off – for, angry as my mother was, she would never have thought of asking me to clean my own boots – I had to admit that I could see her point.

My second economy measure was one she would have understood

even less. In order to save money on food, I explained to Albert, we could help ourselves, when we went shopping, to some of the small crumbs and wastage which was always lying about the counter or the shelves – not stealing, of course, as I was anxious to emphasise, but just picking up the fragments, like the disciples, after the Feeding of the Five Thousand. I propounded the idea when we were taking a walk over The Knott, a rocky outcrop overlooking the Old Church, and the project as I sketched it seemed to be full of daring and enterprise. We would fill our pockets and our bellies with scraps of bread, ham and cheese, and with occasional grapes, nuts or toffees, and so be able to reduce household costs by doing without at least one meal a day. I believe that wild berries, mushrooms and watercress also had their place in my prospectus, but, as it was then the middle of winter, this was not immediately relevant.

I do not know what steps Albert took to carry out our plan, but, after hesitating for some days, I decided to act when next I was sent to the grocer's. It was that shop, in fact, with its bric-à-brac and cornucopia of spilt and spread foodstuffs, which had suggested the idea in the first place. I stood, in the corner of the shop, nervously watching Mr. and Mrs. Walmsley chop, slice, cut, pour out, weigh and wrap up. The cheese-board was close beside me, with its two tall cliff-edges of Lancashire and Cheddar, and, round the base of the cliff, a little detritus of chalky crumbles. Under the cover of my basket, I stretched out a hand, picked up one tiny nugget of Lancashire, about the size of a marble, and put it in my trouser pocket. I was so tense and excited that I could hardly answer Mr. Walmsley when he began to talk to me in his usual genial way, shovelling out polysyllables like a free gift or special offer for the day. I mumbled a reply, made my escape somehow or other, turned into the back street, pulled out the piece of cheese, and looked at it with a glow of achievement, scarcely diminished by the fact that I didn't really like cheese, anyway.

Afterwards, when the glow had faded, I began to have doubts. Was it not stealing, after all? Before long, I was sure that it was, and my conscience began to trouble me like a bilious attack. It was not a thing I could tell my parents; I did not even feel that I could discuss it with Albert; and, of course, confession to Mr. and Mrs. Walmsley was out of the question. The only possible way of putting things right seemed to be by restitution. For days, I worried and wondered how I could pay the Walmsleys back. My first idea was to break off a piece of cheese from our own pantry and drop it on the shelf, or even on the floor, next time I was in the shop. But this seemed to involve the anomaly of stealing from my own parents. Then I thought of going to the Walmsleys' door, after dark, when the shop was shut, and pushing a ha'penny through the letterbox. But I rarely went out after dark, and, anyway, I was scared of being caught. In the end, I think, my conscience quietened down, and the whole plan of *Ekky* was abandoned altogether. Today, Chris Walmsley's great-granddaughter is my goddaughter, and I still feel, at times, that I owe her for that piece of cheese.

Yet, fortunate as I was, and fortunate as – in spite of *Ekky* – I knew myself to be, I was beginning to have some misgivings about my father's calling.

"Give me an example of a hypocrite," said Mr. Wilson, in the course of a Scripture lesson.

"A shopkeeper," suggested one of the boys.

I stiffened at my desk and even Mr. Wilson looked surprised.

"Why?"

"Because he buys things at one price and sells them at another."

Mr. Wilson tried to explain the economics of the retail trade and I suppose I was pacified. But the sting remained, and, a few years later, when I first came across the term "petty bourgeois", I cringed to think how aptly it applied to my father. Eventually, however, I began to realise that, far from living on the labour of others, he had exacted from himself a standard of industriousness such as no employer would have dared to demand. I realised, too, that the provision of trousers is at least as vital to the running of a community as the making of pig-iron, and that a town without shops is no more practicable than a town without work.

Yet the shop worried me as a boy. It was partly because I hated having to wear new clothes: I felt that everyone would know that I had got them out of the shop. My mother did not make things easier. Whenever she saw me with my tie not straight or my jacket unbrushed or a button loose, she would say:

"You want to be an advert for your dad" – which, of course, was the last thing I did want to be.

The very way in which clothes reached me removed any possible pleasure they might otherwise have given. My father would come into my bedroom, braces hanging loose from his trousers and with a pyjama jacket pulled over his vest:

"Your're putting this shirt on this morning," he would say.

Or these socks, or that pullover. And I put them on. It did not occur to me to thank him for them, though I was good mannered enough, and would certainly have thanked him if he'd given me an orange. Nor did it occur to him to ask what sort of shirt I'd like or what colour socks. Clothes were not a matter on which I was expected to have an opinion.

When I was due for a new suit, my father would show me the patterns, but the choice would be limited and my parents had already decided what I would want. Indeed, my father regarded it as mere affectation to take too much time considering such matters.

"Make up your mind," he'd say. "I can't stand here all day."

He'd look down at the patterns, with mildly contemptuous impatience.

"They're all the same, if there's any difference."

Then, when the choice had been made, the impatience would pass from him to me, as I was twisted and turned and taped, made to hold out my elbow like a teapot handle or pull my trousers up tight. My father, like most small-shop outfitters, used a postal tailoring service, sending in the measurements, receiving the unfinished garments for try-on, returning them for adjustment, and so on. I seemed to have to undergo measurement after measurement for the same suit. It is no wonder that, when friends of mine were given a jacket or an overcoat for a birthday present, I felt that their parents were cheating. Even today, I dislike having to buy clothes for myself: I expect them just to come.

It was not until my father was an old man that I began to understand something of his quiet contentment. As a boy, I saw the shop merely as small, dark and stuffy, a place I was expected to keep out of. Later, I began to see it as my father must have seen it.

For, small as it was, it, too, was made to measure. Everything was in its place. My father claimed that he could walk into the shop in the dark, and "put his hand on" any article required, almost to the precise colour and size. The two sides of the shop were fitted with shelves, all of them packed with labelled boxes, tight and neat as a beehive. Not one cubic foot of space was wasted. There were green boxes for the shirts; deep brown boxes for the caps; narrow boxes for the ties; shallow, square, white boxes for the collars – plain, high, starched collars, butterfly collars, pointed turn-downs and rounded turn-downs, and even a few clerical collars. The hats were kept separately in oval-shaped boxes which, piled one on the other, made a fine Solomon's temple pillar from floor to ceiling, while overcoats and raincoats and ready-made jackets hung in a tall showcase on the wall opposite the counter. When a customer wanted to try on a suit or a pair of trousers, my father would snap the lock and hang a green paper blind over the glass window of the door, turning the shop temporarily into a private fitting room.

By the time I had reached my teens, the old rolls of cloth for suitings and the old-fashioned tailor's dummies, which my father had inherited from his days with Seth Slater, had all been thrown out at my mother's persuasion. She was responsible, too, for the new, lighter, less cluttered and, as she would have said, "more artistic" appearance of the shop window. And how greatly my father came to rely on her, in such things, became clear when she was ill and went into hospital for three months. My father was seventy-five at the time, still reluctant to give up the shop, but he now found himself needing to dress the window without her help for the first time for many years. He went upstairs to the store-room and there dug out three or four old mufflers of a type which had not been worn for at least a quarter of a century. These he carefully folded into a kind of Chinese lantern shape, which he had learned from Mr. Slater around the turn of the century, and hung them confidently along the back of the shop window. The date was 1953.

My father's daily routine was as methodical as the lay-out of his shop. He used to keep open from eight-fifteen to seven o'clock in his early days, and from nine to five-thirty after 1945. And the shop really was open throughout those hours: no closing for lunch, except, again, in later years. When he came into the house at meal-times, he would switch on a little battery-worked bell, which rang when the door opened, and when the bell rang, he would drop his knife and fork and go immediately to the shop. Often, he had taken only a couple of mouthfuls when the bell rang, and by the time he had served his customer, the meal was cold. During the Christmas shopping week, it was almost impossible to eat at all.

The blessed respite from all this came on Sundays and Wednesday Early Closing. Sunday, of course, was everybody's day off, but Wednesday afternoon was the tradesmen's own privilege. I learned, as a very young child, to look forward to the peace which came over the house on Wednesday afternoon. To other boys, holiday times meant bustle and stir, the shops lit up and the streets crowded; to me they meant quietness. Even today, when I visit a town for the first time, I prefer to go on an Early Closing Day. I enjoy seeing the shops empty, the shop doors shut, the streets un-crowded. In later years, when I was lying ill in the bedroom two storeys above the shop, I would often start up with a little thrill of pleasure when I heard the yale lock click into place at twelve-thirty on Wednesday. "Early Closing", I would say to myself, and lie back on the pillow, determined to enjoy it. After my father died, in 1954, the shop was let to various tenants for a period of nearly twenty years, and when the last tenant left, and the shop became once more part of the house – which, after all, is what was intended when it was built in 1880 – I felt as if the week had become a perpetual Bank Holiday. I used often to go and sit in the old empty shop-space, just for the pleasure of thinking that the room was now my own, and that people would not crowd it up for the Christmas Eve or walk in at any time of the day to ask the price of a handkerchief.

For Wednesday seemed to be a quite special kind of Red Letter Day – one not shared by the public, but private and peculiar to my father and me. If Sunday was the Lord's Day, Wednesday was *our* day. I could not, of course, foresee that many of my adult years were to be a succession of Early Closing Days, a life on short-time, but my father and his eager anticipation of Wednesday afternoon had already begun to prepare me for it. He taught me to enjoy the quiet.

Not many one-man shops remain today, even in the small towns, and few tradesmen still live above or behind their own shop. Economically, my father was an anachronism, belonging to the tail-end of a tradition which went back right to the time of *The Shoemaker's Holiday*. The independence he prided himself on was always precarious and, perhaps, even an illusion, but it seemed real enough to him. He could do as he liked in his own shop. He had to kowtow to nobody. And he had his own way of running the business which not even my mother understood. No article on the counter or in the window had a price tag, except in code, and I fancy that my father often adjusted the price to suit the customer, charging a country gentleman more than one of his fellow tradesmen. There is a story – which I can scarcely believe! – of three men, a bank manager, a local industrialist and a shopkeeper, who once met in a pub and found that each had bought exactly the same kind of hat from my father but at three quite different prices. I do know, however, that he would sometimes enter less in his ledger than the amount he had actually received, and that the extra unaccounted five or ten shillings gradually added up to enough to pay for our week at Blackpool in the summer. I think he managed to persuade himself that the holiday cost him nothing!

One moment is engraved deeply on my memory because I know it was engraved on his. It was when I was still quite a young boy, and a plump, cocksure commerical traveller blustered into the shop.

"I want to see the boss," he said.

My father tilted back his head, peering condescendingly over his pince-nez.

"I'm the boss," he said. "I'm my own boss."

He had disciplined his life for fifty years in order to be able to make that reply. He had worked ten and sometimes twelve hours a day as a young man, Saturdays included; he had refused the offers of a multiple firm; he had run all the financial risks of the Depression and the two wars. And he had no doubt that it had been well worth it. At one time, when she wanted to move to the south of England, my mother tried to persuade him to ask her wealthy cousin to find him a situation in the large Bournemouth shop of which he was part owner, but my father would not hear of it. He wanted to be his own boss.

If it comes to that, so do I.

The switch from Holborn Hill to the Secondary School was made without too many bumps. Donald and Billy had alarmed me with stories of the ragging of new boys – putting their heads in the wash-basin, and the like – but all was calm and peaceful on the first day. (I learned afterwards that Jimmy Sharp, who knew how to deal with boys, had had a word with the sixth form:

"If you see any of those beauties in Form IV trying to bully the little ones, just give them one under the ear, and tell them it's from me!")

At the beginning, I was self-conscious about the girls in the class and went to a lot of trouble to avoid having to sit next to one of them. Albert, who had been instructed by a girl cousin, had already informed me, fairly accurately, of the basic method and anatomy of sex, but, though I was immensely curious, I scarcely associated this with girls at all. The beautiful and disturbing feminine shapes which I sometimes saw in the photograph section of *The Sketch* and *The Tatler*, turning over the pages furtively in the Public Library, did not immediately strike me as being what might lie beneath a gymslip. I still thought of sex mainly as a process married people had to go through to get children, and I felt, on the whole, that it was rather hard on them.

Once I got used to the girls, however, I was grateful for the new gentleness, the kitchen cosiness, they brought into the classroom, something which had been missing from my sisterless life. Midge, the Headmaster's daughter, Marjorie, who became the wife of a professor, Dorothy, who became the mother of another, Bessie, a lifelong friend, Mary, who married a parson, Shelagh, Rene, Muriel. I was not the kind of boy of whom girls took much notice, being neither tough enough nor cheeky enough, but in my quiet, stay-in-my-own-corner way, I took notice of them and they enlarged my view of life.

Millom, too, was beginning to grow. Our legs enlarged it for us. Albert and I attended different Sunday Schools – he, the United Methodists, and I, the Wesleyans – but we would arrange to meet, later on in the afternoon, for what was supposed to be a well-behaved, gentlemanly, Sabbath-Day walk, each dressed in his Sunday best, and Albert carrying an elegant, silver-headed cane. One March day, on a walk to the Old Church, we turned off beside the beck that runs through the field, and began, on some fancy or other, to make a little camp fire. It was late winter – the grass bitten to the quick by the sheep, the thorn hedge, beside the beck, spiky and bare as a bunch of nails. We could not reach the hedge because of the water, but we gathered up the sticks and twigs that were scattered about, built them into a wicker pyramid and soon were able to set a match to them. The flames belched up, crackling and spitting, like a little volcano, and, in next to no time, the whole pyramid was collapsing into flickering, grey ash. We looked about distractedly for more fuel, snatching at everything we could see, and tossing it into the fire. Suddenly, at the side of my eye, I caught sight of a beautiful, slender branch, lying on the grass. I seized it with both hands, cracked it across my knee, and, almost before the sound of the split had reached my ears, I recognised the silver-headed cane.

"Oh, choc!" said Albert.

Three days later, my parents, who had been asked by Albert's grandmother to pay for the cane, told me that a policeman had called and warned them that, if I was seen trespassing on the fields again, I would be summoned to court. I passed on the news to Albert.

"I don't believe it," he said.

I was flabbergasted at this reaction.

"Why should they go to your house if they haven't been to our house?" he went on, indignantly.

I could think of no satisfactory answer.

"Well, why should they?"

It was the last time anyone was going to scare me with stories about policemen.

Albert left Millom after less than a year at the Secondary School, and the next time I met him, he was a congregational minister, and has since, I believe, become an immensely successful psychologist in the United States.

When he had gone, I made friends with Dudley, and learned to ride a bicycle. I'd been promised the bike when I passed the Scholarship, but my mother found an old one with no brakes, which, she said, "was good enough to learn on". I was a slow and awkward learner. I lacked confidence and I lacked gumption, and, for hours and hours, I trundled round the flat, empty gridiron of Albert Street, Market Street and the rest, until the boys cheered as I passed along. The trouble was that I did not know how to get on and off the machine. I could use a wall or a railing as a mount, but, when I wanted to get off, I had to let the bike run slower and slower and then thrust out one leg as I fell off.

One day, when Dudley had been to see me, I set him half-way home, to the top of the railway bridge. I said good-bye, and turned to wheel my bike back to St. George's Terrace.

"You may as well get on," he said, steadying the machine for me.

I climbed on with some misgiving, having been warned not to try to ride downhill without brakes, but the road was empty and there seemed nothing to worry about. Dudley gave me a shove off and I sailed happily down the bridge, taking the steeply banked left-hand turn, opposite the Church Gates, to find myself aimed straight at a herd of cows that blocked the whole road from side to side. I had two seconds to choose between the wall of the West County Hotel and the horns of the cows. I chose the wall. The bump can still be faintly seen on the right side of my forehead.

The bike, when it came, enlarged my territory still more. Dudley lived high up on the slopes of Holborn Hill, near John Slater. I could mount my bike outside his house, push off and free-wheel the whole half a mile home. Together, we visited Silecroft Shore and the Whicham Valley, while his father, who owned a car, took us as far as Seascale and Carlisle, and gave me my first sight of Wastwater and Ullswater.

Yet Millom was still the centre of my world. Even school was, as yet, only a part-time occupation. I enjoyed it, of course, except for gym and games. Gym I resented, because I thought it was a waste of time–you did not go to school, it seemed to me, to learn to jump over a vaulting horse, which I never did learn, in any case. Yet gym could be endured so long as you kept quietly out of the way, and gave no cheek to the visiting gym instructor. Games were another matter. I detested them with all my heart and the only really miserable times I can remember in the whole of my Secondary School years were those spent on the playing fields, being continually knocked down and stamped on and rolled in the sodden grass, while a cold, damp, grimy wind screeched over from the slag bank. To be taunted and yelled at and kicked and thumped and to be quite unable either to run away or to appeal to anyone for justice seemed to me to epitomise all the unfairness in the world. Afterwards, there was the mile-long trudge back to school, through the mud of the lonning, with my face bruised, my shins scraped, my boots caked in cow dirt, my socks torn and the prospect of being nagged when I went home for letting all these things happen. For nearly two years, I loathed and feared Friday afternoon games, until I was often physically sick and vomited at the very thought of them. Later, I began to invent excuses – colds, headaches, sprained ankles – and stayed in the comfort of the school, doing my weekend homework. Later still, I simply sloped off home. My absence was rarely remarked on. After all, I was reliable and co-operative enough in other respects. But if any headmaster wants to induce a lifelong indifference to, or intolerance of, almost all sports and athletics, then compulsory games is the best way of going about it.

For the rest, school was almost too easy during those first two years. I was the kind of boy who cottoned on to new subjects and new ideas quicker than most – French, Latin, algebra, geometry, chemistry – so that more than one of the teachers thought they had a brilliant pupil. Later, when the novelty rubbed off and I began to lose interest, they realised their mistake. For, in the first six terms, Dudley and I occupied the first two positions in class, as if we held them on a permanent lease. We each collected a George Moore Scholarship, worth ten pounds, in 1926, and, the following year, I won a George Moore Exhibition, one of two, worth a hundred pounds, which were open to pupils from schools in Cumberland, Westmorland and North Lancashire. We went to Carlisle for the examination, sitting it in the Cathedral Choir School, and I had almost forgotten about it when, one morning, we were all called into the gym. We stood there, the boys on one side and the girls on the other, wondering what was up. Mr. Sharp made the announcement and I was completely surprised by the applause with which the school greeted the news. I felt stunned, my eyes dimmed, and I had to clutch at the wall-bars to stop myself from fainting. Dudley, to his credit, was the first to shake hands with me.

I came in late for the first lesson and excused myself to Mr. Siddle in the precise, rather pedantic manner I affected when I addressed the staff:

"Mr. Sharp gave me permission to go home and tell my parents, as we had had no previous word."

But going home had been the least part of my little triumph. What really mattered to me was the applause of those upper forms. For nearly two years, I had been at the bottom end of the school, ignored or pushed about by everyone but the teachers. Suddenly, I had become someone to be noticed. From now on, it would be free-wheeling all the way.

CHAPTER NINE

ALL thoughts of free-wheeling were dispersed like mist in an autumn wind when we returned to school after the long vacation of 1927. We had assembled in our classroom, above the Public Library, and I was congratulating myself on having now reached the middle age of Form III, when Mr. Sharp walked in. He nodded to Dudley and me and a boy called Cyril, son of a policeman, who had only been in the school about a term, but whose ability was already obvious.

"Pick up your things," said Mr. Sharp. "I'm taking you down to Form IV."

Form IV lived in a classroom on the ground floor, divided into two by a wooden partition. Today, it is the setting of the town's Folk Museum and a hand-driven wooden threshing-machine occupies the place where my desk once stood. In Form IV, I found myself with eighteen or twenty boys and girls, most of them a year older than me and at least two stone heavier. For the first time, Dudley and I found ourselves matched against real competition. We had to put in hours of extra work to catch up the year we had missed; we had to struggle hard even to keep in the running. Homework now took up the greater part of the time between tea and bed, and evenings off had to be paid for by twice as much work at the weekend. My little local fame as a reciter was snapped off at the stalk. ("He said 'Cut it out,'" said my father.) For the first three months, I was working at full throttle, straining and striving, with hardly a thought for anything but my school books. Often, the questions and exercises would go on repeating themselves throughout the night, in uneasy dreams. When, at the end of the term, I found myself in the third place, I knew it was the best result I'd ever earned.

After that, the strain eased off. I knew now that I could keep up with the others, and though the regular work was still relentlessly required of us, it was a matter of application, rather than of anxiety. The school had laid its claim on me, however. From now on, until I left, it would be the centre, the purpose, the driving force in my life. So far as I was concerned, the town almost disappeared from view. The concerts and socials and musical evenings were put away as childish things. I no longer wanted the applause I used to enjoy: I wanted another kind of applause. Already, the school was beginning to build a wall between me and Millom. People I had looked up to as a boy now seemed old-fashioned, ungrammatical in speech and narrow in outlook. I could no longer talk to my own parents about my work, or, indeed, about anything that seemed really to matter. They were proud of me, in a bewildered way, but I knew that they could not understand. I was disconnected from the world I was once part of. New emotions, new interests, new excitements were continually being generated, until my senses were charged like an electric battery. I gave off sparks in the dark. To put it in the oversized language in which I expressed myself at the time: I fell in love; I discovered poetry; I discovered Cumberland. All three discoveries were simultaneous and intermingled. A fourth was, perhaps, the sum of the three, even the multiplication of each by the others, the concentration and consecration of them all. It is of this that I must speak first.

In Millom, in those days, it was generally believed, with what foundation I have no idea, that if you wanted to go to college, you had to be confirmed. By college, of course, was meant any form of higher education, including university. The Methodists, as a whole, approved of education. They might be rather less enthusiastic about the Church of England, but few of them would let a matter of formal conformity interfere with their sons' prospects. So, when I reached Form IV and the possibility of college and a teaching career appeared distantly on the horizon, it was decided that I had better be confirmed. Now it happened that, though I had enjoyed the chapel services well enough, I had not liked the Sunday School. At St. George's, however, I found more order, more discipline, more seriousness. The Superintendent, W. J. Atkinson – "Weejee" to the town – was a tall, serious layman, with only one arm, a kind of pious Nelson, who devoted himself with equal zeal to

St. George's Church and the Millom Amateur Operatic Society. He took an immediate interest in me, placed me in my Uncle Jim's class to begin with, and later, occasionally, put me in charge of the youngest boys whenever there was a shortage of teachers. I remember, as clearly as if he were still speaking, the advice he gave me, when he handed over one of these junior classes. The lesson that Sunday was supposed to be on Holy Communion.

"I should put it to them this way," said Mr. Atkinson, leaning forward, his cupola of a bald head polished like marble, his empty jacket-sleeve jack-knifed across his breast:

"When a friend is visiting the house, you say to him: 'Have a cup of tea before you go.' Well, in the same way, in Christ's family, you invite your friends to come to the Lord's Table with you."

I was much impressed with this image and developed it at some length, drawing forth analogies from bread and cake and party jellies. I can still see the wide-eyed, half-incredulous, eager attention of the small boys.

But when, after a few months, I found myself in the Confirmation Class, I heard the vicar, the Reverend H.P.Walton, speak of Holy Communion in quite a different tone.

"Some people are afraid they might catch infection from the Communion cup," he once said.

(I thought of the "individual Communion cups" at the Methodist Church, and how my father, though he was an Anglican, had approved of them.)

"But, I ask you," he went on, "could there possibly be any infection in the blood of Our Lord Jesus Christ?"

Put like that, I had to admit it seemed highly unlikely!

And "like that" was just how he did put it.

Mr. Walton was a lean-faced, swarthy-skinned man, with something of the toughness that came from a chaplain's experience in the trenches. He had had the education of a gentleman, but was greatly aware of the poverty and social misery all around him in his parish, and was as much concerned with the state of his choirboys' footwear as with the state of their souls.

"I used to be a socialist, once," he said to me, and to admit to having been a socialist at all was unusual in the Church of England of the 1920s.

Many a time, as a local grocer told me, he would give a 10/-voucher to one of his parishioners, or even one of his non-parishioners, and once, when he went to the shop to pay up, he found that the 10/-had been altered to £1/10/-.

He was a man of great kindness and quick sympathy, and a man, also, of a simple, uncomplicated and rather true-to-the-letter kind of faith.

"Sometimes boys tell me that they can't understand the Incarnation," he once said, for he would talk to me, even when I was only fifteen, on almost equal terms.

"I explain it like this: 'You have a father and a mother,' I say. 'Everybody has a father and mother. Now Jesus only had a mother.' It's as simple as that!"

For him, it was as simple as that. For me, this simplicity gave a quite new view of religion. At the Methodists, it had mainly been a matter of exhortation: "Do this; don't do that; accept the Lord Jesus Christ as your Saviour." At Holborn Hill, it had been all Bible stories, while in the Secondary School we had had no religious instruction whatever. But now, religion was presented as a straightforward set of statements or propositions, like geography or geometry. Something you could actually *learn*.

"If anyone asks you what you believe as a Christian," said Mr. Walton, "what would you say to them?"

The dozen or so boys and girls sitting in the front pew gaped uncomprehendingly. He turned hopefully to me.

"Recite the Creed," I said.

He was my friend for life!

Yet, of course, it was not what was in the Creed that excited me, not what the words meant, but the words themselves. I was meeting, for the first time, the lovely platitudes of Cranmer, hearing the Flesh taking word. Moreover, Mr. Walton spoke with a kind of intense, yet curiously matter-of-fact, conviction, of much that I had scarcely heard of before – the Catechism, the Sacraments, the Eucharist. A word like "altar" acquired a new glow, both mysterious and taken-for-granted, both other-worldly and *this*-worldly.

For Mr. Walton was an Anglo-Catholic, and if my parents had been church-goers, I would, no doubt, have been aware that there was already a tension between him and his predominantly Low-Church congregation. The fact that I was not aware of it may have made it easier for me to receive and respond, though, looking back, I find it hard to judge how deeply I was influenced by the vicar's words or his views. Perhaps it was much less than I thought at the time, for I was subject to so many influences, so many rays were being focused on my mind and my imagination.

There was, to begin with, the time and place. The Confirmation Classes were held in the church on a week-day evening. At the beginning of the course, we walked up the gas-lit drive, with the last clinkers of a February sunset scattered behind the bars of the churchyard trees. We sat in a dim church, the lights turned up above the front pews, the rest of the building receding, backwards and upwards, into enormous ambiguities of shadow. There, week by week, as the classes went on, we assembled through gradually lengthening evenings, until, the week after Confirmation, the trees and the church steeple were swilled with light and the yellow gas-jets of the crocuses flickered up from the ground.

There was one class, however, when the boys were told to meet separately from the girls, in the Vicarage Room. As it happened, I had a cold that week and could not attend, but Mr. Walton gave my father a pamphlet to pass on to me.

"Now you take notice of that," said my father, as he passed it on.

It was the only sex instruction he ever gave me.

The pamphlet, with its high puritan attitude to sex – 'There was once a boy, who was tempted by a bad girl to do something which he knew was very wrong" – struck me as being just silly, yet, in a way, it pointed to the heart of what was disturbing me. For my body was aware of more than I could understand. I was already boyishly in love, and so much that had seemed solid was now sliding and tottering away, like a collapsing house. I used to dream, over and over again, that I was falling down a mine-shaft or over a cliff-edge or down flight after flight of long, steep, sharply-twisting stairs.

Then, a week or so before Confirmation, all these apprehensions and stirrings grew suddenly still, as when the threat of thunder dies away. The air clarified, leaving me, nevertheless, taut as a telephone wire. For a time, every part of me vibrated with an emotion more intense than anything I had felt before. It is hard, at this distance, to define it. I cannot call it a conversion, for I did not seem to be converted *to* anything. There was no sense of guilt, nothing of the repentance which, for years, I had been taught I ought to feel. It was more like being a piano string when the damper is lifted and the lower notes are struck and the unstruck strings hum faintly in sympathy.

For several Sundays before Confirmation, I would get up at eight o'clock in the morning, to the amusement and half-annoyance of my parents, and go to the early Communion Service, sitting quietly at the back of the church:

"Lord, I am not worthy that Thou shouldst come under my roof, but speak the Word only, and my soul shall be healed."

I prepared myself for that service from a little book of prayers, one for each day of the week, looking forward to Sunday. I prayed every night and, when I woke early enough, every morning, spending, sometimes, half an hour on my knees, and staggering about, stiff and numb, like a lame man, when I stood up again.

Of the actual Confirmation, I can remember very little, except that it was held, that year, in the Old Church. We bounded back after the service, like a herd of young bullocks let out into the fields.

Ten days later, on Easter Sunday, I was upset when my parents insisted that I drank a cup of tea before I went off to take my first Communion.

"You're not going up to that cold church without something hot in your stomach," my mother said.

The following week, her insistence did not worry me so much. The week after that, I did not go to church at all. Like a patient who is recovering from a high temperature, I was returning to normal.

"When you're dead, you're dead," said Tom Morton, my friend of that time.

It seemed to dispose of a number of problems.

It did not, however, dispose of Maureen, nor would Tom have wished to dispose of her, for he had more sympathy for girls than for religion.

Maureen was a small, quiet, pretty girl – "a violet by a mossy stone", though a very healthy flower on a very sturdy stalk. She was a year older than me, like all the girls in Form IV, but, because she was short – "Suffered from duck disease" as we used to put it – that scarcely seemed to matter. She was one of the Train Pupils, travelling in each day from Broughton-in-Furness, so that I saw her only at school. Evenings, weekends and holidays she was out of sight and out of reach, though not long out of mind. For, at ten o'clock every evening, when the Ironworks buzzer blared out at the change of shift, she could hear it, on a quiet and windless night, in her own home, eight miles away, and we used it as a signal to think of one another.

It was a kind of communication, as I now realise, which suited me far better than any out-of-school meeting would have done. Once, when my mother began to question me about my having been seen hanging around the railway station after school, the blood drained from my face, I nearly fainted and had to be dragged out into the back yard for air. It was not so much that I feared my mother would disapprove of my having a girl-friend, but that I did not want the knowledge of it to enter the home at all. I did not want school and home to come into contact.

For at least a year, Maureen and school were almost indistinguishable in my mind. At holiday time, I would count off the days, and at weekends the hours, to my return to school and her. Whatever classroom we happened to be in, I would contrive to sit either beside her or behind her, and, perhaps, one of the reasons why I disliked gym so much was the fact that the girls were excluded. Oddly enough, my school work did not suffer. I seemed to go through the day with my attention alert to every movement, every whisper of the girl in front of me, yet, at the same time, able to concentrate on the lesson with another part of my mind. More than once, when I seemed to be in a day-dream, a teacher asked me, sharply, to repeat what he had been saying, and I did so patiently, precisely and with understanding. In the end, they regarded Maureen and me with a kind of amused contempt but said nothing. All except the Headmaster, who once threatened to make us walk arm-in-arm round the school playground. But there was no malice in Jimmy Sharp, and I laughed as loudly as anybody. Another time, I had on my desk a drawing I had made of a rose in a little vase. It caught Mr. Sharp's eye and I cautiously pushed a piece of blotting paper over the vase to cover up the words I had written beneath it. But Jimmy lived up to his surname. Slowly and with a kind of teasing deliberation, he stretched out his hand, pulled the drawing from under the blotting paper and looked at the inscription.

"Of such is the Kingdom of Heaven," he read.

For a moment or two, I think he was even more embarrassed than I was. But he quickly recovered and slapped down the drawing on Maureen's desk.

"Is that supposed to be you?" he asked.

In a way, he was quite right – the drawing, whatever it was supposed to be, was really a picture of Maureen. For Maureen, to me, was all things bright and beautiful. Sex, as I had heard about it, was still largely a matter of honest smut. We laughed at it and passed the stories on from boy to boy. But not from boy to girl. In my mind, certainly,

Maureen was far removed from all "that sort of thing", as my mother would have called it if she'd mentioned it at all. For, among the people she had grown up with, sex was still un-referred to, un-read about, almost, by a kind of unspoken agreement, non-existent. It was not until several years later that I discovered, to my immense surprise, that the Gay 'Twenties were supposed to have been a period of new sexual liberation.

So that, whatever may have been its deeper cause, the love which filled my imagination was of a kind that seemed, to me, to have little to do with what I meant by sex. "Love" was something I had learned about from *David Copperfield and Under the Greenwood Tree* and from the stories in *The Woman's Weekly*, which my mother occasionally bought. And, of course, from the poetry I was just beginning to enjoy.

I was naively oblivious to the sexual innuendoes of Keats and Tennyson but their romantic raptures set me trembling like a tuning fork. "Come into the garden, Maud" roused nothing of the derision, or even downright ribaldry, that it would surely rouse in a boy of today. I thought it said just what I would have felt in the circumstances. And put it very nicely too.

My love for Maureen was a thing of antique poses and styles, taken from the attitudes of a world which was dead before we were born and has now entirely disappeared. My third discovery, on the other hand, was of a world which, outwardly at least, has not changed much since those days.

> "But there's a tree," says Wordsworth, "of many, one,
> A single field which I have looked upon,
> Both of them speak of something that is gone."

My trees speak of something that is still there.

It was Tom Morton who helped me to discover Cumberland. Tom was the son of the Headmistress of Lapstone Road Girls' School, a widow who, by an odd coincidence, had the same surname as the Headmaster of the Boys' School next door. He was a boy of quite distinguished ugliness, short, short-sighted and beginning to be tubby – a kind of under-drawn, subtler Billy Bunter. He was per-petually in love with some girl or other, always hopeful, always disappointed, and, because he was as useless as I was at jumping, running, kicking or fisting, he was a boy who had been much pushed about in earlier years. But those years were over. By the time I knew him, his calm assumption of intellectual superiority gave him a protection greater than muscle could ever have done. From the time I made friends with Tom Morton, the miseries of the football field and Sports Day ceased to be miseries. They were no longer worth our notice. On the rare days when a school team was engaged in a match, we would be blandly unaware of it; if one of our friends happened to be playing, we would ostentatiously avoid enquiring who had won. On the one occasion I can remember when we had to attend a school match in the Millom Cricket Field, we sat on the boundary, reading a book, until, in exasperation, one of the fielders picked up the ball and threw it at us. We glanced at it, without interest, and went on reading.

Tom was a year older than me and altogether more sophisticated, better read and better informed. He introduced me to Poe's *Tales*, to my first detective stories and to the early novels of H. G. Wells. Above all, he made me walk. I had walked with my parents, but only along roads and footpaths. Tom took me away from the roads on to the shores, the marshes and the fells. Like many boys who are brought up close to the coast, we were not much attracted by the seaside – bathing has always seemed to me no more than an unpleasant and quite unnecessary way of getting wet. But we walked for miles along the sand dunes on bright March afternoons, with the larks trilling like little electric bells and the new green of the sandy turf flecked white with the first daisies and whitlow-grass. We walked up to the tarn on the top of Black Combe and self-consciously kept away from the cairn on the summit because we felt it was rather vulgar to bother ourselves with such things. We climbed Coniston Old Man, and, for the first time, I was able to look down on the Combe from a height greater than itself. It was a memorable moment, all the more so since, as events showed, it was also to be the last time. We wandered through oak woods and fir woods, along rock-cluttered paths and the peaty floors of corries; we scrambled across screes, squelched through fell-side bogs. We crossed becks by natural stepping stones, slithered into the water and sat bare-foot on the bank, while our socks dried in the sun. We ate sandwiches and chocolate and hard-boiled eggs and drank from aluminium beakers, dipped into grooved and sculpted swirl-holes in the blue slate. We added a thirty-seventh sonnet to Wordsworth's sequence on the Duddon, composing it in alternate lines, as we walked beside the tributary Logan, where it skitters down from bare, sprawling moorland to the chasms and sun-shot glooms of the Duddon woods. On one occasion, we cycled the whole length of the Duddon Valley, to Gockley Beck and over Wrynose Pass – then about as rough and nearly as steep as a scree – into Little Langdale, and back by Colwith and Coniston. It was many years before I was able to come again to that elemental, Icelandic, seeming-just-past-glacial landscape of the Upper Duddon, by which time a metalled road had been laid over the Pass, but throughout those years, it remained quite unchanged in my mind and not much changed in reality.

"Now then, Cockley Beck, time to get up," my father would say, as he called me in the morning.

By this time, I was fully caught up in the pull of the stream that was sweeping us along towards Matriculation. There were eight teachers in the school in my day and seven subjects were studied up to Matric level – Eng. Lang, and Eng. Lit. counting only as one. Some woodwork, drawing, singing, and cookery for the girls were taught in the lower forms, and there was a P. T. instructor, who visited the school once a week, but all this, everyone knew, was irrelevant. It was only the cardinal seven that really mattered. The school, in fact, had become a five-year processing-machine for turning out School-Leaving Certificates.

Now I was not one of those who believed in working up to the last minute – "If you don't know it by this time, you never will know it," my father used to say, when he saw me with my books – but I felt the numbing, and rather exhilarating tension as much as anyone. Of the actual examination, however, about all I can remember is that, in the course of, I think, the History paper, a street musician, just outside the school windows, obliged with a rendering of "The Lost Chord" on the cornet, and that Mr. Sharp sent out a boy with sixpence to ask him to go away.

After the examination, when we expected to feel free as hares, we all flopped with reaction. There seemed just nothing that we wanted to do. There were no lessons, and we spent most of the time reading whatever we liked. It happened that my father had picked up at the stationer's a sixpenny copy of Wells's *Kipps* and I began to chuckle over this, as we sat in class.

"What is amusing you?" asked Miss Hobson, sharply.

She was marking Term Test papers and did not want to be interrupted.

I merely raised the book in my hand with the title turned towards her. The often severe face broke into a sudden smile.

"You must read *The History of Mr. Polly* next," she said.

It was my first introduction to what, in 1929, was still called Modern Literature.

The results came out just before we went for our summer holiday – this year to Scarborough. My father and mother came rushing up to my attic bedroom as soon as the morning post had arrived. I was still fairly sleepy but felt a kind of intense calm come over me. The envelope looked small and distant. I opened it, took out the list and turned to the "N"s.

"I've got it," I said, and dropped the list on the bed.

Further details could wait until I went back to school, but I knew, at least, that I could enjoy my holiday without apprehension.

Scarborough was my first glimpse of the leisured elegance of the north, though, the previous year, I had met the more bourgeois elegance of the south on a visit to our Bournemouth cousins. Yet my chief memory of Scarborough is not one of elegance, but of the drawn-out dourness of non-championship county cricket – Yorkshire versus Somebody-or-Other's XI.

The weather was drugged and heavy, pressing like a hot saucepan-lid, as my father and I sat, unmoving, throughout the long afternoon. Then, at close of play, when everybody stood up to leave, I staggered as if I were drunk. For a moment, the field swam round me, and, as if a turban were pushed down over my eyes, first the sky and then the field turned black. Slowly, as it seemed, the darkness lowered itself, like a great weight. I could see only the legs and feet of the people round me, pushing to get out. After a few moments, I was completely blind, and clutched at my father's arm. We could neither sit down nor move backwards, but had to keep shuffling along with the others. Gradually, as we nudged through the gate and the crowd thinned out, the weight began to ease from my eyes. The street bulged and swayed, and I found myself staring, as it seemed, through those knobs and whirlpools of glass you find in the windows of old public houses.

"It's something you must have eaten," said my mother, when I arrived back at our rooms, and, sure enough, I went through the ritual bilious attack with which I greeted any kind of indisposition.

174

But it wasn't something I had eaten; it was something that was eating me.

Scarborough holds one other memory. One morning, immediately after breakfast, I hurried off to the newsagent's to see what reviewers had to say about Bernard Shaw's new play *The Apple Cart*. I had not, at that time, read a single line of Shaw. There was certainly none in the Millom Public Library and there was no school library at all, but I could not help being aware of Shaw for, although he was already at the beginning of his decline as a dramatist, he was still the most publicised writer in the world. Shaw the buffoon, the joker, the iconoclast, appeared day by day in every newspaper like a living comic strip.

"That jackass," my father would umph, half-teasingly, as he read the latest outrageous saying in the *Daily Mail*.

To me, Shaw was almost a new Messiah, for this old man, already two generations out of date, cracking the same jokes he had been cracking for thirty years, pulling the same legs, exasperating the same old humbugs, woke me up to the world I was living in.

All the dogmas, the assumptions, the accepted opinions and attitudes, which had been taken for granted by parents and teachers, at home, at church and at school, were now challenged, not surreptitiously, not by furtive little men in rooms behind cobblers' shops, but boldly, blithely, and with corrosive and cleansing laughter. It was not until I listened to Shaw, in 1929, that I truly realised that the Victorian age was over and gone.

And, when I looked round me, I began to see Millom as I had not seen it before. I saw a town abandoned by the industry which had yanked it into being by a kind of geological Caesarian operation. Slag banks slobbered over acres of salt marsh and meadows, like horrible, grey glaciers of frozen phlegm. The old mines were already four-fifths worked out, with more than a dozen shafts sealed off, and the land, almost everywhere, collapsing like a punctured tyre. One night, the ground gave way beneath one of the little mineral-line locomotives, letting it slump deep into the tunnels and hollows of the mine, going back to the iron womb it had come out of. All around, there were signs of stagnation: huge heaps of unsold ore lay beside the shafts at Hodbarrow, and, at the Ironworks, the unsold pig-iron was stacked like enormous, dirty, grey, bamboo huts. The old unused harbour rotted and crumbled away; railway lines rusted red as the ore they had once carried; long shuntings of empty wagons truanted off into dead-end sidings. Weeds thrust up between the sleepers and thrushes nested on the axle bars.

I saw the people of the town abandoned and seemingly forgotten by the rest of the population of England. Hundreds of men stood about the street corners all day, as if waiting for a funeral that never turned up. Boys hung on aimlessly at school, for want of a job to go to; girls served in shops for five shillings a week. Some of the younger children could not remember a time when their fathers were at work. A dull smother of hopelessness hung over the town like the smutch from a smoking rubbish dump. All the houses at the bottom end, near the slag bank, were cracking and flaking from neglect and age, and only three new ones had been built in my lifetime. The schools were half-falling-down, half-shored-up, waiting to be condemned; the churches and social institutes were all in debt; the shops clung on to existence like Old Age Pensioners on their ten shillings a week. "This," we said to ourselves, in Form V, "is what we have to get away from." Matriculation, in fact, amounted to a Free Pass out of the town.

Then, suddenly, as if an abscess had been lanced, a fierce mixture of feelings burst out from inside me – anger, resentment, compassion and a paradoxically exhilarating sense of disgust. With emotions as intense as any I had felt in St. George's Church, I went through a new kind of conversion and proclaimed myself as Socialist. It was the year when Ramsay MacDonald's party was elected to office, and the Labour candidate from the Whitehaven division, to which Millom belonged, was the late Morgan Philips Price, a distinguished member of the Trevelyan-Macaulay tradition of high-minded, middle-class radicalism.

When the news of Mr. Price's election came through, his supporters gathered themselves together and began a Victory March round the town, waving red flags and scarves and scraps of red material. As they clumped and cavorted up St. George's Terrace, it came home to me, as never before, how sheer poverty had hit the people of Millom. This procession was the nearest thing I had ever seen to the rabble described by Dickens in *Barnaby Rudge*: women in appalling old coats and jumpers, carrying babies, wrapped in rags; children hopping along, with their toes burst out of split boots; old men, their faces little more than skin-covered skulls, pinched and black from years of work and worklessness.

With a gush of what I now know was pure adolescent romanticism, my heart went out to them. These were my fellow townsmen, every bit as much as the more respectable audience which had applauded me at the Methodist concerts. The crowd clog-danced up the street in a grotesque reel of triumph, and flaunted their red badges at Miss Danson, as she sat beside her window, holding herself as proud and disdainful as Lady Bracknell.

We watched from our shop doorway.

"Miss Danson's sticking to her colours," said my mother, with much approval.

"Silly old fool," I said.

"She's having no truck with that riff-raff, anyway," she said.

My eyes blurred with a hot spurt of pain and frustration.

"They're as good as you," I said to her. "Every single one of them." My mother fountained out into tears and ran back into the house.

Later that afternoon, when M.P.Price, M. P., arrived by car, on a tour of his new constituency, I went up to the Market Square and stood on the edge of the crowd, like a bystander, curious but uncommitted. For even at that moment of excited and trembling conviction, I could not entirely disrespect my father's principle of strict, outward neutrality.

"I'll vote on my own two feet," he would say, when any of the political parties sent a car for him at an Election.

And if people pressed him harder to declare himself, he would play the trump which he was convinced would shut everybody up.

"I've voted for all sides," he would say, putting an end to the conversation, though I knew for certain that he had been Liberal at heart, true as Reckitt's Blue – the Liberal colour in our constituency – since long before Gladstone died.

So I held myself back, at the corner of the Square, beside Mr. Dixon's chemist's shop, just close enough to hear the voice of the new Member when he addressed the gathering under the Market Clock.

"It's the red blood of the people," he shouted, pointing to the party flag. "That's where our colour comes from. It's the red of the blood."

He shook the hands that were thrust up at him from all sides and then drove slowly out of the Square towards the railway bridge, the crowd running beside the car and cheering all the way.

I joined in neither the cheering nor the running, but stepped slowly along the pavement, speaking to nobody, like Peter, following afar-off.

When we returned to school, that autumn, I found myself in what, I believe, was the largest Sixth Form entry, up to then, in the history of the school. There were, in fact, six of us. Three – including Cyril, who later became a Professor of Inorganic Chemistry – chose to take up science, and, so far as I was concerned, were lost to human conversation. The other three of us opted for arts – English, French and History. There was no choice of subjects and it was only by careful planning that the staff could be spared for a Sixth Form at all. My two companions were the two boys of my own age who had entered the school a year earlier than me – Bob Morton, son of the Headmaster at Lapstone Road Boys' School, though no relation of Tom's, and Ted Fisher, son of a retired police sergeant, whose family had farmed the Duddon Marshes for several generations. Our Form-mistress, as we discovered with some apprehension, was to be Miss Hobson, who taught History throughout the school and was also to be responsible for Sixth Form English. We had long been acquainted with Miss Hobson as the most formidable character in the school – a strict disciplinarian, who could subdue a noisy class with a whisper, and would ram her pupils through the examination machine, year after year, with ruthless, organised efficiency. You had to have greater ingenuity than we could claim if you wanted to fail in History. Every minute of her lessons was work, work, work: a high-speed condensed talk and then the copying of notes from the board, struggling hard to keep up with the chalk.

We had not been in the Sixth Form more than a couple of days before we realised that, so far as we were concerned, the Miss Hobson we had known for four years – "Cow Hobson", to those who liked her least – was gone for ever. In her place, was the genial, plump "Hobby", as efficient as ever, but obviously delighted at being able, for once, to teach the subject she loved to three intelligent and receptive pupils. Even the old-fashioned bun on the nape of her neck seemed to be hanked and plaited with an almost girlish enthusiasm. She gathered us round the table and beamed across it, like a well-contented, middle-aged cook, handing out plates of savouries.

English Literature was now no longer just the books we happened to be studying at the time. Suddenly it broadened, took on the perspective of the centuries. Our syllabus was large, covering at least twelve set books: two plays of Shakespeare's, two volumes of Milton and two of Keats; Chaucer, Sheridan, Lamb, Scott's *Old Mortality*, and the first book of *The Golden Treasury*, with its marvellous pickings of Coleridge, Shelley, Byron and, especially, Wordsworth, which excited me, at that age, more than any other poetry ever written. I think Hobby would have agreed, though she also had a deep feeling for Milton. She once drew on the blackboard a graph of the progress of English poetry, as she saw it. First, Chaucer jutted up, like a cliff, out of sheer nothingness; then, after a gap, came the towering Everest of Shakespeare, the lesser peak of Milton, and a whole century and a half of fen-land flatness, until the Romantics soared up, nearly as high as Shakespeare, followed by the rolling lower ranges of the Victorians. Of Eliot, Pound and Joyce, I doubt if she knew even the names, and if she'd heard of Lawrence, it was only in the pages of the Sunday newspapers. Drinkwater was her idea of a modern poet, Galsworthy, of a modern dramatist, and when I managed to persuade her to include *St. Joan* in our syllabus, I fancy she saw herself as being quite daringly contemporary.

Yet she was a teacher of extraordinary and, at times, galvanising gifts, who sparked off in all three of us a passion for poetry which has lasted a lifetime. (Twenty-five years after we left school, Ted Fisher, then himself a teacher, found the young Ted Hughes among his pupils at Mexborough Grammar School, and passed on, I believe, something of the same spark.) We read, we discussed, we argued. We would sometimes keep a whole lesson going in a crackle and flicker of conversation, each, in turn, throwing in this question or that irrelevancy, to keep the pot boiling. Sometimes, I fancy, Hobby saw what we were up to but pretended she didn't for the fun of it. At the end of term she would bring a great pile of books for us to read and hand round, one to the other, during the holidays – Hardy, Conrad, Galsworthy, even Kenneth Grahame. I had not heard of *The Wind in the Willows* until I read it during the summer holiday of my seventeenth year!

Much of the time, of course, we were left to get on as well as we could on our own, and, as there was no private study room nor even an unoccupied classroom anywhere in the school, we used to go downstairs into the Reference Room of the Public Library. There we spent, on an average, two or three hours a day in a cramped cabin, with one window like a porthole, high in the wall, giving a view, if you climbed up a ladder to look out of it, of the school dustbin and the darkest corner of the school yard. The place was almost airless, catarrhal from the fumes of the coke-stove, musty and dusty from the half-mouldering, out-of-date sets of *The Encyclopaedia Britannica* and the *Dictionary of National Biography*. We took down pages and pages of what, in the end, proved to be quite useless notes on the lives of Gustavus Adolphus and Richelieu. We sang as we worked, like sailors before the mast, until people in the Lending Library could hear "My Blue Heaven" and "Home in Passadena" wafted melodiously through the doors marked SILENCE. We listened, day after day, to the long, wordy, repetitive jokes of the old librarian, knowing that, unless we kept on his good side, the Reference Library would be closed to us. We squabbled, wrangled, horsed about, and, more than once, Bob and Ted wrestled themselves under the table. At one such time, an encyclopaedia salesman walked in:

"Are you students?" he asked.

Bob and Ted lifted their heads from the floor in some surprise.

"Yes," they said, and went on with their fighting.

By this time, however, I had already begun to cough. I noticed it first in the Reference Library and attributed it to the dust and airlessness. I would huff and splutter over my books and sometimes walk out into the road to draw fresh air into my lungs. As the winter went on, a perpetual cold clamped its damp suckers on my chest.

"He doesn't seem able to throw it off," said my father, as if a cough were a clout to be cast at the end of May.

Yet, in many ways, my health now appeared to be far better than could have been expected from my junior days. During that last year at school, I was absent not even for one single half-day, and, in earlier forms, I had missed only a sum total of one week in four years. The childhood troubles of chicken-pox, mumps, measles, German measles and an annual attack of influenza seemed to be left far behind.

Yet, by Easter, it became apparent that I was not really well.

"I wish you could get rid of that cough," said Hobby, when I interrupted the lesson with a more than usually prolonged buffeting of my bronchial tubes.

I smiled rather wryly, accepting this as the way things were and not seeing that I could do anything about it.

My parents accepted it in much the same way. They were so used to the cough, I think, that it became, for them, just a normal part of my personality, no more than a habit. And, anyway, I was sure to get rid of it when the better weather came. My appetite, however, was poor and I was now having frequent bilious attacks, though this, too, was something they were used to. But, round about this time, I began to develop a symptom which did worry them. Every now and then, often when I was doing my homework, the room would seem to slide away from me, to become strangely distant, and I would feel, as it were, a wind rising up in my head, drowning the sound and sense of the world around me. For a moment, my eyes would blur and the room would grow dark, but, almost immediately, I would take grip and shake myself free of this half-faint. Then, as the world zoomed back into focus, I would begin to tremble. For perhaps a minute I would shudder as if I were standing in a bitterly cold draught. My teeth doddered and chattered; my face went white as a newspaper. Suddenly, the whole of my neck and throat and cheeks and God knows what else under my clothes would turn into goose-flesh, every pore pitted deeply in the skin. It was the goose-flesh that alarmed my father, and, in spite of my protests and assertions that there was nothing wrong with me, he hauled me off to our family doctor. Now, our doctor did not really approve of boys being studious; he thought they ought to be tough and play rugby and hate swotting. So he was convinced that it was all this brain-work that was the trouble. Had I come from a poorer house he might have had other suspicions, but, as it was, he was sure that I only needed plenty of fresh air and more exercise to put me right. Did I play football or cricket? I didn't – the very thought of it nearly brought on the goose-flesh again. Then did I play tennis?

Now, as it happened, during the summer term of 1930, the school had hired the tennis courts which belonged to the cinema, beside the Cricket Field, and the Sixth Form boys were allowed to join in the game along with the girls. The presence of the girls, the flirtatious civilities of the game, the gentle thump and patter, the sun, the larks, the scent of huge, breaking waves of rambler roses on the boundary trellises, even the cheerful clanking of shunted wagons in the railway goods yard – all these appealed to me. So I took up tennis and to everybody's surprise, became not bad at the game. Not good, of course; but even to be not bad was a new experience for me. With a slightly ironic determination, I practised alone in one corner of the courts until I developed a serve which, if it was by no means the fastest in the school, was faster than many. The girls no longer regarded me as a hopeless doubles partner. I was not much good at any other stroke, but, in between bouts of coughing, I served a reasonable number of winners. Why I did not bring on a haemorrhage and serve myself into my grave is something I have never been able to understand.

When July came along, however, and I was removed from the day-by-day stimulus of school, I began to grow listless again. Our holiday, that year, was taken at Harrogate, which is not the most exciting place for a boy of seventeen and seemed even less so from my parents' holiday habit of walking, hour after hour, around the suburban and peripheral parts of the town to see what new houses had been built. I was bored and I could not hide it.

"For Heaven's sake, get a smile on your face," my mother said. "We brought you here to enjoy yourself."

"But I *am* enjoying myself," I said, anxiously straining to convince myself and them.

I went on trudging beside them, hot, tired, almost silent and, much of the time, peculiarly thirsty. The long drinks of cool lemonade are all of that holiday that I can recall with any pleasure.

Something else was beginning to trouble me, too. I had an almost continually sore throat and my voice became gritty and husky – croaking like a corncrake, as my father used to say. My mother said my voice was merely taking a long time to come back after breaking, and that this was a sign that I was going to be a baritone. Still, my cough certainly did seem to have abated somewhat, during the summer months, and I returned to school, in September, with no real suspicion that I was in anything but my normal fair-to-moderate general state of health.

It was the husky throat which gave Hobby the excuse to intervene. We were in the middle of one of our English lessons, when Mr. Sharp came in. He gave Miss Hobson a knowing look.

"Come along with me, Nicholson," he said. "There's someone I want you to meet."

I followed him downstairs into a room where I found the visiting school Medical Officer and his assistant nurse.

"This is the boy Miss Hobson spoke about," said Mr. Sharp.

The doctor examined my chest and throat, made no comment and allowed me to return to my class, but that afternoon, at four o'clock, he called at our house.

"We're a bit worried about your throat," he said. "We think you ought to stay off school for a few days, while we arrange for you to see a specialist."

I looked at him in stunned surprise, shocked, not by the prospect of the specialist, but by the thought of having to miss school even for a few days.

"Then we'll have to think about your career," he added, presuming, as everybody did, that I was going to teach.

My father did not wait for the Medical Officer to make arrangements but took me straight up to our family doctor, who, this time, saw danger, and immediately made appointments with consultants in

Liverpool. My father and I travelled down by train, taking four hours over the journey either way. The throat specialist was non-committal but suggested that he should take out my tonsils. The chest specialist made some show of putting away his stethoscope after he had examined me.

"Well, Doctor?" said my father.

"I can't find anything actually wrong with his chest," said the doctor, "but the very look of him, his shoulder blades sticking out like wings, his flushed face, his cough, a slight blueness of the finger nails – they all point to one thing."

My father gazed at him, tense, troubled, completely puzzled, having no suspicion whatever of what the man was trying, as tactfully as he could, to tell him.

"T.B.," said the doctor.

My father shrivelled up. He did not seem to take in the meaning. He stared straight ahead as if he had had a stroke, but he did not say a word.

"Do you know what I'd do if he were my boy?" said the doctor, after a long silence.

"No," said my father, rousing himself, as from a deep sleep.

"I'd have him X-rayed. And then, if it's positive, we'll have to get him off to a sanatorium."

The word suddenly suggested to me open windows, hills, the sky, long walks in the snow.

"It'll be up to him, then," added the doctor, noticing my reaction. "After all, it's his funeral."

"I hope not," I said.

It was a poor joke, but it helped at the time.

A few days later, our doctor brought down the specialist's report. He also brought the advice which, I believe, saved my life.

"If I were you, Mr. Nicholson," he said, "I wouldn't let Norman go to the County Sanatorium. It's tough up there, like a prison. He'd never stand it. He wouldn't be happy, and if he wasn't happy, he wouldn't get well. I'll make enquiries about a private sanatorium and I think he ought to go down south for a while. It'll only be for about three months and it shouldn't cost too much."

"Never mind the cost," said my father. "I'll do whatever you think is best for the lad."

CHAPTER TEN

THE sanatorium to which I was to go was at Linford in Hampshire, chosen because it would be near our Bournemouth cousins. These cousins, or, at least, the two aunts, as I called them – both born at Haverigg – had reservations about the choice. They thought that my father was getting a bit above himself. A private sanatorium, they seemed to imply, was all right for a Sobey, but far too good for a Nicholson. Once, when they visited me, I happened to say, using the current vocabulary, that there were "some very nice people" there.

"And so they should be," snapped my Aunt Emma, "considering what they're paying."

Nevertheless, they welcomed my mother and me when we travelled south, put us up for several nights and borrowed my Uncle Dick's chauffeur-driven Daimler to take us to Linford in some style. I was excited, tense, nervous yet not really apprehensive. It had not occurred to me that I might die, though, as I now realise, it had occurred to everybody else. I thought of my illness mainly as an interruption and my one aim was to get it over as quickly as possible. There would be three or four months of long walks and open windows, and then I would be able to return to school, pick up my books and begin to chase after Bob and Ted as hard as ever I could.

It took less than a week for that picture to fade. It was not that I lost hope; it was just that the gentle routine of the sanatorium drew me into its self-enclosed sphere. The world I had come from, the world I would, God willing, go back to, began to seem curiously distant. I was locked in a universe of tiny perspectives which yet seemed to take on tremendous significance. In day after day of doing, to all intents, just nothing, I saw myself living through a dangerous and heroic saga.

To get well seemed to me – as, I think, it seemed to most of us – the great moral obligation of our lives.

The routine began as soon as I arrived. My mother and I were met by a nurse, who took me down to the detached wooden chalet, secluded among trees, which was to be my home. She turned down the corner of the bedclothes.

"You'd better get into bed," she said, "and I'll telephone for a doctor."

My mother looked at her in astonishment.

"He won't have to go to bed, will he?" she almost wailed.

"For a day or two, at least," said the nurse, showing some impatience.

My mother said good-bye. I got into bed and soon afterwards Dr. C., the youngest of the three doctors in charge, came to see me. He welcomed me courteously, took my pulse – it was, if I remember rightly, not much below two hundred! – and unwrapped a thermometer that looked to me nearly as big as a poker.

"We take our temperatures four times a day by the rectum," he said.

I looked blank.

"Don't you understand?"

"Not particularly."

He hesitated for a moment, not being used to this difficulty with his class of patient.

"It goes in the hole in the back," he explained, with a certain polite distaste.

The winter night set in early and a gale blew up, hurling rain in bucketfuls against the window by my bed. My chalet stood on the slope of a hill, fifty yards from, and rather below the level of, the main building of the sanatorium from which it was completely hidden by an enormous privet hedge and several overhanging trees. From my bed I faced the two, always-open sliding-doors, half the width of the wall, that gave onto a little porch, screened by the privet. At my bed-side, and on the opposite side of the chalet, were glass windows, which I was allowed to close only in a storm, while only the fourth wall, behind my back, was solid. There was a bed, a bed-table, a chest-of-drawers, a wash-stand, a commode, a wicker reclining-chair, a small chair for visitors, some shelves and an anthracite stove. An electric bell enabled me to communicate with the main building – one ring for a maid, two for a nurse. Compared to the indoor rooms, the chalets, of which there were three or four, scattered about the grounds, were bare and spartan, being intended for patients who were up most of the day, but the bareness was no worry to me, while the separation gave me a privacy, almost a freedom, which I soon learned to value.

The first night was strange, with the wind snarling outside and the trees creaking. The faint glow of the stove made the shadowy shape of chairs look as if they were gathered together for a seance. In the morning I woke to my new reality. I was roused, while it was still dark, by the odd-job man, who came in to refuel the stove. Then it began: the quiet, steady, ceaseless, rippling little stream that kept our days turning like a mill-wheel. First, the nurse with the breakfast menu and a cup of tea, which, after a day or two, I did not bother to drink. Then the three meals, the three doctors' visits, the two strict Rest Hours, at noon and at six p.m., the daily washings and bed-makings and clearings-out of the room. Long before we were supposed to switch off our lights, at nine-thirty, I was tired out and fast asleep.

That, at least, was an ordinary day, to be repeated over four hundred times before much variation came my way. But the first two days were not ordinary. I was weighed, carried up to the main building and X-rayed, and all three doctors separately made long examinations of chest and throat. At the end of these, Dr. S., the head of the sanatorium, sat on the edge of my bed.

"We usually find that our patients are more able to work with us," he said, "if we explain to them what we are trying to do."

He went on, then, to outline the principles of rest, exercise, fresh air and food, comparing them – not very felicitously, so far as I was concerned – with the training methods of professional footballers.

"We've got to bring your temperature down first," he said, "and then it's mostly up to you."

He paused for a moment and looked out of the window – a tall, lean, Galsworthian character, already in his sixties, with white hair and moustache so sleek that they looked as if they were distempered on the bare skin. It may have been that the words meant more to him than to his colleagues, for, as a young doctor, he himself had been a patient and from his experience then had decided to devote his life to the care of tuberculosis.

"We can't be watching you all the time," he went on, "but remember one thing. If you're tempted to shirk or slacken or not carry out the instructions we've given you, then it won't be us you're cheating; it'll be yourself and your mother and father."

The next morning, he gave me something else to think about.

"We must rest that larynx of yours," he said. "Whisper."

I gaped at him, struck dumb.

"Go on," he said, whispering himself. "Whisper. Whisper: A noisy noise annoys Noyes."

"A noisy noise annoys Noyes," I half-breathed, half-grunted.

"Whisper properly," he said, "like this."

I soon got the knack.

My mother came to see me that afternoon, before she returned to Millom. She bounced brightly down to my chalet, and then stopped dead.

"Are you still in bed?" she cried out, in surprise. "Haven't you been up at all?"

"Not yet," I whispered.

That was her second surprise.

The following Monday morning I was able to write and tell my parents that I had gained three and a half pounds in five days. This quick response to rest and food was common among the new patients – I heard of one man who put on six pounds a week for several months together – but it gave encouragement, however deceptive, just at the time when we most needed it. My temperature, too, after having been around 102°F when I arrived, had now subsided to what seemed a comparatively reasonable plateau of between 100° and 101°. After that, a drop as little as 0.2°, maintained over several days, was seen as an achievement. So, as the months crept on, my weight nudged up and my temperature eased down and I began to look forward confidently to the summer.

In the meantime, I was exploring my surroundings, though without, of course, actually leaving my bed. From my window I looked down the bushy declivity of the sanatorium grounds, across a wild garden, walled in by massings of trees, where cypresses and spiry evergreens were positioned in the angles of the zigzag path, designed for out-of-breath patients. The trees blocked off any view of the little valley of the Lin, but, through gaps in the branches, I could see heath-land, rising to the low ridge of Picket Post, a mile or a mile and a half away, with the Ringwood-to-London road running along the spine of the horizon. Then, as spring came along, and I was allowed to sit at the door, I could look across the drive, which ran at the back of the chalet, and over the boundary hedge to the hundred or so yards of gorse-and-heather-sprigged common that divided us from the New Forest. Beyond that, and just within my view if I stood up, were black enclosures of conifers, with the ground slowly heaving behind them to a table-land of gravelly heath. The tuberculin-tested herd roamed freely over the common, and, twice a day, I would hear the leading cow's bell, clinking round her neck, as she grazed steadily byre-ward at milking time.

I was not to set foot on that heath or that common for more than a year, nor even to have a distant glimpse of the farm and the forty acres of beech wood within the bounds of the estate. Yet I had no feeling of being shut away from these inviting prospects. It was more as if, in a way, they came to me. For twenty-four hours a day I breathed the air and weather of the Forest. The winds and mists freely entered my room and often I found my breath frozen to rime on the pillow, Some mornings I had to break the ice in my thermometer jar before I could take my temperature. Like nearly all the patients, I soon became almost impervious to the cold. I would stand about in the snow in my slippers, with only a jacket on top of my pyjamas, and not even notice that it was freezing. And when May came in I was often roused from sleep, just as the dews were rising in the first sun, to find myself dazzled by the glitter from every leaf and branch and grass-blade and half-stunned by the sound of all the birds of the Forest shouting their heads off from copse and hedge and furze and heather.

It was the birds, of course, which caught the notice of the patients. From my very first morning I was aware of them: not just robin and blackbird and songthrush, but birds which I was certain I could never have seen before, birds of a brightness and brilliance which I could scarcely believe was to be found in England – chaffinch, greenfinch, blue tit, great tit, magpie, wagtail. They are all, as I now know, among the commonest birds of suburb and farmland and can frequently be seen in my own back yard in the middle of Millom, but, at that time, they seemed to be completely new discoveries. Even the starling, every dark feather faintly iridescent with the rainbow that the sun casts on spilt oil, was a bird I had never really looked at before. They were so clean, close, abundant and tame. The robin accepted my chalet as part of its territory and I would wake in the mornings to feel it hopping inquisitively around my counterpane. It would sit on the corner of my bed-table, as I ate a meal or wrote letters, and, more than once, when the maid brought in my tea and I went on reading for a minute or two,

I found, when I turned to the tray, that the centre of my bread and butter had been pecked away.

The chaffinch, too, and the tits would assemble at meal-times on the spread branches of the spruce tree, and, sometimes, especially in cold weather, would come inside. I remember one occasion when I was having a visit from an old man, suffering as much from bronchitis as T.B., who used often to pop in to see me, partly because he, too, was on whispers. He was, in many ways, an unhappy and frustrated man, who had built up a prosperous cattle-food business and was now desperately trying to run the firm from the sanatorium, snubbing the sons and sons-in-law who were waiting to take over. He was sitting there, saying very little – for, as his whisper was too bad for me to understand and he was too deaf to hear *my* whisper, conversation was restricted – when the birds began to come in. Within a few minutes, there must have been thirty or forty or fifty of them, mostly chaffinches, but with a few sparrows. They perched on the sliding-doors, on the window-ledges, on the tops of the chest-of-drawers, the wash-stand and the chair backs. The old man and I remained silent, watching them with a kind of wonder. Then, suddenly, they began to grow restless, to fly from one perch to another, and down to the floor and up again. Soon, the inside of the chalet was like a cage filled with a swarm of enormous, though friendly, bees. At last, the old man had had enough of it. He pushed himself slowly to his feet, and, with one hand in front of his face and the other waving his walking stick defensively, he shuffled to the door. The birds buzzed and hovered and swooped and banked all about his head, until he was out of the chalet. Then, within another minute, they had all gone.

By this time, new curiosities, new interests had taken hold of me. Soon I could identify all the regular bird visitors to the garden – linnet, yellow-hammer, goldfinch and bullfinch, stonechat and tree-creeper, nuthatch, red-backed shrike, green woodpecker and, in summer, whitethroat and blackcap and all the warblers. I trained myself to recognise the occasional and rarer species, as soon as it appeared. The day that I first saw the goldcrest creep, like a little green mouse, over every square inch of the bark and branches of the spruce was a day burnished with a golden glow. And once the lesser-spotted woodpecker clipped itself onto the trunk of that same tree – a small, straight-necked, vivid bird, black, red and white, and as stiff as if it were fashioned out of painted wood. It posed, pondered and flew off, never to be seen again in forty years, but printed, like a snapshot, on my memory for ever.

In the summer of 1932, when I was first beginning to move about, I found the domed nest of the willow warbler and the coconut-shaped nest of the long-tailed tit, each within fifty yards of my chalet. Even that first spring, though I was limited to my ten-foot radius, I was able to spot and identify at least sixty species. Some of them were like Wordsworth's cuckoo:

> ". . . an invisible thing,
> A voice, a mystery."

There was the chiff-chaff, for instance, which piccolo'd its own name, out of sight in the highest trees, and the nightjar that purred, like a cat, along one of the branches of a small oak in the boundary hedge. And throughout May and June, I woke, night after night, as from one dream to another, to find the moonlight or the pre-dawn darkness freaked and shot through with the flashes and dim, low glimmerings of the nightingale's song.

> "The nightingale, if she should sing by day,
> When every goose is cackling, would be thought,
> No better a musician than the wren" –

I remembered Hobby's systematic underlining of the manifold ornithological inaccuracy of Shakespeare's famous lines, and now I had proof of it. For the wren advertised its musicianship every day of the year, its song sizzling out of its little body, like soda from a syphon, while the cock nightingale sang not only through the night, but for two or three hours of every morning and every afternoon. I have stood on the veranda of the bungalow where we gathered for tea, and stared hard at the bird, perched on the railing, not two yards away, while it stared back at me and went on singing, as if it were wound up like a clock and could not stop until the spring ran down.

I began now to borrow from the Sanatorium Library books on nature and the countryside – Hardy, Hudson, Jefferies, Gilbert White; books on birds, animals, snakes and trees. (I took no interest, at the time, in flowers, and so lost an opportunity which has not returned.) And all these presented a picture of an England which, except in a few secluded spots, no longer survived. Our corner of the New Forest, however, was one of those spots. Except for the few cars which drove in each day, bringing patients or visitors, we were living in a world which was still that of pre-1914. The road outside the boundary hedge was unmetalled: only the farm carts and an occasional rider ever passed that way. The Forest paths were so little frequented that once, when I dropped my watch, I was able to go back to the place, a week later, and pick it up. Even the main roads were comparatively empty and the ponies lived on the heath and not on the grass verges, begging for sandwiches. Jack, the odd-job man, who cleaned the boots and looked after my stove, spoke in the dialect of Hardy's rustics, and the old men I sometimes saw hedging or ditching might easily have talked their way into the lines of Edward Thomas. In our sheltered, anachronistic, artificially preserved backwater, we seemed to be living in the long sunset of a world which, elsewhere, had disappeared into the night. I ate, breathed, slept, dreamed in the climate of a lost arcady; I saw myself as a complete countryman in a country that no longer was.

Yet there were anxieties, questionings. I realised, as soon as I arrived at the sanatorium, that the doctors and my fellow patients belonged, almost entirely, to a class that I had scarcely met before this, a class which seemed to have a completely different set of social values. Perfectly commonplace remarks of mine would be met with surprise or incomprehension. I found, for instance, that in football, the shape of the ball was of such importance that people would groan in sympathy with King George, when he had to attend the Wembley Cup Final, but were extremely interested to know that one of my Sobey cousins was an international scrum-half.

I was surrounded, too, by a new kind of speech, a new vocabulary. I met and chatted to a great many of the patients, since my chalet was on one of the more frequented paths, and soon I had adopted their tone and accent without knowing it. When my parents came down to see me, early in the summer of 1931, I was almost shocked to hear the sounds which came out of their mouths. For their speech, which had been my own for sixteen years, now seemed completely strange, the speech of a people and a part of the world to which nothing in me now wanted to belong. As they walked up the drive, arm in arm together, they looked small and pitifully unsure of themselves. I was embarrassed for their sake and ashamed of my embarrassment.

Up till then I'd always looked forward to the weekly arrival of *The Millom Gazette*. The first few months I read every single item in it – the cricket match reports, the court cases, the concerts and church services, even the whist and billiard scores. Once, in an account of the School Speech Day, I saw, to my immense pleasure, that the Head-master had referred to me as "a boy with a brilliant record, whose health had unfortunately broken down". He went on, not inappropriately, to point out the serious inadequacies of the school buildings. Then, one day, one of the nurses, picking up a copy of *The Millom Gazette*, noticed an advertisement:

> "Jos. Nicholson
> Gents Outfitter."

She read it out and added, teasingly:
"That's your father."
She did not really think that it was, of course, since patients at Linford did not usually have small shopkeepers for their fathers, but, from my miserable and guilty silence, she realised she had accidentally hit on the truth.
She read on, half in amusement and half in a kind of malice:

> "Agent for Battersby Hats
> And
> Dent's Gloves
> Suits and Overcoats
> made to measure."

I squirmed under the bedclothes in a misery of anguished pride. From that day onwards *The Millom Gazette* was destroyed as soon as I had read it.

In my heart, however, I made my reservations and planned my counter-attack. My reading, at that time, was largely Edwardian, since the Sanatorium Library seemed to have been bought, in bulk, in the early or mid'twenties. There was, of course, a good deal of Dornford Yates and P.G.Wodehouse; there was Somerset Maugham and Hugh Walpole and Francis Brett Young. But there was also almost the whole of Wells, Bennett and Galsworthy, to which I added the collected Shaw, my first Christmas present from home. I had not the slightest feeling that what I read was in any way out of date, for Wells, Bennett and Shaw spoke to me of the kind of society I had known before I came to Linford and they confirmed what I had already begun to think about it. I did not, by any means, despise the society in which I now found myself. I liked its manners, its courtesy, its range of interest. I enjoyed, and was grateful for, the comfort of the sanatorium, for the luxury of the Forest air. It was a privilege, I realised, that only my father's self-sacrifice could have bought for me; and it was a privilege, I bravely and romantically believed, that everybody ought to have the right to buy.

"You'll be a Conservative," said one of the nurses – a dark, pretty Welsh girl, who, following an operation, had joined the sanatorium staff as a temporary respite from the heavier duties of general nursing.

"No," I declaimed, in my most vehement whisper. "I'm a Socialist."

"Good boy," she said.

By the spring of 1931 my temperature chart was recording a typical T.B. "swing", with the reading very low in the early morning, rising through the day to a peak at about six o'clock. Slowly, the six o'clock reading began to settle to around 99°.

"If you can keep it below 99 for a week," said Dr. S., "I'll let you sit up for a little while."

The hope, in itself, was enough to send my temperature up again, for it was extremely sensitive to excitement or nervous tension, but, somehow or other, I survived the week and was allowed to sit in my reclining-chair for half an hour.

After that, I watched my thermometer like a mariner taking soundings in treacherous channels. In a few days the half-hour was extended to three-quarters of an hour and then to an hour. Then my temperature began to wobble. I was given the benefit of the doubt for a day or so, but soon there was a sharp rise and back to bed I went. This up-and-down process went on month after month. I was bitterly disappointed the first time, but eventually learned to accept such setbacks like changes in the weather.

"He's a boy who takes disappointment very well," said Dr. S. to my parents.

If only my pluck had been equal to my patience I might have made a far quicker recovery.

There was not much, in the early'thirties, that could be done for a case like mine. Artificial pneumothorax, which worked very successfully with some, was not, apparently, suitable for me, but, in the early summer, the doctors decided to experiment with gold injections. The injections, once a week, seemed, at first, to have no obvious effect, but after about four weeks, there was a rise in temperature, and the treatment was discontinued. A month later, when I seemed to have recovered, it was decided to renew the course, and this time the effect was spectacular.

It was a beautiful June afternoon, and I was lying under a single sheet, hot drowsy but not otherwise very worried, when I noticed that my chest had broken out into a bright red rash. I pushed myself out of bed, went towards the dressing-table and picked up a hand mirror. Face, throat, neck, hands were all covered with the red spots. Remembering, hazily, something I had heard about measles, I opened my mouth and stared in the mirror. My tongue was spotted like potted meat. I reeled back into bed and rang my bell.

I lived, then, through the worst night of my life. I was isolated entirely from the rest of the sanatorium. A special nurse was engaged for me, from an agency at Bournemouth. One maid was assigned to deal with my chalet and was not allowed to mix with any other patients. My temperature soared to nearly 104°. I tossed and turned and sweated all the summer night, while my mind played, over and over again, delirious variations on the Wimbledon tennis I had been listening to on my crystal set:

"Perry-Borotra-Austin-Cochet
Perry-Cochet-Borotra-Austin."

The horrible permutations seemed to be taped inside my head; I had only to close my eyes to switch on the machine.

In the morning, I was weak and exhausted: my head felt as if it had been shaken all night, my fingers were dry, my hair was wet. Yet, in a dazed way, I knew that I had survived. My temperature dropped to about 101°. The nurse, with nothing else to do, blanket-bathed and bullied me all day. I drank four pints of milk. Two days later, I learned that I had not had measles at all. Such reactions to the injections were, it seemed, not uncommon. The other patients, however, were allowed to go on believing that I had measles since it was the best way of making sure that no-one disturbed me.

I entered now into a long period of the doldrums. I do not think I was disheartened, but, in some ways, my effort slackened off. In one way, at least. For now I had lost almost all my appetite and had largely given up even trying to eat. The scales no longer offered me any encouragement. The gains of the first few months had petered out and I was left putting on half a pound one week, losing it the next, perpetually, as it seemed, stranded between eight stone and eight and a half. Food became the biggest bugbear of my life. I loathed the very thought of meal-times. The sanatorium food was, in fact, well cooked and served, with much variety to tempt our appetites, and many delicacies I had never tasted before – brains, sweetbreads, sheep's heart, braised tongue, jugged hare. But they were all the same to me. The birds congregated in the spruce tree at breakfast, waiting for my bread and bacon; the doctor's dog turned up regularly and swallowed half my lunch. Often, when a meal was set before me, I would stare at it for a quarter of an hour, unable to persuade myself even to pick up knife and fork, and when eventually I did so, I found the food cold and uneatable. On such days, if I had been offered the chance of choosing whatever I liked — say, for a birthday treat — I should unhesitatingly have chosen a glass of water.

Yet, I was as happy as usual, most of the time. I read ten or more books a week; I wrote long letters home, and to Ted and Bob and Tom; I chatted and played chess with other patients. Mr. Walton, now a curate in Bournemouth, came over to see me several times; so also did another Millom man, Mr. Willy Yarr, one of the Head Foresters, living at Burley. Dudley and his father looked in, while on holiday on the south coast; Hobby called, when she was staying with her sister in Poole. All of them did their best to hide their dismay at finding me still in bed.

It caused me no dismay, however, for, by this time, the sanatorium had become my entire world. I could not see beyond its horizon. I could barely imagine the time when my life would have to be lived somewhere else. Millom, as I told my father, seemed just a place I had once visited.

He smiled wryly and without much understanding. Then he put the question which, I think, had been in his mind all the afternoon:

"Do you think you'll be home for Christmas?"

I shook my head slowly and was pained to see the look of disappointment and anxiety which spread across his face. I did not understand that anxiety any more than he understood mine.

It was not until about March of the following year that there were signs of any change. I had just passed through a spell of melancholy which had nothing to do with my health. I had fallen in love – as I was expected to do – with a girl of my own age, who, after a few weeks, had very naturally preferred the attentions of one of the young men who were up and about. They took long walks in the Forest together while I languished in my chalet. Eventually, however, I realised that the girl and I had nothing in common but our eighteen years and our temperatures, and, in throwing off the obsession, I seemed to take a step forward. Soon, in the cool, glittering mornings, I was allowed to take my first walks – fifty yards, seventy-five yards, a hundred yards. The change in perspective with every step was as dramatic as if a painted landscape had been turned into a live one, or a photographic still into a movie. Through new gaps in the trees, across new dips in the hedge, I saw cottages, barns, distant fields, woods and heath, of which I had been unaware in all the fifteen months at the window of my chalet. And – though it was almost too good to believe – my temperature stayed steady. I was allowed to dress; to walk as far as the shelter, where the less active patients sat for most of the day; to get up for lunch and then for breakfast. The excitement of eating my first meal in company was so great that I had to go back to bed for the rest of the day! Indeed, the excitement of meeting people, of talking, discussing, enjoying the mild banter, the chess and poker games in the shelter and lounge, was always more likely to upset me than the physical effort of walking.

Not that I walked very far. A quarter of a mile was the longest I accomplished that time – a gentle circling of the immediate environs, which, nevertheless, opened new vistas on every side. I was still far from steady; still subject, day to day, to the verdict of the thermometer; but now I could look up to Picket Post and feel that, if ever I could walk there and back, I would have nothing else to ask for.

Then, early in June, there was a letter from my parents, saying that Dr. S. suggested that they should come down at the end of the month and take me back to Millom.

I gawped at the letter in numb disbelief. It seemed incredible that I should have to leave the sanatorium. I knew I was not fit enough; I felt sure that this must be obvious to everyone. I waited until Dr. W., the second in command, made his mid-day round.

"What's this about my going home?" I asked.

He turned away, staring at the floor.

"You can't stay in these places for ever," he said, at last.

I understood: the money was giving out. It was a possibility to which I had not given the slightest thought in all that time. My father, for his part, had not let drop so much as a hint. He had watched the savings of thirty years slowly seep away, month by month, as he signed the cheques, and never said a word. It was not, indeed, until he died that I came to realise how great had been the sacrifice he and my mother had made, how close to insolvency he had permitted himself to drift. But on that June day, in 1932, I still understood enough to know that I must accept, as inevitable, whatever was to come. I said nothing more to the doctor and nothing at all to any of the patients. I wrote home saying how much I was looking forward to returning to Millom, but I went about those last weeks in a state of stunned bewilderment, not daring to cast my thoughts even a couple of months ahead.

Then, one evening, about ten days before I was due to leave, I gave a quiet, soft cough, reached for my sputum mug and spat out about a teaspoonful of blood. Immediately, I was put back in bed and a telegram was dispatched to my parents, cancelling arrangements. I felt perfectly well. I had no temperature, no headache, no pain; but the doctors took the setback very seriously. I was made to lie flat on my back with a sandbag balanced on my left shoulder to inhibit breathing and all movement on that side. I was not allowed to get out of bed, to sit up, or even, for a day or two, to roll over in bed. Reading became an athletic feat to be accomplished with the absolute minimum of muscular movement. Only my eyes and my brain were permitted any activity at all.

At the end of a week, however, the red stains cleared up, and, after another week, I was allowed, very cautiously, to start sitting up again. And, this time as never before, everything seemed to go right. It was as if, somehow, the haemorrhage had done me good, had been a last hurdle that I had to knock out of the way. I began to get up, to resume my exercise, and, for the first time for eighteen months, to speak in my normal voice. The effort was strange. I was almost embarrassed by the unaccustomed vibration of my larynx. My whole throat seemed to shake and tremble like a rattle or the wheezing fife my father had once played in the St. George's Institute Band. For my whisper, while it had been adequate in the quiet, enclosed space of my chalet, was frustrating and often totally useless in the noisier world of general conversation. I seemed, much of the time, to be surrounded by people who were stone deaf. I was sometimes so exasperated that I took to carrying a policeman's whistle and blowing it whenever I wanted people to take special notice of what I had to say. It was not, as I found, the most tactful way of attracting attention, especially indoors.

The restoration of my voice restored to me a place in everyday company. I could join in conversation instead of having to wait until someone was prepared, as it were, to lend me an ear. About this time, too, I made a new friend. Celia was a handsome, intelligent, young woman, a few years older than me, whose father – a Russian Jew by birth – was busy making a fortune out of the manufacture of furniture. Fortune apart, her background was very different from that of the well-to-do bourgeoisie who made up most of the patients. Her schooling was not unlike mine; her youth, in East London, had brought her up against a knock-about world of shops and small businesses which might have been Millom with a Cockney accent. To Celia, for the first time in two years, I felt I could talk openly about my home and my parents.

My walks lengthened, and usually I took them with her. Steadily, a whole new landscape opened up. We stepped on to the common, and saw the land stripped bare to the sky, stretching and curving and muscling like a torso, with only a dark astrakhan of pinewoods in the crutch of the distance. We explored the beech wood beyond the farm, plunging like divers into the gloom beneath layer under layer of thatching leaves. We entered the old conifer plantations, walking along sun-shot aisles, cut through dark crypts and apses, where the shadows continually flickered with the chucks and whistles of wren and robin, blackbird and cole tit. We walked, at last, as far as Picket Post, and gazed over the long undulations of the Forest, with pine clumps smudging the hollows or lining the ridges like a horse's mane. Less than a hundred yards from the sanatorium itself, we found a thicket of gorse, solid as a sea-wall, with a path gouged into it like a canal. The gorse was so high, and the path worn so deeply into the chalky gravel, that, as we walked along it, we sank below ground level like soldiers in a trench. Stonechats – "vuz-clackers", as Jack, the odd-job man, called them – kept clicking their little castanets, and once, when I was sitting quite still, a bird began to buzz and boil, like an angry kettle with a very sore spout, and I looked up, startled, to see a Dartford warbler, now one of England's rarest breeding species, only two feet above me, among the yellow gorse flowers.

For a year and a half, I had been absorbing the scents and seasons of the Forest, passively, like a perceptive vegetable; now I began actively to explore and discover. Celia was even more ignorant of the country than I was, but she had not been educated into the polite boredom of the boarding-school girl. Her four extra years, plus her own tact, prevented my falling in love – an experience which, as I realised by then, did my constitution little good! – and her natural enthusiasm doubled my delight in all that I was finding round about me. It was a short season and I *knew* it would be short – the letter from home would not catch me by surprise this time. But it was like a gate opening on the world. I did not look very far through the gate, but, at least, I no longer turned my back on it.

There was another way in which Celia helped prepare me for life outside. After my haemorrhage the doctor decided that I was not to stay up in the evenings but was to go to bed at six o'clock and take dinner in my chalet. It was then that Celia persuaded me to listen to the Promenade Concerts on my crystal set. I did not need much persuasion. My actual knowledge of music scarcely went beyond Gilbert and Sullivan and my mother's piano playing, but I was quite ready to believe that, if music had more to offer, then I was capable of accepting it. I began, of course, with the obvious cream cakes of tune – Mendelssohn's Violin Concerto, the "Unfinished", the "New World", but one evening, Celia sent me a note, by one of the maids, saying, "Tune in now and listen."

I tuned in to music the like of which I had not heard before. There seemed, to my untrained ears, to be no obvious melody, but instrument after instrument – violin, oboe, perhaps bassoon – kept running up and down and looping over and over in delicious patterns of dissolving and re-forming sound. It was as if a Persian carpet or a Morris wallpaper had come to life and begun to dance. I had no idea what I was listening to, but I realised that this music would be mine for ever. I learned, the next morning, that it was Bach, one of the Brandenburg Concertos – the perhaps unreliable echoes of memory suggest that it may have been either the first or the second. I searched through the stack of gramophone records in the lounge, found one of an aria from a Bach cantata, and played it over and over again whenever I had the room to myself. Gradually, after many hearings, and a good deal of help from Celia, I began to recognise the patternings and imitations and *obbligatos*, to be aware, however imperfectly, of the delights and complexities of counterpoint. I had become a Bach fan before I learned Bach's name.

The year glowed into a ripe and complacent September. New colours began to ooze back into the landscape. The harvested fields spread out squares and rhomboids of bright-dyed hessian; the trees and hedges were lacquered with ochre and ginger; the willow warbler began its final encore; and it was arranged that I was to leave Linford in the last week of the month.

I was more prepared this time. Quietly, in my mind, I had been re-calling the walks that would be possible for me in Millom – Dowbiggin's Fields, the Old Church, the Knott. I resolved that, whenever I went out of the house, I would turn my face towards the country; I would never go in the direction of the Ironworks or Hodbarrow. I would keep away from the streets as much as I could; I would not be persuaded to enter church, chapel, cinema, places of entertainment or even shops. I would live, so far as it were possible, as if Millom were just a village, as if the mines and the furnaces and the slag banks did not exist. I would try to pretend that I had not really left the sanatorium at all. I found encouragement, at that time, from one of my friends among the patients, a lawyer from Liverpool, who, like me, was on whispers. "The Captain", as I called him, was a man in his fifties, who, though he had been struck with serious tuberculosis of the larynx, seemed otherwise astonishingly fit and vigorous and was able to walk ten or twelve miles a day. He had taken an interest in me from the day he arrived because, as he said, "I came from the civilised half of England." This north-country pride was something I had not met for nearly two years and it gave me new heart. No longer did I need to feel apologetic about my home town. I came from Cumberland, the finest county in England, and that should be good enough for anyone.

"You could take all this," the Captain would say, vaguely indicating three or four square miles of the Forest, "and drop it in Wensleydale, and it would be a fortnight before anybody noticed it."

We discoursed in Cumberland and Lancashire dialects, argued about Lancashire and Yorkshire cricket, and jointly put in a request that Lancashire hotpot should be added to the sanatorium menu. In an up-surge of patriotism, I even asked for a second helping.

The month moved on in a burnish of petal and berry and I went about saying good-bye to all the places I had come to know in the previous six months. Good-bye only for a while, however, since it was now planned that I should return to Linford in the spring for a general examination and check-up. My friends, as I was to learn years later, were warned not to put too much faith on that return.

For my own part, I was determined to make it possible. I listened carefully to my instructions. I was to go to bed as soon as I reached home and stay there for a day or two, to recover from the journey. I was to keep up the same routine as at Linford, watching my temperature, doctoring myself, using my own judgement. It would be advisable for me to continue to retire at six o'clock every night, throughout the winter. If I caught a cold, I was to go to bed immediately.

"He knows how to look after himself," Dr. S. told my parents. "Don't fuss him. Just leave him alone to get on with it."

They called for me in my Uncle Dick's car, soon after breakfast, one Monday morning at the end of September. Half the patients came on to the drive to wave me off. I felt a pang far greater than when I had left home, two years earlier.

I can remember nothing of the journey – not even the taxi drive from Waterloo to Euston. I seem to have travelled through the Midlands and industrial Lancashire in a state of numb apprehension, solacing myself with memories of Linford, but, as we steamed out of Barrow-in-Furness, in the late evening, I began to brace myself to face reality.

"I bet it feels good enough to be coming home," said my father.

I could not find the heart even to pretend to agree.

The Barrow platform, the Furness Railway ironwork seats, the sidings, the slag bank pushed themselves roughly into view, like old acquaintances whom I had been avoiding for two years. The railway carriage clattered and clanked with the voices and accents of all the years of my upbringing. I kept my mouth shut, realising how strange and un-northern my own voice sounded now.

We shifted out beyond the hulk of the Barrow slag bank and I caught my first sight of Black Combe across the Duddon Estuary, looking dark and smudgy in the grey evening: it lifted my heart for a moment as nothing else had done that day. But when we nosed on towards Askam, the chimneys and furnaces of Millom Ironworks spiked up into view, grim, gaunt and bony, and, somewhere behind them, lost in the smother, was the town. The train dragged me slowly nearer. I felt little but resentment. I saw Millom, in my memory, as small, dark, drab, damp and mean. There was not, I feared, a lungful of breathable air in all those streets and back-alleys. When we stepped on to the platform at the station, I was so tired that I could hardly recognise the few people who came up to me to shake me by the hand.

"Glad to be back, you will be, an' all," they said, one after the other.

We climbed the steps from the platform, my parents insisting on carrying all the luggage. There was no Uncle Dick's car to meet us now. We walked down the Bridge, and through Danson's back street – the route I had taken, four times a day, on my way to Holborn Hill School, less than ten years before. Yet this was no return to a familiar country. On the contrary, everything around me seemed unreal. I stood outside the shop, while my father fumbled with the keys, and stared up to the attic window, which, in preparation for my coming, had been turned into a casement, to give me more fresh air. I did not know what was going to happen; I did not know where I really belonged.

Forty years later, in that same attic room. I thank God for a lifetime spent in that same town.